The Avalonians

About the Author

PATRICK BENHAM is a teacher, musician and composer of guitar music. In the 1970s he edited *Torc* magazine, an alternative periodical devoted to Glastonbury matters. The personal contacts established at that time have provided him with much of the archival material which is at the heart of this present study into the lives of an earlier generation of activists in this ancient sacred place.

The Avalonians

by

Patrick Benham

Gothic Image
PUBLICATIONS

First published by
Gothic Image Publications in 1993
as The Avalonians ISBN 0 906362 26 1
This edition published by Gothic Image Publications,
PO Box 2568 Glastonbury, Somerset BA6 8XR, England
www.gothicimage.co.uk

ISBN 0 906362 68 7
13-digit ISBN 978 0 906362 68 6

A catalogue record for this book is available from the British Library

Cover design by Peter Woodcock and Bernard Chandler
Book design and artwork by Bernard Chandler

Printed and bound by the Gutenberg Press, Malta
Text set in Linotype Janson, titles in Cochin

Contents

Acknowledgements

MANY PEOPLE GAVE MUCH TIME and trouble to provide me with more details for the first edition of this book than I could have ever hoped for. Regrettably, some of them are no longer with us. Particularly vital was the help of the following:

Monica Wallace for all her many letters covering the Tudor Poles, the Allens, Letchworth, Ireland, and the background of her parents, Mary and John Bruce Wallace.

Christopher Tudor Pole for Tudor Pole family background.

Bunty Martin for Allen family background and memories of her father John Duncan.

Francis Allen for his Carlyle family-tree.

Ros Pitman for helping to make connections.

Konrad Hopkins for his knowledge of William Sharp/Fiona Macleod.

My aunt, *Phyllis Benham* for her help with my Stanbrook Abbey enquiries and Catholic matters.

D. N. Clark Lowes, Librarian for the Society for Psychical Research, Kensington, for giving me access to the papers and letters of Frederick Bligh Bond.

Abba Seraphim, Metropolitan of Glastonbury, for help with Bligh Bond and Archbishop Francis.

Alan Richardson for his knowledge of Dion Fortune and his welcome encouragement in the early stages.

Simon Buxton, of The Society of the Inner Light, for checking and advising on my Dion Fortune chapter.

Rev. Dr. Gordon Strachan for his kind words and for hearing some of the early chapters at Little St. Michael's, Chalice Well.

Dr G. Krishnamurti for his astonishing knowledge of the 1890s, and for his interest in reading through some of the early chapters with me at my home.

R. A. Gilbert for helping with my enquiries about A. E. Waite.

Lord Grey of Codnor, Chairman of the Chalice Well Trust, and the Wardens at Chalice Well, Leonard and Willa Sleath, for allowing me access to their archive.

J. C. M. Nolan for his knowledge of John Duncan.

S. E. Scammell for his family link to Archdeacon Wilberforce.

Dame Eanswythe Edwards, OSB, Archivist, Stanbrook Abbey, also *Dame Gertrude Brown*, OSB.

David Bromwich of the Somerset County Local History Library.

Antony Bates for his personal knowledge of the Order of the Cross, and for memories of his friend, Mary Bligh Bond - also for the loan of his copy of *Avernus.*

Jane Read, Keeper, Early Childhood Collection, Froebel Institute College, Roehampton, London.

Kathryn Murton, Curator, Manuscript Collections, British Library.

Evelyne Draper of the Science Museum Library, South Kensington, London.

Anthony Burton, Keeper, Bethnal Green Museum of Childhood, London.

Stella Armstrong, Secretary, The Order of the Cross, 10 De Vere Gardens, Kensington.

Elizabeth Doctor, Library Assistant, The Wellcome Institute for the History of Medicine, London NWI.

D. J. Wright, Librarian, British Medical Association, Nuffield Library, Tavistock Square, London.

William B. Evans, Admissions Officer, St. George's Medical School, London.

Deirdre Clarke, Assistant Librarian, Trinity College Library, Dublin; *Pam Burrough* (Chief Librarian, Retd.) and the wonderful staff of the Public Library, Street, Somerset.

The Hon. Mrs Acland-Hood of Wootton House, nr. Glastonbury.

Edith Rice of Glastonbury; *Harry Carter* of Glastonbury.

Elaine and Natalie Campbell.

Ian Boughton of The Rutland Boughton Music Trust.

Michael Hurd; Dr Greg Tillett; David Tudor Pole; Jean, Lady Carroll.

Fr. Jude Daryl Parham, The Church of Christ on the Mount, Woodstock, NY.

Rt. Rev. Aelred Watkin, Abbot of Glastonbury.

Michael Holroyd; Dick Snelling; Rowland Handley; Hooper & Wollen, Solicitors, Torquay; *Joan Allen; Brendan Ashe; David Jenkins; Alfred Moore; Elizabeth Sutherland; Michael Denton and Linda Renoth* of Berwick St. John.

Bishop Seraphim Sigrist.

Stan Nicholls of Street, for photographic processing; *Hank Harrison*; *Stephen Morland*; *Nick Farrell*; *Helen Clark* of Street; *John Michell*; *Frances Howard-Gordon and Jamie George* of Gothic Image, Glastonbury.

FOR HELP WITH THIS SECOND EDITION:

Steve Sneyd for picking up a point or two regarding his kinsman
   R. de Tunstall Sneyd.
Dr Tim Hopkinson-Ball for valued help and advice on the Bligh Bond
   chapters and some other points.
Paul Ashdown for his insights and sanity.
Gerry Fenge for discussions on Tudor Pole and sight of his manuscript
   biography.
Guy Robins for his kind gift of *The Reality of Music* by Rutland Boughton.
Geoffrey Ashe for his encouragement and kindly writing the new Foreword.
John Owen Smith for his literary and historical knowledge of the
   Headley and Haslemere area.
Bernard Chandler for working closely and patiently on the text with me
   and for formatting this volume.
Peter Woodcock and Bernard Chandler for the excellent new cover.
Frances Howard-Gordon for inviting me to do this new edition and the
   free rein she has given me.
Abba Seraphim for his knowledge and his wise and measured approach
   to the ecclesiastical claims of others.
The late *Michael Rubinstein* for directing me to his father's Glastonbury
   play and his correspondence with Dion Fortune.
Hilary Rubinstein for his interest in this new edition and allowing me to
   quote from his father's work;
Yvonne Brown of New Zealand for further information on Felkin's
   activities there;
John Kemplay for his work on John Duncan and help with related issues.
Michael and Catriona Blaker for making possible the connection with
   Francis and Libby Dineley.
Francis Dineley for documents and information on Rev. William
   Goodchild.
James P. Carley for his update on the Maltwood Museum.
Lone Bang of Friends of Bride's Mound.

ACKNOWLEDGEMENTS

THE FOLLOWING HAVE KINDLY GIVEN
PERMISSION FOR THE USE OF THEIR MATERIAL:

The Incorporated Society for Psychical Research, 49 Marloes Road,
Kensington, W8 6LA for the extracts of Bligh Bond letters and
the photographs of F. Bligh Bond and Capt. and Mrs Bartlett.
Robert Hale Ltd. for the extracts from *The Heart of Scotland* by Charles
Richard Cammell.
Weidenfeld and Nicholson for the extract from *Memoirs* by Israel Seiff.
The Society of the Inner Light, 38 Steele's Road, London NW3 4R5 for all
quotations from works of Dion Fortune and the photograph of Dion
Fortune with her husband.
The Chalice Well Trust for the photographs of Alice Buckton and the
Blue Glass Bowl, and the extracts from their records and papers.
The National Gallery of Scotland for the photograph of the painting
St. Bride by John Duncan (code G510A2).
The Rutland Boughton Music Trust for the photograph of Rutland
Boughton, the photograph of Gwen Ffrangcon-Davies, the cover of
the 1922 Festival programme designed by Christina Walshe and the
extract from *The Glastonbury Festival Movement* by Rutland Boughton.
The Archivist at Stanbrook Abbey, Callow End, Worcester, WR2 4TD for
the extract from the House Chronicle.
The Somerset County Museums Educational Service, Weir Lodge,
Taunton, for making available copies of the group photograph of
Alice Buckton and children's dance group at Chalice Well.
R. A. Gilbert for extracts from the Diaries of A. E. Waite.

Thanks to the following for supplying, or helping to supply, or offering
to supply, photographs:
*Christopher Tudor Pole, Monica Wallace, Bunty Martin, Leonard and
Willa Sleath, Antony Bates, Ian Boughton, Simon Buxton, Paul Branson,
Bill Knight, Sara Benham, David Walker, John Bainbridge, Abba Seraphim,
Bernard Chandler.*

Foreword to the Second Edition

by Geoffrey Ashe

M Y EARLIEST MEMORY OF Glastonbury is of something that didn't happen.

The story begins in Ottawa, Canada, where I used to read in the parliamentary library. I was already familiar with some of the works of G. K. Chesterton (who, I am glad to see, is having a revival). In Ottawa I discovered another one, his *Short History of England*. This is not so much a history as a series of historical essays, some of them wonderfully perceptive, some highly inaccurate, but all brilliant. Near the beginning of the book is a chapter headed 'The Age of Legends'. And here I read about Glastonbury, the Grail, and the traditions of Arthur.

Back in England some years later, during a stay in Devonshire, I noticed a bus station with a sign advertising a day excursion to Glastonbury, Wells, and Weston-super-Mare. Of course it was Glastonbury that mattered. My wife and I boarded the coach. It crossed the country and approached Glastonbury over the Polden hills. We were struck instantly by the Avalonian hill-cluster in the middle distance, and by the Tor – the 'Royal Tor' as Thomas Hardy called it in a poem, seen from the same angle. Our vehicle approached closer, reached the town, and turned along what I now know was Magdalene Street. Expectation was high. It passed the Abbey and . . . DIDN'T STOP. We had a brief glimpse of grey stone walls, and that was it. The subsequent stops at Wells and Weston-super-Mare were of long duration.

It's one of the signs of change and progress that the omission of the Abbey would be unthinkable today.

My next step, quite a while later, was the reading of Christopher Hollis's little-known but forceful book *Glastonbury and England*. Hollis is almost the only author who quotes the reputed prophesy in 1587 by Austin Ringwode, the last member of the community, about Glastonbury's future rebirth, when 'peace and plenty will for a long time abound'. This rare quotation leapt out at me and I was committed. I wrote my original Glastonbury book *King Arthur's Avalon* soon after.

That was a long time ago, and the book led me into other topics besides Glastonbury – the Arthurian Legend, of course, and the archaeology of Britain in what is now rather less often called the Dark Ages. However, when someone interviews me, I've always made a point of saying that I'm not an Arthurian monomaniac. I've read widely, and written and lectured and taught widely. But the commitment to Glastonbury with all it implies remained, and still remains. 'All it implies' has turned out to be a great deal. Perhaps 'implies' is not quite the word. One of the most impressive things to happen since I wrote *King Arthur's Avalon* has been the proliferation, not only of the basic Christian matter (and it *is* basic, not incidental), but also of fresh mythology, New Age speculation, and theories of various credibility. And of course there is the Festival, which began more than thirty years ago and is now internationally famous.

Glastonbury, which people used to assure me was 'dead', has become extraordinarily lively and active. The change, even over the past ten years or so, has been phenomenal. Is it right to see all these things as fulfilment – or, at least, the beginning of fulfilment - of Austin Ringwode's prophecy of rebirth? He wouldn't have approved of some of the manifestations, or even understood them. I have reservations myself. But there has been far more to welcome than to reject.

Patrick Benham's exploration of the developments over the past century or so, and his depiction of the people involved, is by far the best presentation there has been, and it's very good now to see this book reappearing. Patrick has not only unearthed fascinating facts that no one ever brought together before, or even knew about; he has managed to stay sane while examining them, and to keep the reader sane as well. In Glastonbury, this is more of an achievement than you might think. The rebirth can be viewed from various angles, and its future course is impossible to predict, but *The Avalonians* will remain an indispensable part of it.

The Glastonbury Mystery
(Foreword to the First Edition 1993)

by John Michell

THE COUNTRY WHICH PATRICK BENHAM is inviting us to enter is reputed to be the oldest and holiest of our native sanctuaries. It is a very beautiful country, the image of an English paradise, with streams, meadows, apple orchards and green, rolling hills grazed by sheep. At certain times the play of clouds and sun casts a peculiar, wistful, transient light upon it, stirring the imagination and waking up old dreams and memories. Glastonbury is a place of great spiritual intensity. That is a fact of nature, confirmed by every age and generation, from the earliest times up to the present. Those who care to can discover it for themselves. It is a strange phenomenon, and if you have an active, impressionable mind you are naturally inclined to look further into the matter. Thus you are infected by the spirit of Glastonbury and drawn inwards, as if through stages of initiation, towards the heart of its mystery.

Everything about Glastonbury, the landscape, the light and atmosphere, its archaeological relics and its accumulation of unique legends, contributes to the mystery of the place. Its special quality is made obvious at first sight by its most prominent feature, Glastonbury Tor, the central pivot of its mythological landscape. Steeply uprising in the middle of a watery, hill-fringed plain, it is one of the natural wonders of England. Its shape and position relate it symbolically to Mount Meru, the world-centre mountain, and this is emphasized by the lore and legends which have settled upon it from prehistoric times. In the Celtic tradition it was a place of initiation, a centre of Druid enchantments, the entrance to the underworld and to paradise. Terraced paths around its slope form the traditional pattern of a labyrinth, symbol of the Celtic Mysteries. Its summit was no doubt sacred to the Celtic deity who judged the souls of the dead and led the forces of light against demon armies in the upper air, for with the dawning of Christianity these attributes were assumed by the Archangel Michael, in whose name a monastery was established upon the Tor's summit.

In legends of King Arthur, Glastonbury Tor was his fortress and, according to some, his place of burial. His mythological influence extends over the surrounding countryside, where several of the episodes in his adventures are traditionally located. This suggests that the wheel of country around Glastonbury was once linked with and made to illustrate the Arthurian cycle as a whole. Such was the practice in ancient Celtic realms, where the country and people were divided into twelve sections, each with their own characteristics, their note in the musical liturgy and their particular episode in the mythic cycle of King Arthur. This was a land beneath the spell of priestly enchantment, whose central symbol was the Holy Grail.

The entire mystery of Glastonbury is likewise centred upon the Grail. Christian legends associate it with the mystical relics of the Crucifixion, brought to Glastonbury soon after that event by St. Joseph of Arimathea. In earlier accounts it was the healing, nourishing cauldron of the Celtic goddess. It has been represented by many images, none of which reveal its true essence, for it is not so much an object as a state of being, a state of perfect harmony, whether in one individual or in society as a whole. From its natural position at the centre the Grail influences all around it, like the core of a magnetic field or the code of eternal law at the centre of a perfectly ordered universe.

Spiritual involvement with Glastonbury leads inevitably to the question of the Grail, so it is appropriate here to consider the nature of that elusive talisman. As indicated by the esoteric scholar, René Guénon, it has two principal components, the "primordial vision" and the "primordial tradition". The meaning of this can be found by anyone who chooses to seek it; neither is there any secret about the supreme function of the Grail. It is the way or means by which eyes are opened to recognition of the terrestrial paradise.

All that is generally known about the Grail today is that it is lost. It is indeed so thoroughly lost that its very existence is denied, and only a few people in modern times have acknowledged it. Many of those people have followed tradition in making Glastonbury the centre of their Quest. In the same tradition some have died and been buried there, adding unconsciously to the vast collection of religious bones that gave to medieval Glastonbury its reputation as a 'heavenly sanctuary upon earth'.

Much has been written about the great saints and Christian Fathers who feature in the legends and early histories of Glastonbury Abbey: St. Joseph who founded there the first church in Christendom, St. Patrick its first abbot, St. Gildas the chronicler, St. Brigit of Ireland, St. David of Wales, St. Dunstan the alchemist and a host of royal and religious notables from Celtic and Saxon times. Unknown to history are the countless pilgrims who, having made the Journey to Glastonbury, settled around the sanctuary and continued there to pursue their Quest. Such people's lives are rarely recorded, and those of us today who are attracted by the mystery of Glastonbury are thus deprived of the experiences of our predecessors. We have reason, therefore, to be most grateful to Patrick Benham for filling a gap. The people he describes in this book were not particularly distinguished or widely famous, but their lives and mentalities were all deeply affected by their experience of Glastonbury, and they left their mark upon Glastonbury's ever-evolving legend.

The story begins almost a hundred years ago, when Dr John Goodchild, acting through inner guidance, concealed a mysterious antique vessel in the holy well of St. Bride on the outskirts of Glastonbury. Years later it was rediscovered, and from that event came some very amazing consequences. The development of an era that shaped the future course of esoteric and mystical-religious studies is the subject of Patrick Benham's quietly sympathetic, factual account. He writes as an insider, with deep, personally acquired knowledge of Glastonbury and its 'Avalonian' characters. We are not asked to believe anything, but we are certainly not invited to be sceptical or scornful. These old Glastonbury questers were not - though with the inevitable odd exception - cranks or fanatics, but sensitive, cultured people, whose common aspiration was not towards self-indulgence but to serve the best interests of humanity. They did not always succeed; their story has its share of tragedies and failures, but its overall effect is encouraging and inspiring. Anyone who has had experience of Glastonbury, and is curious about how that experience has been received in the past, will be specially delighted by this book. Those who have not yet been there are forewarned about the spiritual power of the place and its ability to transform the lives of its favoured pilgrims.

Introduction

ALL STORIES ARE INCOMPLETE; something always continues. This is even more true of the Glastonbury story. Why? Because the principal character of that story is the place itself – a point well-noted by John Cowper Powys when he framed his novel *A Glastonbury Romance*. If humankind should ever disappear from the face of this planet, the chances are that some form of this landscape will remain, brooding on the passing impact of the dreaming, foolish biped that once worked and played and sated its appetite for God, or the Gods, within its bounds.

Our Avalonian story is therefore one segment of a larger narrative. We are looking at a period from around the close of the Victorian age through to the early 1970s, by which time most of the original people had gone and the events they had set in train had been assimilated into a new phase of activity.

Inevitably, in the thirteen years since the first publication of this book, and as new facts have emerged, I felt I wanted to revise and re-phrase parts of the text to improve the meaning or give a different emphasis here and there. I am pleased I have now had the opportunity to do that. There is some new material, but enough remains of the original for it still to be essentially the same book, hopefully enhanced. During the same period since 1993, several new books have appeared dealing with some of the people in this account in greater detail. In fact nearly all our characters are now well represented in print apart from Dr John Goodchild and Mary Bligh Bond, and I therefore give that as a reason why the text may seem unduly weighted in favour of information currently unavailable elsewhere, particularly with regard to Dr Goodchild and the story of the blue glass bowl.

I became involved in Glastonbury after an employment opportunity opened up for me in 1969 that chanced to be nearby. It was a time of interest in 'alternative' lifestyles. There was an emphasis on 'small is beautiful', and a desire to get back to human-scale forms of living, to rediscover a sense of *real* community and *real* communication. In the

1970s, Glastonbury seemed just the place where the 'alternative dream' might achieve a measure of realization. To this somewhat vague end, a small group of us started a local magazine called *Torc*.

As we began to feel our way with *Torc*, we soon became aware that another group of people had been drawn to the 'other side' of Glastonbury a couple of generations before. Remarkably, some of them were still available and approachable. One was Kitty Tudor Pole, sister of Major Wellesley Tudor Pole, founder of the Chalice Well Trust. I think she contacted me after someone had told her of the interesting things the 'young people' were doing at Glastonbury. Soon after this, WTP's son David got in touch, and became a frequent and supportive visitor. The more we found out about the past events the more we became very aware that there was little documentation of what had obviously been a critical stage in the unfolding of the latter-day Glastonbury mystique.

During those few years, 1971-75, I collected all sorts of snippets of information - and then sat on them for rather a long time, unsure how I would ever make good use of them.

It was more than ten years before feelings of guilt got the better of me, and I persuaded myself to get down to the task of telling the story of a particular phase of Avalonian history. I had a lot of 'leads', but nothing like enough material to convey a full picture. I had to research, seek out relatives and friends of the subjects of my proposed collective biography - and start writing!

What you will find in these pages is a mixture of the ordinary events of the lives of the people involved in the spiritual rebirth of Avalon in the first thirty years or so of the twentieth century, along with their *ideas*.

It has not been my intention to try to prove or disprove the theories or spiritual claims of anyone in this study. It would be just as unreasonable to try to prove that something was, or was not, a *true* work of art. In fact, much of it occupies a sort of 'borderland' realm between art and the spirit - with political and social repercussions thrown in, to boot. There is no dogma here, but simply an account of people's inner perceptions, their psychic *reality*. They might say that they can see into other planes of existence, other 'dimensions'. We might question their conclusions about what they see, but we cannot deny that, to them, what they have experienced is absolutely real.

Vision and prophecy have always had a respected place in human affairs. It is recognized as a gift even within institutional religion. It is also a field wide open for charlatans to abuse for the exaltation of their own egos - or for material gain. But I can, with a clear conscience, state that I have no reservations whatsoever about the total sincerity of every person whose life comes under scrutiny in this study.

The other predictable insinuation is that all these people who see visions and hear voices must be mad, mentally unstable, seeking some sort of escape from the responsibilities of normal life. Be assured that they were all active in worldly affairs; reasonable, kindly, responsible social beings and in no way psychotic or deluded in the clinical sense.

This book may introduce you for the first time to Dr John Goodchild. It transpires that, in many ways, he is the key figure of the piece. He is less known than most of the others, all but forgotten except for some very small references in Tudor Pole's writings. If nothing else, I hope this account will help to give him his due recognition. I regret that I have neither been able to find a portrait of him nor discover where he went to school. Ironically, my enquiries about his brother, William, were satisfied on both these counts. Unfortunately, they did not share the same place of education.

Certain characters have been omitted on the grounds that they do not quite fit the Avalonian credentials proposed by Dion Fortune! One such is the Rev. Lionel Smithett Lewis, vicar of St. John's, Glastonbury for some thirty years after the Great War. This would seem to make him more of a Glastonburian, as DF described the locals. He is best remembered for his book *St. Joseph of Arimathea at Glastonbury or the Apostolic Church of Britain*. A friend of Bligh Bond, although he did not approve of his psychic activities, he was much respected for his pastoral care of the town over a long period. He was something of a Celtic enthusiast and had a great appreciation of the contribution made to the local community by Alice Buckton, overseeing the erection of the memorial to her inside St. John's church on the south wall just east of the entrance.

In all this we should not forget the townspeople of Glastonbury who have maintained the fabric of the place for generations. How they responded to the ways of the newcomers perhaps depended on their religious allegiance or the extent of their own book-learning. The fairest judgement is that they were divided: some were for, some were against and not a few were indifferent. Rutland Boughton, who suffered opposition to his musical and dramatic activities in the town, reported that it had been "...rather trying to be met with refusals from parents who seek to save 'the eternal souls' of their young from satanic influences of the arts in general, and of the Glastonbury Festival in particular".

My look at the 'New Era' at Glastonbury has been brief and limited to evidences of a continuing Avalonian awareness. Although inevitably very connected with what went before, it is really another story.

CHAPTER ONE

Avalon

T HE NAME AVALON has become associated with Glastonbury to a point beyond question. It is everywhere: in house-names, businesses, a school, and more. It has long had a sort of vague acceptance among the local people as something to do with legend, King Arthur and the Grail and all that sort of thing. But to dig deeper, to try to find out why this is so, or how it happened, is to get into a very complicated area indeed. Perhaps we shouldn't worry. Might we not just as well content ourselves with Avalon as a 'feeling', recognized subjectively as a magical point of fusion between the known and the unknown applied to a small area of semi-rural England?

All places breathe their own atmosphere of destiny, hinting at some future deliverance coloured by a nostalgia for a once-known, but lost, past. Glastonbury's is writ larger than most.

The fact of it all lies in the landscape itself: nature has set the scene to allow our myth-making faculties full rein, opening a gateway, a bridge, to another world.

Every nation has its chief holy place. We can think of Jerusalem in the Middle East, Delphi in Greece, Tara in Ireland. For England it is Glastonbury. The name itself is a thing to conjure with, as John Michell shows in his *New Light on the Ancient Mystery of Glastonbury:*

> "It is possible that the first syllable in 'Glastonbury' derives from an old British word for oak or woad, and it has also been linked with Glasteing, a legendary early settler at Glastonbury... but there is no reason to doubt the obvious explanation, that it is a simple translation from Glastonbury's former Celtic name, Iniswitrin, Isle of Glass or Crystal Isle. A glassy isle is mythologically a place of enchantment. Within it is Caer Wydr, the Glass Castle, and Caer Siddi, the Fairy Fort, also translated as the Spiral Castle. The country where these places are to be found is Annwn, the Celtic land of Faery. In *The Spoils of Annwn*, a poem attributed to the sixth-century Welsh bard, Taliesin, is described how Arthur

sailed there to rob its ruler of his magical, pearl-rimmed cauldron which gave sustenance to all who were worthy of it. This vessel seems to have been an early version of the Holy Grail, and Arthur's quest for it in Annwn foreshadows the location in Christian times of the Grail Quest at Glastonbury."

There is little doubt that Glastonbury was a pagan centre long before it became the prime Christian shrine of the West. In ancient times it was a tidal island, a sea-shore place, and, as Geoffrey Ashe has suggested, may have been venerated as one of the 'Isles of the Dead' from which souls passed on into the other world.

From a distance, the landscape is dominated by the strange conical hill known as the 'Tor'. A lone church tower caps its summit, dedicated, as such places nearly always are, to the Archangel Michael. Apart from the lesser hills scattered round and about, the land westward towards the Bristol Channel is flat as far as the eye can see, the shelf of the Mendips to the north and the less dramatic ridge of the Poldens to the south-west. Near the side of the Tor, set in a well cared-for garden, is the ancient chalybeate spring known as Chalice Well. Water pours from it at all times even in periods of long drought.

Glastonbury itself is ranged around the square of roads which frames the extensive grounds of the ruined Abbey, once the largest and grandest in the country. These days there is nothing 'quaint' about the town. There are supermarkets, filling stations, bookshops, cafés, tourist shops, inns and car-parks. Some eight thousand people live there.

To the west, towards the long-closed railway station and these days intersected by the relief road, runs Benedict Street, passing an ancient church bearing the same dedication. More correctly this should not be Benedict at all, but Benignus, a Celtic personage whose name ought not to have been so blatantly expunged from memory. A half-mile further on, within a system of fields known on old maps simply as 'Bride', is the site of a hermitage and chapel, no longer visible, said to have been occupied by the Irish saint, Bridget, with her community of nuns. Nearby was once a spring known as St. Bride's Well, of which more later. On the southern edge of this area, close to the road leading to the neighbouring shoe-making town of Street, the whale-back shape of Wirral Hill rises up and falls sharply towards the crossing of the River Brue at Pomparles Bridge. This is the 'Weary-all' Hill of the Joseph of Arimathea story, the place where it is said he struck his staff into the ground. This took root, to become the famed Glastonbury 'Holy Thorn' which flowers remarkably every year at Christmas.

It is known that prehistoric settlements existed here. A hundred years ago a local antiquarian, Arthur Bulleid, discovered the foundations of two ancient lake villages, built for security on wooden piles in the sea-marshes a couple of miles or so outside the town.

In more recent times the suggestion has been put forward that the dominant prehistoric culture here was matriarchal – making it pre-eminently a 'goddess' place. This dovetails well with the theory, which we will explore later, that a women's druidic 'college' may have existed at Beckery, on the site of St. Bridget's settlement, in early Celtic times.

There are two linked traditions at Glastonbury. The first is that Christianity came to Britain immediately after the crucifixion, with Glastonbury the chosen site of its foundation. The second is that Glastonbury is the ancient 'Isle of Avalon' where, as legend has it, King Arthur and Queen Guinevere lie buried. The two are connected by the story of the Holy Grail. One tradition has it that the uncle of Jesus, Joseph of Arimathea, brought the Cup of the Last Supper with him to Glastonbury, and disposed of it by either, as some say, burying it on Chalice Hill (near Chalice Well), or delivering it to the safekeeping of a secret priesthood. In time its location was forgotten, and this was deemed the cause of the many misfortunes that befell the Kingdom. In the Arthurian romances, the Quest of the Knights of the Round Table is for the recovery of the vessel leading to the restoration of the Waste-Land to life and fecundity. The trouble is that none of these stories comes into any kind of focus before the chronicles and other literature of the eleventh and twelfth centuries. It is not before this time, either, that there is any reference identifying Glastonbury with Avalon.

There are indications that point to a pagan origin for much of the later, Christianized material. This conclusion need not destroy anything for us if we are primarily apprehending these stories on the level of the 'soul', as atmosphere, as poetry. With Christianity came a sea change, an adjustment of the psyche, collectively and individually, which *extended* but did not demolish, the pagan rapture of the Celtic heart. So, too, the storytelling flowed on the inner currents. There was a new promise of Divine Love, of Transcendent Being, of Deification - but ever the battle with the forces of opposition, of destruction. It is not the place here to discuss the historical complexities of the development of the Glastonbury Arthurian and Avalonian lore, nor is it in my power to do so. The whole ground has already been thoroughly worked over by that greatest of latter-day Avalonians, Geoffrey Ashe, who has lived for more than thirty years in Dion Fortune's former home at the foot of the Tor. In his *King Arthur's Avalon,* all these questions are carefully sifted through and discussed sympathetically at length.

We should hold it as our basic premise that 'Avalon' is something spiritually real and valid, something that can be recognized by those whose destiny it is to travel close to the heart of 'inner' things. We can allow that it has both an identity with the location known as Glastonbury *and* a meaning on a level which transcends it. During the nineteenth century, an awareness gained momentum of what might generally be called 'The Matter of Britain'. Precisely where this revival began, if it had ever wholly died, is debatable. Possibly with certain poets; possibly within certain Masonic, Rosicrucian groups; certainly with William Blake. In his writings Blake foresaw a spiritual destiny for Britain, personified as the giant Albion, and the birth of a new awareness in men and women.

The idea that the sleeping Arthur might return, and that this represented something, took hold. Tennyson was the most notable exponent of the Arthurian myth, and its connection with Glastonbury, in his *Idylls of the King*. There was also a bevy of socialists and 'New Thought' radicals who saw it all as an allegory of the birth of the 'whole man', unexploited and emancipated with nature in useful toil.

This period saw the emergence of new occult and esoteric movements which taught that myth has meaning for our inner evolution. Initially, the impulse was from the East and the Theosophy of Madame Blavatsky, but first with Anna Kingsford, then with Rudolph Steiner, and finally with Dion Fortune, a sense of an indigenous western 'mystery tradition' saw light of day, giving credence to both Pagan and Christian elements.

These developments bore in an interesting way upon aspects of the Celtic revival being witnessed in Ireland and Scotland at that time. While much of this had to do with politics and the overthrow of the English oppressor, there were, within the cultural engine of the endeavour, key figures who were fellow-travellers with our fore-mentioned occultists. We can think here of William Butler Yeats and George William Russell (aka AE) in Ireland, and William Sharp (aka Fiona Macleod), Lewis Spence, Patrick Geddes, and the painter John Duncan in Scotland. All had connections with the Theosophical Society. However, there were qualitative differences between the aspirants in the two countries: Yeats and Russell were prepared to invoke the powers of the Old Gods and heroes to give zeal and inspiration to a call to arms in Ireland, while the Scots preferred to confine themselves to fostering a more pacific spiritual awakening of the ancient Celtic spirit chiefly through the medium of the arts. The Welsh, too, should not be ignored here. Their arising ran on different lines with a highly successful restoration of their language and a reinstatement of the Bardic tradition with the *Eisteddfod* as the focus for its celebration.

Even if perversely, there was a minority in England that found it could easily identify with the developments happening just beyond its borders to the north and west, mindful that it had once itself been a Celtic land in ancient times. We can fairly identify this seeming anomaly as the "English Celtic revival"; if it requires a venue, then we need look no further than Glastonbury, with its green hills and apple-orchards. This is the God-given stage-set on which our *Dramatis Personae* now enter.

CHAPTER TWO

The Doctor

THE HEALTH OF THE POPULATION in Victorian England was not good. Tuberculosis and pneumonia were rife, and often terminal, and not confined to the poorer classes. With the onset of winter the misery increased. Those who could afford it made their escape to the Mediterranean coast of France and Italy. By November its villas and guest-houses were well-stocked with ailing expatriates. It was a self-contained community, preferring the services of its own kind to those of its hosts. English medics were in much demand.

Dr John Arthur Goodchild made the journey south for some thirty years to his lucrative winter practice in the Italian resort of Bordighera. He saw the season through and then returned to spend the summer in England. He usually passed this time at his father's home at Hampstead, London. After the death of his father he became a regular guest at the Francis Hotel, Queen Square, Bath.

It was the pattern of his whole working life. Immediately after qualifying in 1873 he began his first term of service at Cannes, on the French Riviera. Here the authorities were becoming resentful of the increasing numbers of foreign doctors in business on their soil. Goodchild explained the position in the following despatch which appeared in the British Medical Journal for January, 1877:

"In the midst of the floods at home, the members of the British Medical Association maybe glad to know that we have had a sample of English rainy weather upon the French Riviera, the rainfall being the heaviest known for some years past; still the weather, if not quite equal to that of San Remo and Alassio, beyond the Italian frontier, has been on the whole warm and enjoyable, and many very serious cases have greatly benefited by the climate since their arrival. Nice has, I believe, been freer than usual from typhoid fever this year, and I have only heard of one case amongst the English residents; but there has been a good deal of wind there, and, on one occasion, the sea rose so high as to wash away the seats on the Promenade des Anglais… Probably these French health-resorts will present a very altered appearance next year, if the present Bill for excluding English practitioners be brought forward; for English consultants will naturally resent the insult, and send their patients on to San Remo, Bordighera, and Alassio, a proceeding they can indulge in with easy consciences, as the climate is better, and the *mistral* less deadly on the Italian Riviera."

True to these expectations, the next winter found the doctor working from Bordighera. Not that he had moved all that far; the Italian shoreline is continuous with the French, passing on its way the little principality of Monaco, with its gambling haven at Monte Carlo. From the Italian side the white casino could be seen sun-lit beneath the giant headland.

However good his reputation in the Italian resort, Dr Goodchild had talents and interests far beyond his professional responsibilities. He was fascinated by all manner of antiquarian and mystical subjects. He was the author of several volumes of poetry, drama and prose. When his collection of poems, *Somnia Medici,* was published in 1884, even the great Tennyson was impressed: "I judge these poems to be the work of one who is far more than a mere follower of my own."

The mythic realm was never far below the surface of Goodchild's creative work. Even in his own life there were times when unseen forces seemed to be shaping the course of events. Never was this more so than in an episode which had its fairly insignificant beginnings in Bordighera in the February of 1885. An artist friend of his reported finding two unusual glass objects in a tailor's shop down on the Marina. He described them as a 'bowl' and a 'platter'. Feeling curious, Goodchild accompanied his friend back to the shop. It was more the shallow bowl that drew his attention. It was quite primitive, yet some skill must have been involved, for within the glass was a silver leaf pattern of interlining blue, green and amber floral designs.

Having little knowledge of glassware, he was unable to judge its age or place of origin. Perhaps a forgery? Glass making was a traditional craft in Italy; copies were often being made of antique glass. According to the tailor, the objects had been found bricked-up within the walls of an old building which was being demolished in a vineyard which his father had bought at Albenga, a village between Bordighera and Genoa. Interesting finds had been made there before. Goodchild knew it as the site of an early Christian settlement, having a church dating no later than the fourth century. Accepting that these seemed to be genuinely old articles, he agreed to buy them.

Not long after this, with the winter season over, Dr Goodchild packed the bowl and the dish among his effects and made the customary journey back to London. Once there, he showed the bowl to his father, who became quite excited and seemed convinced that it was a vessel of some significance. He felt the need for an informed judgement on it as soon as possible. He sent his son off to see Sir Augustus Franks, Keeper of British and Medieval Antiquities at the British Museum, an expert on glass, who had at one time overseen the work of Italian craftsmen, brought to England to make copies of antique ware.

Disappointingly, Franks' findings were inconclusive. The vessel bore no resemblance to any known example. He did feel that it was probably ancient, as there were no modern craftsmen capable of understanding the special process by which it seemed to have been manufactured.

For the Goodchilds there was at least some comfort in the suggestion of an origin in antiquity. For the time being they laid the matter to rest: the bowl and the dish were locked away in a cupboard in the father's house, where they remained for some ten years.

As a single man Goodchild had more time at his disposal than others of his profession with domestic and family responsibilities. It would have been impractical for a man with a wife and children to have a summer address in one country and a winter one in another, let alone pursue a whole range of additional interests. The attractions of this nomadic life may have kept Goodchild a bachelor. He found time to exercise himself in writing fiction, poems and a play, even while continuing in his medical work.

There was one item in his creative output which drew specifically on his working experience in Italy. *Chats at Sant' Ampelio* charts the course of the formidably undramatic after-dinner discussions of a group of winter emigrés in an Italian villa. The characters must have had their models among the typical types that Goodchild found around him. There is the Narrator, a doctor - ostensibly Goodchild himself, but much more one-dimensional. Also on hand are: the Rhymer; the Chaplain; the Socialist - his credibility flawed by his dependence on the income from invested capital; the Hostess, and her younger Sister. It must be pretty well all fiction, but quite good fun in its way, and not nearly as dull as this brief account might suggest. Goodchild writes well and can hold the reader's interest. He uses this convivial frame-work to float what are, patently, some of his own ideas and theories. His Socialist, for example, expounds for a whole chapter on his grounds for believing that there were early civilizing contacts between Middle

Eastern seafarers and the people of Britain and Ireland. This runs close
to the opening theme of his later work *The Light of the West*, and also
parallels many points raised by the Irish film maker Bob Quinn in his
book *Atlantean*, published nearly a hundred years later.*
Chats at Sant' Ampelio first appeared in 1888, and did well enough
to be published again in 1890, bound in one volume with its sequel
The Sage of Sant' Ampelio.

Goodchild's *Sage* turns out to be yet another of the visitors, but
distinguished by owning his own property. He is accorded this title, not
by dint of any special knowledge, but more as 'one who has discovered
the equilibrium of life'. He manifests a kind of down-to-earth spirituality. For him, communion with God is a day-to-day affair. Each ordinary
meal is held to be taken in the spirit of community with his fellow men
and God:

> "Your friend (the Chaplain) reverences the bread and wine which he
> consecrates. I hold that the same respect is due to all our food, being the
> common food of God and man, and God's gift to man as a needful part
> of the temporal life which he has given..."

The Doctor visits the Sage with greater frequency as the old man faces
his last days. There is much searching between them on the question of
the after-life. The Sage, or Mr Logan, as he is called, confesses that he
has revised his childhood dream of a heaven where he and all others
might be equally happy and at rest:

> "That great and terrible division which weighed heavily upon me as
> a child, has no terrors for me now. I see that in such a heaven as I then
> pictured, I should have suffered annihilation, and that some new exis-
> tence would stand in my place. I think that I shall be suffered to remain
> myself, and shall have duties to perform in my new shape of existence for
> which I have been but imperfectly prepared by my life here. Some will
> be more perfect than myself, some less so. Some of us, no doubt, will be,
> with Christ, subject to no further death. That means heaven, as I once
> held it; and as I fancy it now, it means a moral existence in which time
> and matter, as our learned know it chemically and physically, can have
> no part. Some of us will be unfit for this heaven in which death and Hades
> have no portion. They have fitted themselves by animalism, or unbelief,
> or self-seeking, for a further temporal and material existence only."

---

*Quinn also makes a rare reference to the work of John Foster Forbes, friend of Mary Bligh Bond.

In spite of its reference to Christ, the foregoing leans towards the Eastern doctrine of Karma. In this the soul is held to have to endure a succession of many earthly lives until it frees itself by righteous action. The reconciliation of such ideas with the Christian belief in redemption is common to many occult and theosophically-inclined groups in the West. Goodchild may be using his 'Sage' to pronounce his own opinions, which could have come to him through contact with some kind of esoteric teaching, or perhaps by way of his interest in the Greeks and the philosophy of Plato.

There is a further example in the following verse, presented as having been found among Mr Logan's papers after his demise.

THE BRETHREN

Jesus, Thy brethren, sons with Thee
Of Life which was and is to be
Who fain would sit to left and right,
Of Thee upon thy throne of light;
May this be theirs? Shall some, found just,
Clothed yet again with mortal dust,
Live perfect; die once more to save
Young brethren spirits from the grave,
For orbs which now to mortal ken
Are many as the sons of men?
Shall those that live obedient here,
And live the love which casts out fear,
Walk yonder 'neath Thy crown of thorn,
The Christs of planets yet unborn,
Which far beyond our thought extend,
For service of Life's endless end?

What we have here are three questions which beg to be accepted as possible fact. The saving power of Christ is perceived as a dynamic requisite of every inhabited body in the greater universe, to be called forth a myriad times again and again, to infinity. Those who fulfil the spiritual demands of our present dispensation will rise and share with Christ the Sonship of God, and from that estate find themselves appointed Redeemers of worlds yet to exist. The reincarnationalist element is again implied here, but with a new twist.

Goodchild was an original thinker. There is a characteristic piece in *The Sage of Sant' Ampelio* called 'The College of St. Sophia'. This

'College' is no less than the School of Life: a spiritual and intellectual complex of everything mankind has built up over the past ages. Human weakness and folly are there too. It is a fantasy, full of light-hearted comment on serious matters. Rooms and halls exist to serve every known discipline, philosophy or creed; but the students, representing ourselves, typically fail to take up all the opportunities for knowledge available to them: "Most are idle, and learn little; but all take something away which *may* be of use to them in their future career."

The 'Department of Moral Pathology' is the most curious, bordering on the surreal with its display of preserved hearts. Among the exhibits are the hearts of all the most famous and significant people who have ever lived, as well as examples from different races and cultures reaching back into prehistory. There are even what he calls the 'Autobiographical Preparations' - hearts which have been dissected by their former owners. Most of these only exhibit the best side of their hearts, the ventricular side, dealing with purified blood.

"What a firm-fibred, little, rotund heart is John Bunyan's; and what a mere bladder, from dilation, is Byron's! I can see right through the latter whenever I pass it. Shelley's, though terribly thin in places, is much better constructed as a whole. Perhaps the heart which shows the least sign of disease here, as in the Biblical Series, is that of St. John."

So much for the 'College'. Let us take just one more extract from *The Sage of Sant' Ampelio*. The authentic voice of Goodchild the doctor comes through here, and the quality of the writing shows up well. This is from the chapter, 'The Passing of the Sage'. The old man is nearing his end:

"There was something weird either in the garden that night or in my own fancy, when the dying man slept on so peacefully; and I, healthy and in my usual strength, stood almost afraid to move in chill night air, beholding nothing, save, as it were, the skeletons of trees, which yet lived and would show themselves covered in foliage ere the sun-rising. I cannot analyse my thoughts sufficiently to set them down here; but I felt myself more under the oppression of the mystery of death than I have often done in my life, or than I did in the quiet room above."

There is worth in these literary pieces, but today hardly anyone knows anything about them - or much else about Goodchild himself for that matter. It is only through his Glastonbury connection that he is remembered at all, and then only in passing. Nevertheless, he had quite a few works published. In 1890 a tale called *A Fairy Godfather* came out, followed by two more in 1893: *Tales in Verse* and *Lyrics*.

The following letter to the editor of the *Review of Reviews* shows him keen not to pass over the chance of a good notice in the right place.

23 Thurlow Rd
Hampstead
July 16th

Dear Sir
I fancy that the little copy of *Lyrics* which I mentioned when I called at your office may not have reached you. The *Review of Reviews* was certainly upon the Publisher's list, and I will see that another copy is forwarded if they failed to send it.

Yours very sincerely
J. A. Goodchild

The critical journal named here was started in 1890 by William Thomas Stead, a powerful and influential figure of the times. He was a journalist and author who saw fit to expose the many injustices of society wherever he found them. He was a leading light in the peace movement of the day - a stand which generated much opposition towards him in Establishment circles. From 1893 he also edited *Borderland*, a periodical devoted to psychic matters. His *Letters from Julia* (1897) were said to have been dictated by the departed spirit of a young American woman whom he had known shortly before her death. He met his own end on that fateful day, 15 April 1912, bound for New York on the maiden voyage of the *Titanic*. He was last seen by survivors helping women and children to make their escape from the vessel.

Another illuminatus of the London scene known to Goodchild was the Canadian-born scientist and novelist Grant Allen. Much of what he wrote was social satire and he was a strong upholder of women's rights. Around 1895/6 his nephew Grant Richards was working for Stead on the *Review of Reviews*. The following note may well relate to Goodchild's verse-drama *The Two Thrones*, which appeared in 1895.

(dated Sept. 24, Hampstead; no year)

Dear Sir
Mr Grant Allen has invited me to send you a copy of a work in which he
and Mrs Grant Allen have been kind enough to interest themselves, and
of which the present complete edition will be issued early next month.

Yours sincerely
J. A. Goodchild

Goodchild wrote again to Richards on October 25, from Casa Eldreda,
Bordighera, enclosing an original verse. This gives some idea of the
time when he normally made the move south to Italy.

Throughout these years, alongside his undoubted concern for his
patients' wellbeing and his efforts to promote his own literary offerings,
Dr Goodchild became preoccupied with a much larger quest: to seek
out the true roots of the spiritual life of the West.

Much had been made in those days of the notion of the 'Mystic
East'. Numerous anecdotes and 'strange tales' arising out of the British
Imperial experience, together with the emergence of the Theosophical
Society in England in the 1880s, helped to fuel the myth. The West
languished in a material darkness while the East shone with wisdom
and spirituality. The idea still persists.

While some happily abandoned themselves totally - robes and all -
to Orientophilia, a good few of the seekers after the deeper things of life
found themselves struck with an identity crisis which they alleviated by
returning to ponder upon the rich harvest of spiritual lore available,
so to speak, in their own back yard. Perhaps the first was Dr Anna
Kingsford, who spurned the Himalayan Masters said to inspire the
writings of Madame Blavatsky, and went off with a section of the London
Theosophical Society to form the Hermetic Society as a platform for
her esoteric reappraisal of Christianity and classical mythology. Clearly
they all felt more at home operating within the continuum of their own
tradition. Others later followed, moving into magical groups, such as
The Hermetic Order of the Golden Dawn, or that curious amalgam of
Theosophy and liturgical ritualism, the Liberal Catholic Church.

The appeal of the East lay in its open tradition of techniques
designed to lift the individual consciousness out of a hostile environment where a merciless sun beat down on lives often cut short by
famine and disease. Where such practices existed in the West, they had
largely been the prerogative of small, often secret, underground groups,

and as such easily forgotten. Dr Goodchild sensed that there were many lost gems of inspiration and enlightenment awaiting rediscovery in the Western world, and he was wise enough not to overlook the heart of the Christian tradition in his researches.

From his copious reading of ancient manuscripts and modern commentaries on early texts, a pattern was coming into focus. Ireland figured more and more in his investigations. Everything pointed to a high culture existing there even before the coming of Christianity. Drawing from these sources he embarked on a new work, to be called *The Light of the West*.

CHAPTER THREE

The Light of the West

ONCE THE IDEAS ON HIS NEW THEME were worked out, Dr Goodchild began to organize them into a form suitable for publication. It was quite a task, but he still found time to put out just one final item in verse, which he called *The Book of Tephi* (1897).

At this point it would be well to consider the essential character of the thoughts that played through his mind as he went about his everyday duties. The spiritual forces which he tapped in his enquiry into ancient beginnings could be very pervasive and compelling. His historical perspectives had an archetypal quality that readily harmonized with the powers and attributes of the individual psyche. He perceived that ancient Ireland had been the centre of a cult venerating the female aspect of the Deity. This found its embodiment in the person of the High Queen, or Mor Rigan, whose memory has only passed down to us in corrupted form as a supernatural denizen of the battlefield. She was a real person, not just a mythic figure. At least, that was Goodchild's contention. It was not a view likely to be acceptable to academic historians, but that didn't bother him too much. Neither was it all fantasy without proper scholarship. Far from it; he made some telling observations about the machinations of the Celtic church to subvert the growing Roman influence in its midst. His references were substantial and accurate. Yet ultimately what he was formulating was a spiritual story. He believed that the occult lore surrounding the High Queen and her cult became attached to the figure of Bride, the poetic embodiment of the Gaelic folk-soul in legend and bardic teaching.

The people of Bride prophesied and anticipated the coming of Christ. Goodchild held that her mysteries were known throughout the ancient world even as far as the Holy Land. It was no accident, therefore, that the Christian message was carried to the islands of Britain soon after the crucifixion, along with certain relics. It was understood that here was the truest and most proper ground on which to sow the seeds of the new faith. Goodchild believed that it was ordained that the two should be conjoined: the High Queen and her teaching 'as to Woman' with Christ in His aspects of both 'Child' and 'Man'. He deemed the union successful in so far as it found its expression in the Celtic Church up to the time of St. Columba, in the sixth century. Thereafter it suffered a decline in the face of disputes from within and the effects of the proselytizing endeavours of the Church of Rome.

Now what happened next can be looked at in two ways - either Goodchild had become so heady and 'book-happy' that his ideas had got hold of him and taken on a life of their own, or his labours on *The Light of the West* had suitably prepared his mind for use as an instrument of higher and spiritually progressive forces.

It was 1897. The manuscript was with the publishers, and the book due to be available to the public some time the following year. In the autumn Dr Goodchild set off once again for Italy, breaking the journey at Paris, staying at the Hotel St. Petersbourg.

He was no stranger to psychic experiences, occasionally having the power to see and hear things on a paranormal level. This usually occurred during sleep, in a dream. But here, in his hotel room, he was quite awake when he experienced something far stronger and more defined than anything he had known before.

The first intimation of anything unusual happening to him came as a sudden feeling of paralysis - he was immobilized, quite unable to get up. He then started hearing a strange disembodied voice giving him instructions in a rather commanding tone. It seemed familiar; he fancied he had heard it before, some while back, in a dream. That time it had been more argumentative, and he had been able to answer back, even getting it to make concessions on his behalf. Now, however, he was powerless to act against its specific directions. Although afterwards he could not recall everything that was said word for word, he remembered the sense of the instructions very fully.

It started by referring to the cup in his father's possession, indicating that the vessel had once been carried by Jesus, and that as the question of a Jesus-Cup had occupied people's minds so much in the past century, it had been resolved to produce it openly so that through it certain facts about the life of Jesus might be known. Also, it was to be a powerful influence in shaping the thought of the century to come.

The voice then told him that he would have to take the cup to Bride's Hill, an area known as the Woman's Quarter, at Glastonbury, Somerset, as soon as possible after his father's death, but not until further instructions were given. Ultimately, it should end up in the care of a woman, as women were not bound to keep its secrets in the way that men were. He remembered just the closing words: "Later, a young girl will make a pure offering of herself at the spot where you lay down the Cup, and this shall be a sign unto you."

The message ended. The speaker had been unseen, but at the end of the address Goodchild was aware of a rosy light around him which condensed itself into an oval form, palpitating with brighter golden sparklets above his head. It gave the sensation of a kind of electrical warmth to the touch, and moved off towards the window, only to disappear as he tried to follow it.

After a day or so, he moved on to Bordighera to resume his winter commitments, with the memory of the strange visitation still very much in mind.

As it happened, a few weeks later news came from England that his father had died. Quite possibly Goodchild was unable to get to the funeral, as we know, from his own account, that he sent for his sister to bring the 'bowl' and the 'platter' to him in Italy. That was in the spring of 1898. He kept the Cup (Goodchild and others have always awarded it a capital 'C' when written) but sent the dish, according to certain 'instructions', to a prominent Italian family - one report suggests to a member of the Garibaldi family. For the while, he had to bide his time regarding the business of getting to Glastonbury and Bride's Hill.

Meanwhile *The Light of the West* had appeared. Whatever significance we now like to attach to the work, it seems that it made little impression at the time. Falling as it did between an argument in favour of the virtues of spiritual womanhood and an appraisal of the early history of Ireland, it addressed itself to an uncertain readership.

The book follows a chronological outline. It opens with an account of the various waves of settlement in Ireland, according a historical status to the supposed mythical tribes of the Nem-idh, Firbolgs and Dannites (the Tuatha De Danann). The key is with the Dannites, under the secular and spiritual leadership of their High Queen. From her cult stemmed all the druidic and bardic teaching of Britain. She was the embodiment of wisdom, the all-sustaining one, the source of all knowledge. With the eclipse of the Celtic Church, Christianity became the adversary of the Old Faith. Lest we question the truth of his scheme, Goodchild is at pains to show that any remembrance of the old order was deliberately distorted and obscured for political and theological purposes over many centuries. Even the bards disguised the stories for their own preservation. The bountiful nature of the High

Queen is given in an old tale in which she is described as a 'black-maned heifer', known as Glas Gounach in Connacht:

> "Glas Gounach travelled three provinces of Erin everyday, and gave milk to everyone on her journey each day; no matter how large the vessels were that people brought, or how many, she filled them. She was sent to give food and comfort to all; and she gave it, but especially to poor people."

According to Goodchild, even the High Queen herself was separated in the 'revised' stories, away from her own people, renamed Cessair, and relegated to the time before the Flood.

The chief centre of religion was at Grellach Dollaid, north-west of Tara, the site of the High Queen's funeral games. As the earthly representative of the Queen of Heaven, her psalms and speeches were venerated, even by Christians, in the sayings of Amerghein. This was a concealed identity, as Amerghein was a man, the name having been mutated by stages from Mor Rigan, through Mur Rigan (Sea Queen) and Murghein (Sea Birth), to Am-er-ghein (the marvellous child of Am). The embodiment of God, imminent in all things, was known as AM, or, the Mystery of Amerghein. This was poeticized in such references as: "AM is the rushing of the wild beast; AM is the Wisdom (Eo or Salmon) which dwelleth in deep waters."

The book progresses from the pagan to the Christian era. The story is one of the old and the new faiths blending happily together. Many priests were also druids, with no conflict in their ministry. Many teachers went out from Ireland across the continent of Europe and beyond, preaching a form of Christianity strongly imbued with the mysteries of Erin. Goodchild points to their influence on such individuals as Simon Magus, Hermas Pastor, and the writers of St. John's Gospel and the Revelation of John. Of the writings of the fourth century Welsh heretic Pelagius, he considers that "enough remains to show that he understood Our Lord's teaching as to children, and that of the High Queen as to women."

The Celtic Church reached its highest point with St. Columba in the sixth century. He is shown to be thoroughly Christian while still protecting the older mysteries:

> "Columba himself, both in right of his royal birth and his extensive learning, was probably more initiated into the mysteries of the Prime Story of Ireland than any, except those to whom their maintenance was

primarily entrusted... And even in his day the higher religious tenets were matters for the instructed alone. The introduction of Roman custom by Adamnan in the century following that ruled by Ireland's greatest native saint did not for several centuries put a stop to the private harmonising of the older faith with Christianity even in the monasteries. In fact, it evidently existed amongst individual monks long after the Synod of Cashel, 1160, put an outward finish to the work inaugurated by Adamnan, nearly five hundred years earlier. Later on, the cruelties of Elizabeth's governors and the unworthiness of most of the reformed episcopate, did much to render the external conformity of the Celtic Churches with that of Rome an inward reality."

Columba, of course, eventually moved on to found his monastic community on the Scottish island of Iona, in the heartland of the Gaelic-speaking people who have preserved so many memories of Bride. Goodchild quotes the tale in which she is *Muime Criosd*, or the Foster-Mother of Christ, as retold by the Scottish writer Fiona Macleod. This story offers itself as a clear allegory of the bringing together of the two faiths. Bride is portrayed as nourishing the infant Jesus at her breast. In another tale she is cast as the midwife at his birth.

The Light of the West is not just a history book; it seeks to restore the female element in all life. Goodchild sums it up:

"The Light of the West is the beauty of womanhood. It inculcates the hatred of warfare, and of empires established by the greed of nations or rulers. It preaches woman's desire for the empire of love. Let man, indeed, be manly in the defence of wife and child; but if uncalled to such warfare, let him apply himself to God and his works. God will give him out of such knowledge defence, and if he wrong no man, empire also."

The book also offers us a small clue about Goodchild's early upbringing. There is an allusion to his Buckinghamshire nanny teaching him and the other children of the family the 'names of their toes'. From the smallest these were: Eeny Peeny, Para Ludy, Lady Whistle, Loddy Whostle, and the Great Odurman Dod. He suggests that the last three correspond to Lady Waeshael, Lord Waeshael and the Great Ealdorman God, Saxon translations of the Celtic Bith, Ith and Amith. As to the first two, they might be addressed to the babe as 'Little being, little soul, prepare your praise.' In light of the fact that Goodchild's mother unfortunately died when he was eight, the nanny must have had a special significance for him. It seems he went to live with his maternal grandmother in the town of Buckingham while the rest of the family remained with his surgeon father in Ealing. Possibly this loss had a bearing on his subsequent preoccupation with spiritual womanhood.

Goodchild's later thought and activities cannot be satisfactorily understood without some knowledge of the themes proposed in *The Light of the West*. To that end we have made our brief excursion through its contents. There now remained the matter of getting to Glastonbury with the Cup.

It was August before he eventually journeyed to fulfil this crucial part of his mission. With the help of an old map he managed to locate the spot just outside the town known as Bride's Hill, or the Woman's Quarter, at Beckery*. As with all things to do with Bride, the name is taken to refer to St. Bridget of Kildare. But the Irish saint was only a later heir to the traditions of Bride, from whom she took her name. There are several forms: Bridget in England; Bride in the Western Isles; Brigid in Ireland. Nevertheless, we often find St. Bride in England, including here at Glastonbury.

Dr Goodchild remained in Glastonbury for three weeks before he got any indication of what he had to do. Then, early in the morning of the first Monday in September, he was awoken from his sleep by the sound of a voice urging him to get up and take the Cup with him.

Before long he was making his way across the fields to the west of the railway station, the voice still offering its calm, firm directions. He arrived at the well, knowing with certainty that he had to conceal the Cup within its murky waters. He achieved this by lodging it in a hollow beneath a stone. The deed done, he returned to the town. The destiny of the object was out of his hands - at least in so far as it was no longer in his physical care.

From now on the doctor's annual summer itinerary would include a pilgrimage to this spot - an observance duly carried out each year from 1899 until 1906, apart from 1905. Each time he went there he must have wondered what kind of sign he might ever be given to fulfil the prophecy of his unseen guide. Yet for most of those years he strongly suspected that the Cup was no longer there. This fear arose during his visit in 1900, when he was perplexed to find that the well had been thoroughly cleared out, presumably by a farmer or land drainage workers. He could find no trace of the vessel in the place where he had left it. Undaunted, he still had faith in its destiny, even if it had been taken somewhere else. It was a matter of watching and waiting.

---

*In recent years this historical place has been under threat from development. On April 28 2005, a group called Friends of Bride's Mound successfully purchased part of the site. They are working to save and protect the rest of it. See their website: **www.friendsofbridesmound.com**

CHAPTER FOUR

Kindred Spirits

D R GOODCHILD WAS LOOKING AHEAD to new things. He had done all that seemed necessary regarding the Cup, and *The Light of the West* was now in the public domain. It had been his intention to produce another book exploring the European aspect of his Irish investigations. For some reason this plan never materialized; but even so, the year 1899 found him pursuing a likely line of enquiry in that direction.

A trip to Rome from his winter base at Bordighera gave him the chance to investigate the recently discovered ruins of the palace of the Roman Senator Pudens, reputed to have been a sanctuary for the first apostolic emissaries from the Holy Land. According to the *Epigrams* of the pagan writer Martial, Pudens had had a Christian wife called Claudia. It was also recorded that their children were raised as Christians in the company of the Apostles. Goodchild felt there were good reasons for believing that this Claudia might be the daughter of the defeated British king Caractacus (Caradoc), exiled with his family to Rome. His son Linus had been consecrated first Bishop of the first Church in Rome at the hands of St. Paul. The British connection here obviously appealed to Goodchild. Caractacus was of the Silurian Royal Family that held sway over territories which included the religious centre at Glastonbury. Eventually Caractacus and his family were pardoned and allowed to go free, some choosing to remain while others returned to Britain.

If the Matriarchal-Druidic centre at Glastonbury had assimilated a form of Christian teaching very soon after the Crucifixion, then might not Claudia have been a Christian even before being taken to Rome? It was an appealing theory, but so far the evidence was lacking.

In the grounds of the Palace of Pudens was the Church of St. Pudenziana, dedicated to Pudentiana, one of the martyred daughters of Claudia and Pudens. In the apse of the church Goodchild found something rather intriguing. Unfortunately the light was not good at the time, but he was able to make out a mosaic portraying a group of the earliest Christians in Rome. The view from the body of the church was unsatisfactory. It was prohibited to enter the area right in front of the mosaic; neither was it possible to gain access to a good vantage point on a balcony as both of these had to be approached through the adjacent buildings of a community of nuns. Even clerics had to apply to the Holy See for permission to go there.

Time was short. He was only in the church for a few minutes on this occasion. He concluded that what he saw there might well be a representation of Claudia in her role as Church-Mother in the company of her children and Christ and the Apostles. Some of the symbolic images, particularly that of a dove, impressed him greatly. It was only in later years that he began to build a really substantial theory on the basis of this possible evidence. We will return to that in due course.

The Celtic revival in the arts did not escape him. It had been going on for some years and inevitably drew his sympathy. Scottish, Welsh and Irish writers and artists of the Celtic 'fringe' were all asserting themselves boldly in the quest for a modern identity against the threat of an Anglo-Saxon cultural and political hegemony. It was an uprising of the soul that was mostly victorious and certainly left the world the better for it.

Among the writers was one with whom Dr Goodchild felt very much in accord. This was Fiona Macleod, already mentioned in connection with *The Light of the West*. Convinced that they shared a common muse, he sent her a copy of the book. A reply was forthcoming:

Edinburgh, 1898

My Dear Sir

I have to thank you very cordially for your book and the long and interesting letter which accompanied it. It must be to you also that I am indebted for an unrevised proof-copy of *The Light of the West*.

Everything connected with the study of the Celtic past has an especial and deep interest for me, and there are few if any periods more significant than that of the era of St. Columba. His personality has charmed me, in the old and right sense of the word 'charm': but I have come to it, or it to me, not through books (though of course largely through Adamnan) so much as through a knowledge gained partly by reading, partly by legendary lore and hearsay, and mainly by much brooding on these, and on every known saying and record of Colum, in Iona itself. When I wrote certain of my writings (e.g. *Muime Chriosd* and *The Three Marvels of Iona*) I felt rightly or wrongly, as though I had in some measure become interpretive of the spirit of 'Colum the White'.

Again, I have long had a conviction - partly an emotion of the imagination, and partly a belief insensibly deduced through a hundred
avenues of knowledge and surmise - that out of Iona is again to come a
Divine Word, that Iona, the little northern isle, will be as it were the
tongue in the mouth of the South.

Believe me, sincerely yours
Fiona Macleod

The exchanges continued. In November 1900 Goodchild wrote
congratulating her on her short drama *The Immortal Hour*. But along
with his praise he felt moved to warn her of the danger he perceived
in the kind of beauty she was seeking. She replied:

Nov. 15 1900

Dear Dr Goodchild
I am glad that you have found pleasure in *The Immortal Hour*. I wonder if
you interpret the myth of Midir and Etain quite differently, or if you,
too, find in Midir the symbol of the voice of the other world; and what
you think of Dalua, the Fool, here and elsewhere. Your earnest letter,
written in spiritual comradeship, has been read by me again and again. I
do not say that the warning in it is not justified, still less that it is not
called for: but, on the other hand, I do not think I follow you aright. Is
it something in *The Immortal Hour* (or in *The Divine Adventure* or more
likely *The Dominion of Dreams*) that impelled you to write as you did: or
something seemingly implied, or inferred by you?...

We seldom know how or where we really stand, or the mien and
aspect we unwittingly bear to the grave eyes of the gods. Is it the lust of
knowledge, of Hidden Things, of the Delight of the World, or the
magic of Mother Earth, of the Flesh - to one or all - that you allude?
The matter touches me most intimately.

You have (I had almost said mysteriously, but why so, for it would be
more mysterious if there were no secret help in spiritual comradeship)
helped me at more than one juncture in my life...

Most sincerely
Fiona Macleod

Goodchild would have read *The Immortal Hour* in its original form in the *Fortnightly Review*. At the time it seemed one small item among many others in the output of Fiona Macleod. Ultimately it became the best known by far, after the great popularity of its musical setting by the composer Rutland Boughton. It took London by storm in the 1920s, receiving 216 consecutive performances. Yet the first production was a much more modest affair with a cast mostly of dedicated amateurs. They gave the music-drama its first public performance in 1914 in Glastonbury. The outline plot is uncomplicated:

Weaving in and out of the tale is the strange and terrible dark-cloaked figure of Dalua, the Fairy Fool, enemy of reason and bringer of madness. He seems to be manipulating the fates of the other characters in the drama. The King of Ireland, Eochaidh, finds Etain, a fay princess caught up in the mundane world, sheltering in the primitive cabin of the hunter Manus and his wife Maive. He woos her and takes her as his bride to his castle. One night a stranger, Midir, a prince from the Other World, enters the castle and challenges Eochaidh to a chess game. Midir outplays Eochaidh and wins the right to kiss the hand of Etain. She falls under his spell and he reveals to her that he has come to return her to her rightful home in the Land of Youth. They depart, leaving Eochaidh pleading with Dalua for the dream-life he has lost. Dalua answers with the touch of Death.

Goodchild's reply to Miss Macleod's letter brought with it a hint of male gallantry - a helping hand 'from the opposite side [of] the spring'. It also gives an indication of the different quality of spiritual aspiration between the doctor and the dramatist. FM is more backward-looking and melancholic while Dr G. seeks to progress forward into light and redemption. Disquiet over this must be at the root of Goodchild's warning in his previous letter. As to FM's suggestion that Dr G. had helped her 'at more than one juncture' in her life, that must remain as unanswerable as it is enigmatic. Goodchild returned more thoughts on *The Immortal Hour:*

Bordighera
Nov. 19 1900

My Dear Miss Macleod
I left one or two of your questions unanswered in my last. I am no Celtic scholar. It was your 'Prayer of the Women' which suggested to me first how far you might feel for your sisters, and how far you might journey to find succour...
A woman who gazes into Columba's Well and sees how far the

bubbles burst on its surface, needs all her own wisdom lest she be dizzy, and a hand held out from the opposite side the spring may help her gaze more steadily. *Midhir*, I believe to be the same as the oriental *Mitherd*, the Recipient of Light, and its translator in the *Midhc-Myth*, a voice from the 'Otherworld' as you say, but the wearer of the Mitre, speaking not from the *Under*world, but the *Upper*world i.e. He is a High Priest speaking in the full light of the Sun.

Etain is difficult, and my own ideas by no means formulated. I merely suggest that ere your Etain was born, her name typified the strong hope of the singer, his immortality, his knowledge that the Sun not merely creates but re-creates in renewed beauty.

If you remember Cairbre, the son of Etain, you may also remember those other Ethainn who sung before the Ark in a far country. The Father is put on one side for the Mother, by the singer, the Mother for the Bride. Even Milton, puritan though he was, must invoke a woman to the aid of 'adventurous song' and is careful not to change the sex when in the Muse of Sinni and Silva is seen the Spirit of the Creator.

As regards Dalua, I know nothing of him by name except what you yourself have written. Is there any connection between the name and Dala (the Celtic) which is sometimes found in company with Brat and Death, in your Celtic genealogies?

At the same time I have dimly guessed all my life how folly might be better than the wisdom of wise men, and remembering dimly how much wiser I was myself as a child than after I had grown up, I have incessantly desired a return to that state of childish thought, and tried to learn from children, when I had the chance, the secrets of their folly which carried them so near to divinity, if they were not hurried away from their vision by those around them.

JAG

And so the correspondence went on between them. Yet they never met - and meeting would have been difficult. With Fiona Macleod things were not as they seemed to be. Even Goodchild at the time of these early letters had no knowledge of the truth about the writer for whom he had such regard. The fact was that there was no Fiona Macleod at all in the literal sense. 'She' was the skilfully guarded alias of the Scottish writer and literary critic William Sharp. Pseudonyms are common enough, but this one was different. It came out of an inner necessity: out of a need for Sharp to take on an alternative identity when creating in a certain deeply reflective mode. Even in his earlier working life when he was concentrating his best efforts on sharpening his critical and analytical faculties, there were moments when a more intimate emotional self would overwhelm him, sweeping aside all conscious control. At these times he found he could write with great rapidity while being hardly aware of what he was setting down. This was before he evolved the pseudonym.

The need to give a separate identity to this 'mind within a mind', as he called it, came about gradually. The spark came from his friendship with an American lady, whom he met on the Continent, whose classical beauty so entranced him that she became the model for his own, spiritual identity. Some while later, during a stay of a few months in a cottage in Sussex with his wife Elizabeth, he took the further step of actually naming this other self: Fiona Macleod was born.

As the mood came and went, almost of its own volition, the exceptional repertoire of the extensive Fiona Macleod writings began to emerge. Sharp used to say that if the secret of Fiona ever got out, then the inspiration would cease. In the event, save for a few honoured confidantes, he was successful in keeping the truth to himself right up until his death in 1905. So as to justify his handling of the inevitable correspondence and business negotiations of Miss Macleod, he put it about that she was his cousin. It was all very tricky, and there were some very close shaves indeed. Sharp even arranged two separate entries in *Who's Who:* a genuine one for himself and a bogus one for 'her'!

The geographical focus of many of the Fiona writings was the tiny Scottish island of Iona. It was a kind of northern counterpart of Glastonbury, similarly steeped in romantic traditions, both Pagan and Christian. Sharp drew freely from these local sources in the poems, plays, essays and fables published under the pseudonym. When writing about 'herself', Fiona claimed Iona as the place of her birth and upbringing. This caused much head-scratching among the islanders as none of them could remember anything about her. As might be expected, the style of the writings has a certain strangeness and takes some getting used to, but the rewards are there for those who make the effort. The following is a characteristic extract from *The Dominion of Dreams:*

"These sun-bathed cliffs, with soft hair of green grass, against whose white walls last year the swallows, dusky arrowy shuttles, slid incessantly, and where tufts of sea-lavender hung like breaths of stilled smoke, now seem to me merely tall cliffs. Then, when we were together, they were precipices which fell into seas of dream, and at their bases was for ever the rumour of a most ancient, strange, and penetrating music. It is I only, now, who do not hear: doubtless, in those ears, it fashions new meanings, mysteries and beauty: there, where the music deepens beyond the chime of the hours, and Time itself is less than the whisper of the running wave. White walls, which could be open, and where the sea-song became a spirit, still with the foam-bells on her hair, but with a robe green as grass, and in her hand a white flower..."

Unlike his imagined Fiona, William Sharp was not of the Isles nor a pure Celt, having been born at Paisley, near Glasgow on 12 September, 1855 of partly Swedish extraction. He once wrote to a friend: "By blood I am part Celt, and partly so by upbringing, by spirit wholly so..."

That this unusual man should have been an unusual child is hardly surprising. In his boyhood he was lucky to spend long summer holidays in the West of Scotland, where his family had a house on the shore of one of the Lochs. William was high-spirited and adventurous - it would be wrong to imagine him as a docile introvert. He would go off on his own for hours into the woods, which seemed an enchanted world to him. Even at the age of six he was touched by a sense of the infinite. He wanted to become part of the Spirit of Nature. He built a little secret altar in the heart of the woodland on which he laid white flowers in offering.

One summer his cousin Elizabeth came up to stay from London. Did he guess then that she would one day be his wife? Later she recalled William's early dream-life:

"He soon realised that his playmates understood nothing of the confused memories of previous lives that haunted him, and from which he drew materials to weave into stories for his school-fellows in the dormitory at nights. To his surprise he found they saw none of the denizens of the other worlds - tree spirits and nature spirits, great and small - so familiar to him, and whom he imagined must be as obvious to others as to himself. He could say about them as Lafcadio Hearn said about ghosts and goblins, that he believed in them for the best of possible reasons, because he saw them day and night."

He learned early to keep his psychic nature a thing apart, away from the taunts and jibes of others not so endowed. This separate, hidden realm had much bearing on the character of the pseudonym he would adopt in later life.

When he was sixteen he contracted typhoid badly and needed a full summer of convalescence. This took him to the West where he spent

WILLIAM SHARP

much time with an old fisherman, Seamus Macleod, who lived on a remote island and who featured in his essay *Iona*. From then up to his eighteenth year he gained an intimate knowledge of every loch, fjord and inlet in the Western Highlands and Islands.

At eighteen he joined an encampment of true gypsies from Central Europe. For some months he wandered all over the land with them. This 'free life' on the heather saw the realization of many dreams. The memories of the experience remained with him vividly throughout his life.

In 1881 he went to Glasgow University, and worked well although did not stay long enough to take his degree. An unhappy spell in a law office made him so ill that he had to be sent to Australia for two years to get over it. Once there he spent most of his time engrossed in various literary endeavours, limiting himself to just four hours sleep each night - indifferent as always to his delicate constitution, and an attitude which was to play havoc with his health throughout his life.

He returned to Britain to become a prominent literary critic with an exceptional knowledge of the works of foreign writers. But he was ever a restless spirit, and at the drop of a hat would take off anywhere: Africa, Italy, America - even Australia - leaving all who might be dependent on his services high and dry.

Sharp was on close terms with many leading figures of the day and highly regarded by them. These included William Butler Yeats, Dante Gabriel Rossetti and Henry James. He also knew Goodchild's friends, Mr and Mrs Grant Allen, very well. Yeats recognized Sharp's unique qualities and genius and spoke of his 'extraordinarily primitive mind', and how he was fond of speaking of himself as 'the representative of the old bards'. He considered that he was 'imaginative in the old and literal sense of image-making; not like a man of his age at all.' For a while Sharp indulged in some psychic experiments with the Irish poet (using ouija boards and the like). These led to mental and physical exhaustion to such an extent that he had to withdraw from all further activity of that sort.

The Sharps seem to have been a comradely pair with Elizabeth remarkably accommodating of all her husband's whims and fancies. She put her devotion to William's art before anything else - even her own feelings. She described his attentions to the American inspirer of his Fiona-self as a 'fine friendship' - and there is no reason to doubt that she was right. After his death she worked with great dedication to see to the publication of his collected works in several editions. Yet William often used to travel abroad without her. Her commitment to her own writing and the art criticism she provided for several national newspapers often kept her at home. She was another writer that Goodchild mentioned briefly in *The Light of the West;* her *Lyrica Celtica* caught his fancy.

It would be interesting, but difficult, to try to pick out any influence of Goodchild in the later Fiona Macleod writings, notwithstanding their inspirational character. There are bits here and there in some of the notes and commentaries that echo certain ideas in *The Light of the West.* Among the notes appended to the essay *Iona* is the following comment on the Mor Rigan plainly taken from Goodchild:

"This euphemerised Celtic queen is called by many names: even those resembling that just given vary much - Morrigu, Mor Reega, Morrigan, Morgane, Mur-ree (Mor Ree), etc.. The old word Mor Rigan means 'The Great Queen'. She is mother of the Gaelic Gods, as Bona Dea of the Romans. 'Anu is her name' says an ancient writer. Anu suckled the elder gods. Her name survives in Tuatha-De-Danann, in Danu, Ana, and perhaps in that mysterious Scoto-Gaelic name, *Teampull Anait* - the temple of Anait - whom some writers collate with an ancient Asiatic goddess, Anait. It has been suggested that the Celts gave Bona Dea to the Romans, for these considered her Hyperborean."

Communications between Sharp and Goodchild were at best intermittent. Sharp was either working flat out or travelling abroad when not laid low with illness. But Goodchild was no small star on Sharp's horizon; all his close associates had to suffer his inconstancy. It is possible that Goodchild eventually knew the true identity of Fiona, although not apparently by December 1901, when FM wrote to him, ostensibly from Argyll:

"I had hoped by this time to have had some definite knowledge of what I am to do, where to go this winter. But circumstances keep me here... Our friend, too (meaning himself as WS), is kept to England by the illness of others. My plans though turning on different issues are to a great extent dependent, later, on his...
 I have much to do, and still more to think of, and it may be bring to life through the mysterious resurrection of the imagination.
 What long months of preparation have to go to any writing that contains life within it -even the slightest, the most significant, as it seems! We, all of us who live this dual life of the imagination and the spirit, do indeed mysteriously conceive, and fare thereafter in weariness and heaviness and long travail, only for one small uncertain birth. It is

the common law of the spirit - as the obverse is the common law of womanhood."

That same month Sharp visited Henry James at Rye. The visit gave him much pleasure, but he was far from well. Feeling the need to get away from the English winter, he went to Bordighera 'to be near Dr Goodchild'. A short stay there was enough and his restlessness soon got the better of him. He went on, via Rome, to Sicily to spend time with his good friend Alexander Nelson Hood, who also bore the titles Viscount Bridport and Duke of Bronte, at his Castle of Maniace. Through Hood there was yet another connection with the land of Avalon. He came from a noted Somerset family, which took its descent from an eighteenth century Prebendary of Wells, the Rev. Samuel Hood of Butleigh, near Glastonbury.

Two of the sons of the Rev. Hood were awarded titles for deeds of valour as Admirals. One became the first Lord Hood, the other the first Lord Bridport. A branch of the family still holds lands around Butleigh Wootton where the tall column of the monument to Admiral Samuel Hood is conspicuous in a cleft in the woodlands two miles or so south of Glastonbury Tor. The Hood title became extinct in 1901 with the death of Lord Hood of Avalon.

The Sicilian town of Bronte gave its name to a Dukedom bestowed on Lord Nelson in 1799 by Ferdinand IV. The family of Viscount Bridport received the title and estates after one of them married a niece of Nelson. The Castello di Maniace was first founded as a convent in 1173 on the site where George Maniakes defeated the Saracens in 1040.

Here Sharp found himself in delightful surroundings and good company, enjoying the benefits of a more amenable climate. He found time to write to his friend Ernest Rhys:

My Dear Ernest

As I think I wrote to you, I fell ill with a form of fever, and had a brief if severe recurrence of it at Rome; and was so glad some time ago to get on my beloved 'Greek' Taormina, where I rapidly 'convalesced'. A few days ago I came on here, to the wild inlands of the Sicilian Highlands, to spend a month with my dear friend here, in this wonderful old 'Castle-Fortress-Monastery-Mansion - the Castel' Maniace itself being over 2,000 feet in the highlands beyond Etna, and Maletto, the nearest station about 3,000.

How you and Grace would rejoice in this region. Within a day's easy ride is Enna, sacred to Demeter, and about a mile or so from Castel'

Maniace, in a wild desolate region of a lava wilderness, is the lonely heron-haunted moorland-lake wherein tradition has it Persephone disappeared...

WS

Elizabeth went out to join him in February and they stayed for another month of sunshine and flowers. They then moved on to another favoured spot: the island resort of Taormina on the East Coast. Sharp wrote to Goodchild just before they went:

Friday, 7th March, 1902

Tomorrow we leave here for Taormina... And, not without many regrets, I am glad to leave - as, in turn, I shall be glad (tho' for other reasons) when the time comes to leave Taormina. My wife says I am never satisfied, and that Paradise itself would be intolerable for me if I could not get out of it when I wanted. And there is some truth in what she says, though it is a partial truth, only. I think external change as essential to some natures as passivity is to others: but this may simply mean that the inward life in one person may best be hypnotised by a wavering image or series of wavering images. It is not change of scene one needs so much as a change in these wavering images. For myself, I should, now, in many ways be content to spend the most of my life in some quiet place in the country, with a garden, a line of poplars and tall elms, and a great sweep of sky...

Your friend affectionately
William Sharp

At Taormina Sharp wrote that "it would take a thousand pages to describe all the flowers and other near and far objects which delight one continually. Persephone has scattered every treasure in this her birth-island." It was a popular place for artists and writers from America and all over Europe, and was held to have the right conditions to make it the venue for the second initiation of the young Indian, J. Krishnamurti, into his coming role as the new World Teacher. That contentious father-figure of English Theosophy, C. W. Leadbeater, took him there in 1912 at the behest of his Himalayan 'Masters'.

The year that the Sharps were at Taormina was also one in which Goodchild thought he might be on to something with regard to the

Cup. In the summer of 1902 he met a lady in Bath who told him that she had had the site at Bride's Well described to her in some detail by an old clergyman when she was a child. Was this the person called to take charge of the Cup? He lost no time in taking her down to Glastonbury to see how she reacted at the spot itself. Unfortunately she drew a blank - no influence reached her. They returned to Bath without Goodchild divulging anything of his true purposes in taking her there.

But had Sharp any part to play in this business of the Cup? Goodchild longed to take him there, but the time was not yet right. The years of his friendship with the bard of the north had seemed to coincide with the period since leaving the vessel in the well. Goodchild was inclined to the belief that all associations of any depth must have an ultimate spiritual purpose. There was not only Sharp's involvement to consider; great national events were taking place while the Cup was hidden. A new century had been ushered in; the Queen had breathed her last and a coronation was in the air; the Boer War had been won in South Africa; a Tory government had come to power with the curious Arthur Balfour as Prime Minister. This highly unpragmatic individual had at one time been President of the Society for Psychical Research. He had the gift for rhapsodizing eloquently at length in an intellectual stratosphere without really saying much at all. In other hands his 'Balfour Declaration' might have been a better document and the Palestinian question more resolved at the present time.

Sharp's health was deteriorating. He had to summon all his powers to complete the final collection of Fiona Macleod writings. These were published in 1904 as *The Winged Destiny,* and dedicated by the author to the one friend who understood more than any other the direction and feeling of his inner life. Dr J. A. Goodchild was honoured indeed.

To JAG.

To you, dear friend, let me dedicate this bindweed of thoughts and dreams, which had their life by the grey shores you, also, love. Have you not wandered there often, seeking forgetfulness, and, wandering, found peace?

You are in your southern home, by calm waters where mine are foam-white, and under blue skies where mine are dark with cloud and wind: and yet, of all I know, few do so habitually dwell in that fragrant, forgetting and forgot, old world of ours, whose fading voice is more and more lost in the northern seas. The South is beautiful, but has not the secrets of the North. Do you, too, not hold Iona, motherland of all my dreams, as something rare and apart, one who has her own lovely solitude and her own solitary loveliness that is like no other loveliness? In your heart, as in mine, it lies an island of revelation and peace. For you, too, is the enduring spell of those haunted lands where the last dream of the Gael are gathered, dwelling in sunset beauty.

You who know the way of the wind in my mind know that I do not, as some say, 'dwell only in the past', or that personal sorrow is the one magnet of my dreams. It is not the night-wind in sad hearts only that I hear, or the sighing of vain futilities; but, often, rather an emotion akin to that mysterious Sorrow of Eternity in love with tears, of which Blake speaks in *Vala*. It is, at times at least I feel it so, because beauty is more beautiful there. It is the twilight hour in the heart, as Joy is the heart's morning. Perhaps I love best the music that leads one into the moonlit coverts of dreams, and old silence, and unawakening peace. But music, like the rose of the Greeks, is 'the thirty-petalled one,' and every leaf is the gate of an equal excellence. The fragrance of all is Joy, the beauty of all is Sorrow: but the Rose is one - *Rosa Sempiterna*, the Rose of Life. As to the past, it is because of what is there, that I look back: not because I do not see what is here today, or may be here tomorrow. It is because of what is to be gained that I look back; of what is supremely worth knowing there, of knowing intimately: of what is supremely worth remembering, of remembering constantly: not only as an exile dreaming of the land left behind, but as one travelling in narrow defiles who looks back for familiar fires on the hills, or upward to the familiar stars where is surety. In truth, is not all creative art remembrance: is not the very spirit of ideal art the recapture of what has gone away from the world, that by an imperious spiritual law is for ever withdrawing, to come again newly?

You wrote to me once, 'Beware of the beauty that you seek.' You would have me bow down only before the beauty that is beyond the last careful words of ivory and pale gold, beyond even the airs of the enchanted valleys where Music is...

Beauty is less a quality of things than a spiritual energy: it lies not in the things seen but in harmonious perception. Yet, also, it can dwell apart, in the sanctuary of this flower or of that woman's face. But in itself it is as impersonal as dew, as secret and divine and immortal - for, as you remember, Midir, the lord of sleep and youth and love, the son of Angus, lord of death and the years and the winged passions, was made of dew, of the secret dews: Midir of the twilight, of the secret and silent peoples, of the veiled immortalities. It can exist for us in one face, one form, in one spirit, on the lifted waters, on the hills of the west, in trampling marches of sound, in delicate airs, but it is in all of these, and everywhere: wherever the imagination is become light, and that light the light of flame. To each the star of his desire: but Beauty is beyond the mortal touch of number, as of change and time. Has any spoken mo deeply of this than Plato, when in that vision of Perfect Beauty in t *Banquet* he writes: 'It is not like any face or hands or bodily thing; i not word or thought; it is not in something else, neither living thing, earth nor heaven; only by itself in its own way in one form it for ever

Is it not he also, the wise and noble dreamer, who makes Socrates in Phædrus, 'Beloved Pan, and all ye other gods... give me beauty in inward soul.'

The vision of the few. Yes, but a handful of pine-seed will c mountains with the green majesty of forest. And so I too will set my to the wind and throw my handful of seed on high:

> Cuiridh mi m'aodann anns a' ghaoith
> 'Us tilgim baslach caoin an aird.

But you - you are of the little clan, for whom this book is: you wh gone upon the dark ways, and have known the starless road, and perchance on that obscure way learned what we have yet to learn. For you, and such as you, it is still a pleasure to gather bindweed of thoughts and dreams; still a pleasure to set these dreams, these thoughts, to the airs and pauses and harmonies of considered speech. So, by your acceptance of this book, let me be not only of your fellowship but of that little scattered clan to whom the wild bees of the spirit come, as secret wings in the dark, with the sound and breath of forgotten things."

This text is a thanksgiving for spiritual kinship. For Fiona Macleod - or William Sharp, if you will - John Goodchild stood apart, almost more than any other, as one who had delved into the near-forgotten soul of the past, and who had "...perchance on that obscure way learned what we have yet to learn." Sharp had a tremendous and deep regard for Goodchild. He acknowledged his considerable intuitive and creative gifts to a degree that suggests he deserves more than the total obscurity that the passing of years has bestowed upon him. After all, praise from one who had been so praised by such notables as Yeats and Rossetti was praise indeed. And Sharp was not inclined to give praise casually. The least he could offer was the dedication of *The Winged Destiny* - and offer it with a glad heart.

It was the summer of 1904. Goodchild acknowledged the dedication, shortly following this with another letter:

Author's Club
July 1904

Dear Friend
Yesterday I read your preface to a friend of mine, and afterwards a lady
(a clever woman I believe) came into the room. I had never met her
before, and she had never read anything of yours, but she picked up the
book and asked what it was. 'Just read the introduction', said my friend.
The reader had an expressive face, and I wish you had seen it. 'But this
is something quite new. I never read anything like it before' she said as
she finished: and I fancy that many will do likewise...

JAG

Something else was in the air. At last Sharp was free to journey to Bath
to see Goodchild and from there take a day trip to Glastonbury. It was
to be a highly auspicious occasion and successful on more than one
level. The following day Sharp wrote to a friend about the events of...

"...one of the loveliest days of the year, with the most luminous atmosphere I have seen in England - and the afternoon and evening divinely
serene and beautiful.

I had a pleasant visit to Bath, and particularly enjoyed the long day
spent yesterday at Glastonbury and neighbourhood, and the glowing
warmth and wonderful radiance.

As usual one or two strange things happened in connection with
Dr G. We went across the ancient 'Salmon' of St. Bride, which stretches
below the hill known as 'Weary-All' (a corruption of Uriel, the Angel of
the Sun), and about a mile or less westward came upon the narrow water
of the ancient 'Burgh'. Near here is a very old Thorn held in great
respect...

He put me (unknowing) to a singular test. He had hoped with especial and deep hope that in some significant way I would write or utter
the word 'Joy' on this first day of August (the first three weeks of vital
import to many, and apparently for myself too) - and also to see if a certain spiritual influence would reach me. Well, later in the day (for he
could not prompt or suggest, and had to await occurrence) we went into
the lovely grounds of the ancient ruined Abbey, one of the loveliest
things in England I think. I became restless and left him, and went and
lay down behind an angle of the East end, under the tree. I smoked, and
then rested idly, and then began thinking of some correspondence I had

forgotten. Suddenly I turned on my right side, stared at the broken stone of the angle, and felt vaguely moved in some way. Abruptly and unpremeditatedly I wrote down three enigmatic and disconnected lines. I was looking curiously at the third when I saw Dr G. approach.

'Can you make anything out of that,' I said - 'I've just written it, I don't know why.' This is the triad:

'From the Silence of Time, Time's Silence Borrow.
In the heart of To-day is the word of Tomorrow.
The Builders of Joy are the Children of Sorrow.'

This disavowal of Sharp's conscious intent is instructive. Could Fiona have fleetingly taken him over that afternoon in the grounds of the ancient Abbey? He often used to speak of her as if she were a separate being, of having a sense of her entering his room. Any too precise interpretation of the meaning of these three lines is risky. The mood or mode is maternal; of something waiting for a joyful awakening or birth still held within the heart - or womb? - of the present time; and those who feel for the loss of the old mysteries shall labour for its realisation. Certainly FM and not WS.

It was what Goodchild had hoped for. Things were well-set right from the start of that particularly brilliant day. It was a Monday - a Bank Holiday. There were some clouds about in the morning but by midday these had quite dispersed. They arrived to find the town of Glastonbury nearly deserted. Most of the townsfolk had gone off to the seaside. They had made their way to Weston, Burnham, Minehead - even the Dorset coast - by whatever means available: train, bus, car, motorcycle or bicycle. True twentieth-century style even in 1904.

Something else happened that day: William Sharp became the only person to whom Goodchild revealed the secret of the Cup in the well. As Sharp wrote to his friend, they went across 'the ancient Salmon of St. Bride'. Goodchild was fond of talking about this fish effigy that he believed was laid out over some distance on the ground. He pointed to local traditions which supported this view. It was this same source that led Katherine Maltwood into mistakenly identifying Weary-All Hill as the place of the Salmon when piecing together her landscape Zodiac theory many years later. It is difficult to know how widely the Salmon story was spread around or where it came from. Some support comes from a letter to *The Spectator* in the summer of 1909 from a Rev. F. G. Montagu Powell* of Christchurch:

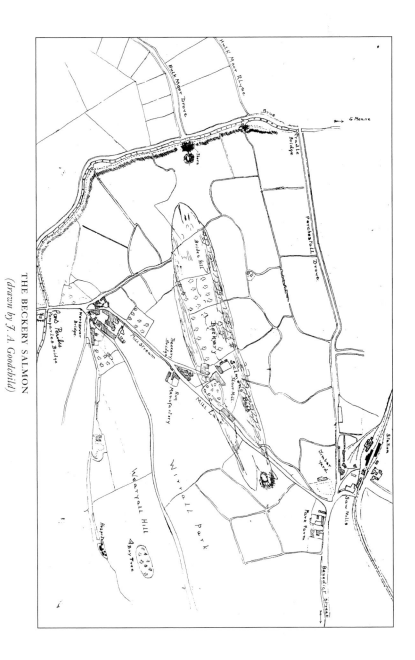

THE BECKERY SALMON
(drawn by J. A. Goodchild)

"...I think it is fairly established that in Europe, if not the world over, most ancient religious sites mark the position of sites more ancient still. At Glastonbury there was such a site, to which the Druids from Western Europe made pilgrimage, where they held their rites and sought interment. This site was indicated by a vast salmon, the fish renowned for wisdom celebrated in the *Mabinogion*, and upon whose shoulders Arthur's knights rode to the city of Gloucester. The outline of this huge fish, some three thousand feet long, is still to be seen, extending from the Isle of Beckery (Little Ireland) on the banks of the Brue towards the ruins of the Abbey, and skirting Wearyall Hill. The outline was probably lined out with flints; but the richer grass can still be noted by the light of the evening sun from the station. The one spot that can be indicated as still remaining is a holy well (not the Chalice Well higher up, but another) called the Salmon's Eye, and where the 'women's quarters' of the Druid priestesses were located. However much of unauthentic tradition may be involved, it is good, I think, to see in Glaston and its precincts, the possibility at least of a site, sacred to such religious objects, far antedating Christianity, and thus comforting to the heart with the conviction that at no time in the history of the human race has God left Himself without witness, even if that witness be of the nature we call pagan."

We have to be wary of claims that something might be 'a local tradition', particularly if the 'tradition' has become quite forgotten in subsequent years. Even Mr Powell introduces a cautious note in his final sentence. But Goodchild went so far as to say that the Glastonbury Salmon was a monument equal in importance to Stonehenge.

Be that as it may, the two of them walked over the land they believed was occupied by the fish effigy to arrive at Bride's Well, Goodchild all the while watching to see if Sharp might pick up any sort of spiritual influence there. Here they found the thorn tree bedecked with its usual array of ribbons and prayers on scraps of paper. One in particular caught Goodchild's eye, and, as will be shown later, was to have a special part to play in the eventual recovery of the Cup.

Sharp's three lines of verse were his contribution to the occasion. His use of the words 'sorrow' and 'joy' was evidence enough for Goodchild. He believed that the vessel he had placed in the well was a 'Cup of Sorrow' which must be transformed when retrieved into a 'Cup of Joy'.

After the Glastonbury trip the two friends went their separate ways, the Sharps visiting America to call on various acquaintances and

---

*Montagu Powell wrote *Studies in the Lesser Mysteries* (1913) which has been reprinted several times. (see p39)

Goodchild preparing for his winter ministrations in Italy. The weather in New York became severe, such that William and Elizabeth decided to sail directly to Italy. They spent Christmas Day at Bordighera. Then they toured around to Rome and elsewhere until striking north to be in Scotland by springtime.

William's health was giving much cause for concern. The cold of that year had got into his delicate system, so much so that he had to spend some time at Neuenahr receiving treatment. He knew it had been a close thing and the outlook for the future was not good. He wrote to his good friend the Hon. A. Nelson Hood that he had had a 'narrow squeak' and that he had been at the 'brink of Cape Fatal' and across 'the Swamp Perilous'.

Elizabeth could not go with her husband to Neuenahr. He wrote to her from there on the 16 June:

> "...I could see that Dr G. can't understand why I am not more depressed or, rather, more anxious. I explained to him that these physical troubles meant little to me, and that they were largely the bodily effects of other things, and might be healed far more by spiritual well-being than by anything else: also that nature and fresh air and serenity and light and warmth and nervous rest were worth far more to me than all else. 'But don't you know how serious your condition may become at any moment, if you got a bad chill or setback, or don't soon get better?' 'Certainly,' I said; 'but what then? Why would I bother about either living or dying? I shall not die before the hour of my unloosening comes'."

He had found an inner peace, but he was still quite ill. A return to London, as usual, did him harm. A letter to Dr G. of 30 July gave more than a hint that his days were numbered; he had dwelt on the darker side of life often before but never so much as a force weighed against him as here:

> "...August is always a 'dark' month for me - and not as a rule, I fancy, a good one: at any rate an obscure and perhaps perilous one. But this time I fancy it is on other lines. I believe strong motives and influences are to be at work in it perhaps furtively only: but none the less potently and far reachingly. Between now and September-end (perhaps longer) many of the Dark Powers are going to make a great effort. We must all be on guard - for there will be individual as well as racial and general attack. But a Great Unloosening is at hand."

Yours ever
WS

A Great Unloosening was at hand - but not quite yet. The Sharps visited Scotland again to see his mother and old friends. On that trip William confided to Elizabeth that he knew it would be his last visit there. One evening he stopped their carriage to get out and walk in the oak-woods. He stood touching the trees in the fading light and was heard to say, "Ah dear trees of the North, dear trees of the North, goodbye".

After their travels of that autumn they arrived at Sicily, and the Castle of Maniace of their friend Alex Nelson Hood, Duke of Bronte. Here on 8 December while out admiring the view in the changing light, a turn in the road brought them into an icy stream of air straight off the snow covered cone of Mount Etna. William had no resistance to the chilling cold that cut through him. By the next day he complained of pains that grew steadily worse. Elizabeth recorded his last moments on the 12th:

> "...About 3 o'clock, with his devoted friend Alec Hood by his side, he suddenly leant forward with shining eyes and exclaimed in a tone of joyous recognition, 'Oh, the beautiful Green Life again!' and the next moment sank back in my arms with the contented sigh, 'Ah, all is well.'"

On that day, for Goodchild and many others, a light had gone out, or, more precisely, two lights. But with the passing from this life it became generally known that the two were really one. The world was told that Fiona was William. But a mystery remained - and still remains - as to how even for William, Fiona had a life and independence apart from his own power of will and intellectual control.

On 14 December 1905, William Sharp was buried in the small woodland burial ground of the chapel at Maniace. There in the winter sunshine his own 'Invocation to Peace' from *The Dominion of Dreams* was read over the grave by Alex Nelson Hood.

A solitary Iona cross carved from the volcanic lava of Etna marks the spot to this day. In 1981 the Commune of Bronte took over the running of the estate and the lands were broken up and sold in separate lots. There are now conducted tours available, and, if requested, the grave of William Sharp can be included in the itinerary.

There are two inscriptions on the lava headstone: one by William and one by Fiona:

Farewell to the known and exhausted,
Welcome the unknown and illimitable.

- WS

 Love is more great than we conceive,
and Death is the keeper of unknown redemptions.

- FM

CHAPTER FIVE

Seekers Finders

THROUGHOUT THE YEARS FOLLOWING the placing of the Cup in Bride's Well, Dr Goodchild remained in touch with events as best he could, watching for any sign of its recovery. He wondered, too, about the measure of his own involvement. Should he have faith in whatever powers might be controlling the operation and leave matters to take their own course, or should he help things along and seek a response by dropping the odd hint in likely quarters? As far as his own feelings were concerned, the latter solution probably seemed more favourable. The question was, how far to go with giving small clues without prejudicing the inspirational influence which had to prevail in the end. There were several possibilities, among them, the seeking out of sympathetic individuals of the right kind of receptivity. As we have seen, he tried taking an interested lady friend from Bath to the well in 1902, mindful of what he had been told about the need for a woman to reveal its secrets. The visit alone, he felt, would try the spirits far enough; he made no suggestion to her about anything being hidden there. Then there was the successful little test he devised for William Sharp, taking him to the well in August 1904 to see if he was inspired to utter the word 'joy'. He also tried another tack, actually letting it be known to some people that he had heard that a precious object had been buried in the Glastonbury area. He was careful not to associate himself with this story, nor did he profess to know the exact location.

Another opportunity, mentioned earlier, came his way during that day-trip to Glastonbury with Sharp. When he later found it necessary to write to the editor of the Daily Express in 1907 to put right certain errors in a report about these happenings, he described how he and Sharp had come across what he called a 'token', left at the well by a young woman from Bristol. Curiously, he goes on to say that they returned it to her the next day with such 'tokens of thanks' as they deemed suitable. Presumably, we can deduce from this sketchy account that the young woman must have left some sort of note with at least her name on it. The name would have been enough: Katharine Tudor Pole had a brother, Wellesley Tudor Pole, whom Dr Goodchild had met several times before. Whatever they 'returned to her' must have included the poem already quoted, composed by Sharp in the Abbey Ruins.

If any of this is seeming to suggest that Goodchild might have been casting clues around a little too freely, it must be emphasised that at no time did he make any direct reference to anyone, apart from Sharp, that a cup, bowl, or anything else, could be found in Bride's Well. Indeed, his actions may have been prompted by his suspicion that the Cup had been taken from the well in 1900, after the site had been cleaned up. This gave grounds for believing that someone already had the vessel in their possession. Doubts, and an understandable attachment to its destiny, can explain his concern.

Dr Goodchild must have often thought back to the unseen voice that had given him guidance in the past, and wondered if some new sign might come to him at this uncertain time. At 5 o'clock in the afternoon of Sunday 26 August 1906 a sign did indeed appear: not a voice this time, but apparently a vision of a sword, suspended in the eastern sky. He duly made a colour sketch of it, naming it 'The Sign of the East'. The meaning of this became clearer when he found himself witnessing a similar phenomenon eight days later. This time it was a cup in the western sky, with a pattern of balls of light over it - three just near it and two more a little above these. He drew it as before, giving the time very precisely as 5.43 pm 3 September 1906 - 'The Sign of the West'. Symbolically, there is a clear enough pattern: Sunday (Day of the Sun), the East - a Sword; Monday (Day of the Moon), the West - a Cup. Whether we care to regard it as chance or suggestion, an obvious Male/Female opposition can be inferred here.

The subliminal contents of Goodchild's unconscious are surfacing once again, to reveal themselves as, seemingly, outward projections of psychic processes. We are back with the thesis of *The Light of the West*, of the Light of Christ, the Sword of the Spirit, coming from the East to awaken the Cup, or Cauldron, of the Mysteries of the Celtic West to renewed life. Whatever the analysis, Goodchild now did an interesting thing: he. sent the cup drawing to Wellesley Tudor Pole in Bristol. A report of the time has it that he asked that the drawing be passed on 'to the pilgrims who have just been to Glastonbury'. Was he being exceptionally clairvoyant here, or did he already know that two friends of Wellesley's had been to Glastonbury on the day that he saw the sign?

With Goodchild, the answer could lie either way - we have now no means of knowing.

With his anticipation now running high, this middle-aged bachelor doctor must have been agreeably surprised to find two attractive young women waiting to see him at his hotel on Tuesday, 26 September. Plainly, they had something quite vital to convey to him. He settled them down and listened to their story. The two were sisters, Janet and Christine Allen, friends of the Tudor Poles, and also from Bristol. What they told him surprised and pleased him even more.

They explained how their friend Wellesley Tudor Pole had received a psychic intimation that they should search in the water at St. Bride's Well during their visit to Glastonbury just over three weeks earlier. It was while doing this that they retrieved a curious primitive-looking blue glass bowl. They washed the mud from it in the river nearby, and sensing its sanctity, had replaced it in the well and returned to Bristol to report back to their friends.

While they were recounting their tale, they noticed that the older man seemed deeply moved. Much was going through his mind, not least that the Cup had not been taken away during the clearing operation in 1900, as he had feared, but must have been pushed to one side into a crevice. Moreover, things were coming about as foretold. Here were women - and maidens, no less. He understood that it was his Cup Sign drawing that had prompted them to see him. The chance of mere coincidence had been too small to pass by.

On this occasion Dr G. gave no hint about his own involvement, and simply stated that he felt sure they had found a very holy object, and that he had grounds for believing that it had once been carried by the Master, Jesus.

When Wellesley and Katharine heard about Goodchild's comments when the two sisters returned to Bristol, they lost no time in arranging a visit of their own to try to get to the bottom of this somewhat guarded response. On the 29th they went over to Bath, just four days after the Allen sisters. This time Goodchild was more forthcoming. He told them the whole story from the time he first saw the bowl in the tailor's shop in Bordighera, through to its concealment in Bride's Well. But he still disclosed nothing about his experience in the Paris hotel. What they learned that day served to confirm and amplify their feelings about the significance of the vessel which the Allen sisters had seen at Glastonbury. In return they told him about their own pilgrimages to Bride's Well and other venerated spots in the area.

To Goodchild, these young and dedicated enthusiasts from Bristol were emerging as the rightful heirs to the Cup and its destiny. It was a position which they had come to accept too.

For his part, Wellesley Tudor Pole had been visiting Glastonbury for some years, and had in that time been given many indications that something special was waiting to be discovered there. The circumstances surrounding the finding of the Cup in the well now made sense of all this. An experience of the Allen sisters in the previous year seemed all the more remarkable in the light of what they now knew. That had been on the occasion of Janet and Christine's first excursion to Glastonbury together, in November 1905. Fortunately, they have left a detailed account of this visit.

It was not the best time of year to choose for a pilgrimage to an open place. The two had alighted from their train at Glastonbury railway station at 4.30 in the afternoon of 11 November. Darkness had fallen early that day beneath a heavy sky; the bells of St. Benedict's church were ringing out above the hiss of steam as they made their way down the station platform and out into the road to make their booking for the night at the nearby Temperance Inn.

That evening they went into the ruins of the great Abbey, undeterred by the torrential rain which was now falling on them. These grim conditions only added to the desolate feelings of sadness and loneliness which came on them there. They returned to the comfort of the inn with minds very much attuned to the wrongs of the past.

Back in the privacy of their room, Christine was determined to break through the mood of darkness which had prevailed on them so far. Taking pencil and paper in hand she endeavoured to subdue her own thought processes to the point of allowing herself to become the instrument of whatever presences might be watching and waiting to communicate some relevant truth through her. Automatic writing, as it is known, was something she had tried before, but never coming so easily as during that wintry evening in Glastonbury. It was a lengthy screed of which the following is just a part:

"I am with you, a monk of the Abbey called Guiseppi."
"Did you see us in the Abbey?" Christine asked.
"Yes, you helped me so I will help you. I am here to guide you. Your pilgrimage will be successful. I will come with you as I am the one that guides... I will show you that the Kingdom of your Father is in Nature, and in your inmost self. Cleave the rocks and you shall find him... We are here to help you. Prepare, for the time is at hand... In the Love of God we go forth to heal and uplift humanity. Keep all this in mind and all things shall be revealed..."

Brother Pietro in God

In association with this message, Christine also had a vision of an old man leaning on a staff. Also present there seemed to be many pilgrims, each one holding a daisy.

The second day came full of continuing promise and a sense of unseen guidance. They decided to follow a route which passed through certain places in the locality which they understood had been venerated by local people from ancient times. As they approached Bride's Hill, Christine was aware of the figure of an old pilgrim walking ahead of them. By the time they reached Bride's Well there was such an atmosphere now upon them that they felt compelled to remain there in silent meditation. It was then that another visionary experience came to Christine, this time of a beautiful saucer-like object being lifted out of the water towards her by a woman's hand. The vessel was full of clear water which was offered her to drink. It was then withdrawn back into the well. The vision faded and they went on their way, not at that time aware that anything special might actually be hidden there. Later, nearer the Tor, in Maiden Croft Lane, Christine heard words which seemed to come from the Virgin Mother herself:

"...I, the Mother of Life, am now with you. Here you learn the Divine Lesson of the Creation. Here is created in you, all Divine Things. Here the Mother Soul seeks to find expression. Return down Paradise Lane, and do not forget the brief span in the Maiden's Croft."

From that day their life had a new direction, a greater sense of purpose as yet not fully defined. It had not been long before this visit that they had first met Katharine and Wellesley Tudor Pole, in what were reported to have been 'rather unusual circumstances'. What these were has now been forgotten - not that there was anything particularly 'usual' about some of the other events in their lives after that time.

Of the team of four, most of the psychic direction seems to have come through either Christine or Wellesley. As mentioned earlier, Christine and Janet had been encouraged to recover the Cup from the well after Wellesley had had such an experience. On that occasion he had been in his office in Bristol engaged in a thoroughly mundane business discussion when he noticed an image of the spot he knew as Bride's Well, seemingly projected on to the wall opposite him. A kind of pulsating light was coming from within the well. To his mind, this suggested a spiritual potency, perhaps emanating from something buried there. On the strength of this vision he asked the Allen sisters to search in the well. This successful mission had led to the meeting that

Wellesley and Katharine were now having with Dr Goodchild.

After hearing the doctor's story, the next step for the Tudor Poles was clear: the vessel that Janet and Christine had replaced in the well must be retrieved and brought to Bristol. Wellesley was not free, but two days later Katharine went to Glastonbury alone. It was the first day in October, and cold and wet. In those conditions the moors on the edge of the town can be as bleak and God-forsaken as anywhere.

Bride's Well itself was more like a rather muddy pond, into which the water from nearby fields used to drain through a sluice. However, it was certainly an ancient spot. An old thorn tree grew next to it on which generations of Glastonbury folk used to hang ribbons and other offerings to St. Bride for the help of the sick or the barren. By the time she reached it, Katharine was already wet enough not to be too bothered about having to wade into the mire at the well, picking around with her hands and feet until she found the bowl-shaped object. Fortunately, this did not take too long.

Soon the strange relic was travelling back with her to Bristol and its new home at 16 Royal York Crescent, Clifton, where Katharine lived with her brother. Here an upper room was turned into an oratory and hung with white drapes. At one end was an altar table on which the vessel was placed in a casket. Candles were lit, and members of the public invited in to meditate or receive healing. There were several reports of cures and mystical and revelatory experiences in the presence of the Cup. As time went on, forms of service were evolved which had points in common with church practices while giving a greater emphasis to the feminine mode represented by the Cup and the teaching of Spiritual Womanhood passed on to them by Goodchild.

Even if they did not actually regard themselves as priests (or priest-esses), one thing is certain: these young women were officiating at services - and that included communion services in which the Cup was used as a chalice for the consecrated wine.* They even undertook to perform baptisms and marriages on occasion. Plainly, they felt they had inaugurated the Church of the New Age, a church in which woman was in the ascendant and Bride, the Celtic embodiment of the Universal Feminine, was restored and harmonized with a mystical understanding of the tenets of the Christian faith. This extract from their service book seems to have more than a touch of Goodchild about it:

---

* Interestingly, the very first Church of England service of Holy Communion to be conducted anywhere by women priests was held at Christ Church Clifton, just around the corner from the location of the Clifton oratory, on the morning of Sunday, 13 March 1994, Mother's Day.

SAINT BRIDE'S WELL STONE

To the Bride:
O Thou Most Holy Virgin Bride, we greet thee.
Thou who comest robed in the Greater Glory of the Holy Spirit
Bride of Supreme Wisdom, Beauty and Truth.
Come on Wings of Deliverance, bearing the shield of a Dove.
Whisper to the saddened heart of My Humanity that Redemption
draweth nigh.
Come, 0 Bride, My Servant to Wait
Come, 0 Bride, My Servant to Wait
Come, 0 Bride, My Servant to Wait
Come in the Light of the Shining Moon,
Come in the Dawning of the Day,
Hear our cry, 0 Bride. Most Glorious Virgin of Supreme Loveliness
be gracious unto thy servants.

The communion service included much that was familiar along with
the new emphasis:

...Let us drink in remembrance that Christ's Blood was shed for us and
be thankful.
  Hail Cup of Joy!
  Hail Cup of Joy!
  Hail Cup of Joy!
  I here in the name of Joy drink from this Holy Cup and offer and
present myself, my soul, my body, to be a reasonable holy and living
sacrifice unto God.
  Bless me that I may be an instrument fitted for the holy work of
turning the Cup of Sorrow into the Cup of Joy.

Amen

A church with young female celebrants; where the Cup brought from
Italy played a central role in the rites; where something of the mystery
of gematria, or spiritual numbers, was revealed: it was all Dr Goodchild
could have hoped for, and more. He advised and prompted, but never
dictated to the keepers of the Oratory. According to one of his many
letters of encouragement to Janet and Christine, the shrine at Royal
York Crescent had a unique purpose:

"...Remember this, at the present moment it is probable that the Oratory
at Clifton, is the one Church in which the Name and Number of the

Master, are exhibited and taught openly. I gave this word on Sharp's authority to KTP and her brother, before she went over for the Cup. OPEN! is a hard word, but there are keys which will open all doors..."

This allusion to a word given on William Sharp's authority is curious. The only conclusion that can be drawn is that Goodchild had been, in some sense, Sharp's apprentice in matters of magic and spiritual invocation. It makes it more likely that it was Sharp who was the inspirer of Goodchild's preoccupation with gematria in his later years.

While the women handled the spiritual side of things, Wellesley was taking every opportunity to show the vessel to scientists and religious leaders in an effort to confirm his belief in its sanctity and ancient origin, and also to present the facts about it to the public at large.

Goodchild finally revealed the details of his Paris experience when Katharine went over to see him in Bath in June 1907. Likewise, eight days later, Wellesley broke silence to members of the triad about the vision of Bride's Well he had had in his office the year before. Two weeks after this they found themselves the centre of attention after the whole story of the finding of the Cup received unexpected, if inaccurate, coverage in the national press.

CHAPTER SIX

The Pilgrims

THE FAMILIES OF THESE YOUNG Glastonbury seekers were of the solid and comfortable Victorian middle class. The Tudor Poles' father was a partner in a large Bristol grain business; the Allen sisters' father was head of operations (Superintendent of the Line) of the Great Western Railway.

There were five children in the Pole family. Their father, Thomas, was born and raised at the family home, Egrove Farm, near Williton in Somerset. He married his cousin, Kate Wansbrough, and moved away from the country to be near his work in Bristol. Their children were Mary, Dorothy (who died in childhood), Katharine, Wellesley and Alexander. The name Tudor, given to some of the children, came from the Wansbrough side of the family. Kate's great-grandfather, the squire of a Pembrokeshire village, had claimed direct descent from the Welsh rebel and patriot, Owen Tudor.

In those days in the West Country, it was not uncommon for someone of Thomas Pole's station in life to espouse such causes as Fabian socialism, Theosophy and the Garden Cities movement. Thomas and Kate raised their children in an atmosphere of respect for the manifold forms of religious expression in the wider community around them. For themselves, they were Anglicans with a leaning towards the Quaker sentiments of spiritual fellowship with an emphasis on social responsibility and good works. Thomas was in touch with some of the leading 'new thinkers' of the day, ultimately enjoying books and ideas to a degree detrimental to his business commitments.

Life, for the children, was full and happy enough despite the sadness of losing Dorothy to scarlet fever just before Katharine was born. Among them was one the others found a little 'odd'. From a young age Wellesley would tell of seeing such phenomena as 'the colours of prayers' rising upward from the congregation in church. He was scoffed at and teased for being so fanciful. Yet later, the others looked back on this attitude of theirs with some shame as they came to know the reality of their own psychic powers. It was perhaps a natural progression for the offspring of idealistic and unmaterialistic parents. Kate and Thomas would talk at length with visiting friends on the after-life, reincarnation and their vision of a new social order. This home atmosphere left its mark on all of them.

After the birth of Katharine the family had moved from Bristol to Weston-super-Mare, where Wellesley and Alex were born. Although radical in some ways, Thomas Pole was conventional enough to insist that his sons attend one of the established public schools. Wellesley was utterly devastated and distraught when the time came for him to be packed off to Blundell's in Devon. He suffered physically, mentally and emotionally at the hands of the older bullies in the school, and never came to terms with the place for all the years that he was there. His father dismissed his pleadings and complaints when he was at home in vacation time. It fell to his older sister Mary to soothe him in his distress.

Mary was an active campaigner for animal welfare; she enlisted the help of the others in canvassing the borough in order to draw attention to the unsatisfactory conditions in the slaughter-houses of those times. Her younger sister Katharine had become a proficient violinist by then, and looked well set for some kind of career involving music.

At school, Wellesley fell in with the prevailing Church of England ethos for a while, and was commended for the strength of his commitment. In time, his independent spirit took him beyond the accepted view and led to some altercations with his mentors.

He left school with the offer of a place at university, but turned this down in order to help out in the now ailing family grain business. It was during this period with Messrs. Chamberlain, Pole & Co. that he forged his first links with Glastonbury. The call, when it came, was quite unexpected: he had a dream, clear in every detail. In it Wellesley saw himself as a monk in the ancient Abbey. The effect was so lasting and powerful that he felt compelled to take a day trip to Glastonbury as soon as he could. The year was 1902; he was just eighteen.

The visit was a revelation: the ancient features of the town and its surroundings were just as he had seen them in the dream, yet he had never been to Glastonbury before. In fact, he felt he had 'come home'.

From then on he returned as often as he could, each time sensing more of the special quality of the place, and growing in the conviction that something - perhaps some kind of holy relic - was waiting to be discovered there.

At the foot of the Tor hill, on the easterly road out of town, was a seminary for the training of Catholic missionary priests. In the walled

SOME OF THE POLE FAMILY AT WESTON-SUPER-MARE WITH VISITORS.
On the left: Alex, Mary and Kitty on the right.

gardens to the rear was an ancient spring known as Chalice Well, from which iron-laden waters gushed forth even in times of severe drought. It was held by tradition to be the site of the twelve huts of the anchorite disciples of Joseph of Arimathea. Wellesley found it a useful place to call and rest before climbing the Tor. Father Field, the priest in charge, was always ready to listen to the thoughts of his serious-minded young pilgrim-visitor, and took note of Wellesley's belief in some likely discovery in the area, promising to look out for reports of any unusual finds in the future.

In his journeyings around Bristol, Bath and the Glastonbury area, Wellesley began to make contact with people having similar interests - sometimes privately, other times at meetings and lectures. On two or three occasions it is known that he met Dr Goodchild. Glastonbury was discussed in a general way, but nothing was said about the Cup in the well.

While on one of his lone pilgrimages to Glastonbury he received a clear impression that he needed to find a 'triad of maidens' to help in the search for a holy relic.

Soon after this, in July 1904, he took his sister Katharine on a visit to the sacred spots of Glastonbury for the first time. In fact they travelled separately, Katharine cycling down from Bristol having arranged to meet her brother when she arrived. Somehow they missed each other, and Katharine had to spend the night in a guest house before successfully finding him the next morning. They went all over Wellesley's pilgrimage route together. Katharine recalled that 'he showed me the place where the Cup was eventually found. Being so psychic, he was more impressed than I was.' It was while she was there that she left the 'token', perhaps a prayer with her name on it, that was found soon afterwards by Dr Goodchild and William Sharp.

A few months later Wellesley met his sister's friends Janet and Christine Allen and realized that he had found his 'triad'.

The Allen family background was more orthodox than that of the Poles. Thomas Isaac Allen was as much the stern white-bearded Victorian patriarch in his own home as he was when directing the operations of the prestigious Great Western Railway. He had succeeded N. J. Burlinson as Superintendent of the Line in 1894, extending the latter's success in increasing the speed and efficiency of the traffic. He introduced restaurant cars on the service between London and Bristol and Cardiff, and pioneered the first road motor omnibus services, which were run initially by GWR. He was apparently also responsible for launching something described as 'the first steam rail motor car service' on the Stroud Valley line.

Thomas Allen had married Margaret Sophia Carlyle, daughter of Benjamin Fearnley Carlyle of Oakwell Hall, near Leeds. The family claimed direct descent from the line of the Earls of Carlisle, who hailed from the Scottish border region. Margaret's brother, James, had a son, also named Benjamin Fearnley Carlyle, who, as Dom Aelred Carlyle, founded the first Anglican Benedictine religious community, established for some years on Caldey Island, off the coast of South Wales (see Chapter 14).

The Allens had ten children: five girls and five boys. By some quirk of providence, most of the flair and strength of will fell on the female side of the family. The second oldest, Mary, led the way well enough, first as a suffragette, organizing numerous acts of public vandalism all over the country, and later as Commandant of the Women Police of Britain. As can be imagined, it was easy for the children to see their well-ordered, well-provided-for household as a rather awesome embodiment of divine law and purpose. Mary perceived this with characteristic eloquence:

> "I can recall my groping sense of something large and portentous, deeply mysterious and elusive, upon which shifting foundation I built my fantastic dream-universe. In that realm, 'Nannie' was the immediate hovering potentate, while Mother and Father, a step further removed, were the direct interpreters of God. Only they had access to, and were on intimate terms with, the Deity, who was a looming dark-bright shape compounded of benevolence and sternness, who had his direct omnipotence just above the roof of the house, in what was known as 'the Sky' or 'Heaven'. And prayer was directed to the definite spot on the ceiling, through which it shot instantly, beyond recall, like a well-directed arrow."

On the strength of Thomas Allen's position with the railway company, the family was privileged to travel like royalty, anywhere it wished, in its own special coach attached to the train. Even on the continent their way was smoothed by officials, briefed to accord them full VIP status.

Only the very best was good enough for the Allen girls; they rounded off their education at a finishing school in Switzerland and took music lessons in Germany.

Once back in Bristol, Janet and Christine were able to meet up with Katharine Tudor Pole (or Kitty, as she was usually known), whose family had by then returned from Weston-super-Mare to live once more in the city. They seem to have taken on their role as Wellesley's

SOME OF THE ALLEN FAMILY AT BRISTOL.
The girls (left to right) are Janet, Mary and Christine. The brother is Denys.

'triad of maidens', to do his bidding at Glastonbury, quite readily. But there is already an anomaly here - at least, within the scenario for the future of the Cup offered by Goodchild: only a woman was meant to be able to reveal its secrets. How far should a man - or men - be allowed to dominate the course of subsequent events?

How Wellesley judged his position can be best seen in a written statement he prepared in 1907:

"For some five years from the present date I have been interested in Glastonbury, its legendary, its mythology. I never visited its Shrines or its Holy Places from mere curiosity, but from the first, my visits were actual pilgrimages with a set purpose before them.

As the years have rolled by, that purpose has begun to unfold itself and to become more definite - more tangible.

My pilgrimages have taken place either on the first weeks of each year, or around Bride's Day (Feb. 1st) or both. Almost from the first day that I was there on pilgrimage, I have felt convinced that a great find was about to take place and I have dedicated myself to the search for the 'Holy Graal'.

During the past two and a half years my sister Katharine has been working with me on pilgrimage (and in prayer) and has been engaged in her own private dedication.

For the past thirteen months her two friends, Janet Bevill and Alice Christine Allen, the way having been prepared, dedicated themselves as Pilgrims at the Spiritual Shrine of the West. All three have, to some extent under my personal direction, been preparing the Way for the Coming of the Holy Graal. In September 1906 I finally became convinced that the time was ripe and that the search would be rewarded. Two out of three maidens received instructions from me as to the particular spot at which to make their search on the Glastonbury Fens.

Their efforts resulted in the bringing of the Holy Cup, encrusted with mud to the surface of a certain Holy Well, where it was reverently washed and left to wait further instructions. As a result of this, my sister was sent down to bring back the Holy Graal to a shrine prepared for it at 16 Royal York Crescent, Clifton.

From October 1st 1906 to the present date, January 1907, the Cup has been in the guardianship of the three maiden pilgrims, who by their prayers, their work and their pilgrimages at Glastonbury, prepared themselves for this holy task."

signed - Wellesley Tudor Pole February 22, 1907
witnessed - Janet Bevill Allen

At this time Wellesley seems to have accepted that the Cup itself should only be attended by women, appointing himself merely the director and advisor to the guardians of the vessel. Eventually the triad was dissolved and this condition evidently became less compelling as time went on, through to the period in his later years when Wellesley was actually looking after the Cup on his own.

Another notable point in this signed statement is the apparent assumption that the object brought from Glastonbury was no less than the lost Holy Grail of legend. They retained this belief even though they had known by then of its origin in Italy. (Goodchild was careful to distance himself from any such association: for him it was simply a 'Jesus Cup', having no previous connection with Glastonbury.)

Janet, too, set down a record of her experiences:

"It was in 1905 that I first heard of a pilgrimage to Glastonbury and felt strongly a call to visit the Holy Shrines there for myself. The way having been prepared by Katharine Tudor Pole, in the spirit of a pilgrim seeking Light, I went down with my sister on November 12th 1905 and followed the old pilgrims' route shewn to us by Wellesley Tudor Pole, stopping at many sacred spots for prayer and meditation."

After the Cup had been recovered she wrote:

"It was with a deep feeling of reverence and awed feeling of responsibility that I realized that the Vessel we had brought to light was the Holy Graal. I wondered many times why such an event should have come into my life, feeling a keen sense of unworthiness to be called as one of the custodians of this Sacred Relic.

It was too immense a fact to be anything but dimly grasped at first, but gradually faith grew stronger and in earnest prayer to be made more worthy for this Holy Task I dedicated myself to Its work."

In fact - and perhaps surprisingly - all the three members of the 'triad' never went down to Glastonbury together before 10 March 1907; but after that time they went quite regularly.

Even in her nineties Katharine could remember the itinerary of these excursions very clearly:

"We used to go by an early train from Clifton, and after arriving at Glastonbury station we went along Porchestall Drove to Cradle Bridge, over the Brue stream. Leaving that on our right, we crossed over two fields until we came to Bride's Well, in which the water was quite shallow. Offerings were put there, and ribbon was sometimes tied on the Thorn Tree above. The well was really a sluice for draining the field, and it and the thorn tree have since been done away with. There is now a stone marking the place.

After meditating there we continued to Bride's Hill, now called Beckery, where St. Bride and her nuns came in the fifth century from Ireland and built a chapel.

An old friend of ours, Dr Goodchild, said that this spot was called the Salmon's Back, as in olden times it was a fish idol when the sea was there. We then continued along to Wearyall Hill, where we had our picnic. Going along Bere Lane, we used to go into the old Barn there for a little time. Then we went to see Chalice Well, which was shown to us by an RC priest, as the place then belonged to the Roman Catholics.

After climbing the Tor, where we went through a certain ritual, we continued down Paradise Lane and Maiden Croft Lane to the station. At other times we went into the Abbey Ruins and visited other churches, and once I took my violin and played at the Well and on the Tor.

We were certainly very dedicated and I hope we were able to make a channel for the spiritual power."

Not much is known about the reaction of the parents of the Glastonbury pilgrims to their exploits. There was probably little in the way of outright opposition; more an amused tolerance of something that, in time, would pass away as the demands of the practical realities of life became greater. Thomas Pole even made his way to Glastonbury and stayed a day or two to try to fathom something of the hold that the place seemed to have on Wellesley and Katharine. It was soon after the national publicity of the 'find', and he was irritated to find himself being pestered by journalists seeking his opinion on the claims being made about it. As for Thomas Allen, he was to become so vexed at losing his daughter Mary to the suffragette cause, that the antics of Janet and Christine would have been of small concern to him. There may well have been some sympathy with their interest; it is known that a marriage service was held for a member of the Allen family in the Oratory at Royal York Crescent.

When the 'demands of the practical realities of life' did finally press greater on Wellesley and his friends, a sense of commitment to their spiritual vocation remained with them in spite of new and very changed circumstances. Each took a very separate path in life while still holding fast to all that the Glastonbury experience had given them.

CHAPTER SEVEN

Deans Yard

THE YEAR 1907 SAW THE CUP being paraded before numerous academic sages in an effort to substantiate the psychically derived story of its origin. In many ways it was treated more like a person - some potential star whose talent was being surveyed by experts before being launched to a position of influence on the world's stage. For its young provincial finders it was their passport, too, to a fuller rapport with the larger world establishment. The Cup had become the means of a 'rite of passage' toward greater spiritual and social fulfilment.

The first authority of any note to be shown the vessel was Dom Aidan Gasquet, Abbot President of the Benedictine Order in England. Gasquet's opinion on the Cup was the first of many, from that day to this, which have signally failed to throw any really helpful light on its age or place of origin. In his view it seemed unique and was probably of either Imperial Roman or Greek (or Roman) Christian manufacture. He referred Wellesley to a Mr Reed, of the British Museum, who decided that it was 'a clever copy of Imperial Roman work'. Later, one of his colleagues, Mr Wilde, was more accommodating, allowing for at least three possible origins: Phoenician or Roman (about 500 BC); Venetian (in the Middle Ages); or a recent copy.

After some consideration it was agreed to let Dom Gasquet borrow the Cup, first to show it to his brother and then to seek the opinion of several specialist firms in the Birmingham area. All shared the belief that it was of ancient manufacture.

While Gasquet had the Cup with him a rather odd thing happened. He had called in on Mr and Mrs Turville Petre at their home at Bosworth Hall, Husbands Bosworth, Leicestershire. They took the opportunity to ask him to investigate some of the Court Rolls and manuscripts in the library. While he was there he placed the Cup for safekeeping high up on a darkened shelf. He was not a tall man, and when the time came for him to leave he reached up and groped around on the shelf, unable to locate it. Instead his hand came into contact with a volume of very ancient parchment manuscripts. It turned out to be a previously unknown Psalter of about the tenth century, giving the complete monastic form of the Divine Office as publicly said, and a Calendar of the Cathedral Church at Canterbury. There was even a likely connection with Glastonbury, as Gasquet explains in the published edition:

"It is perfectly evident from the unique character and indeed splendour of the Psalter, whether we regard its size, the handwriting or the ornamentation, that it must have been written for some great personage. No person connected with Christ Church, Canterbury, would seem to be more likely to have been the possessor of this manuscript, so notable in its art and execution, than St. Dunstan, the first ecclesiastic of the kingdom. In this connection also it must be remembered that the calender contained in the volume is based on the calender of the monastery of Glastonbury, which is what might be expected in the case of one who had been Abbot of that House."

Dunstan, of course, had been born and raised in the Glastonbury area, a pupil of the Saxon Abbey and later its Abbot. King Edgar made him Archbishop of Canterbury in 959.

The inspirations of psychics were still not ignored. The best of these came from Miss Humphries, a psychometrist and clairvoyant living in reduced circumstances at 44 Elgin Crescent, Notting Hill. Wellesley called on her with the Cup on 27 January, 1907. She took him into an ill-lit back room and, with the Cup on her lap, spoke her impressions out loud as they came to her. She felt that the vessel was of extreme age and proposed an origin in India around 1,000 BC. There then followed a series of images of some intensity - of the Last Supper; of Jesus with St. John and Mary Magdalene; of the Crucifixion and the rock-tomb where Jesus was laid. At this point she confessed herself "too overcome with the power of the Cup to go on". She also reported seeing a female figure standing near the vessel while the sitting was going on. Wellesley saw no concrete image, but was aware of a kind of phosphorescent glow issuing from the Cup, filling the room in the half-light. The whole experience convinced Wellesley that Miss Humphries was a reliable and genuine sensitive. It was not his only consultation with her.

As to the vision of a woman, others had seen a similar figure, sometimes kneeling, sometimes standing by the vessel. Often the face was veiled. The capacity of the Cup to induce such clairvoyance in certain people extended through the whole of its time in the sanctuary at Royal York Crescent. Various symbolic forms were reported. On one occasion Christine witnessed "a very beautiful white dove with outspread wings" hovering over the casket which held the Cup. Another time, while she was officiating at a service, "a very beautiful angel entirely enveloped in its own wings" appeared to her during the saying of the Sanctus.

In the spring of 1907, while Christine and Janet were staying in London, their attention was drawn to a series of lectures to be given by Archdeacon Basil Wilberforce, Canon of Westminster and Chaplain to the Speaker of the House of Commons, on the subject of the relationship of the eastern religions to Christianity. They duly attended and were not at all disappointed; his universalist point of view and the quality of his inspiration impressed them greatly. Surely here was someone of learning and influence who might give serious consideration to the Cup and its story? They did not approach him then, but returned to Bristol to confer with the others. They agreed to contact the Archdeacon. Their enquiry brought a kindly and positive response and a meeting was arranged for a little later on.

It was a time of much anticipation. Other things were in the air: Glastonbury Abbey was up for auction; there were even more visitors to the Oratory, among them a rich American, Mrs Garrison, who intended to bid at the Abbey sale. On 6 June, Wellesley, Janet and Christine went down to watch the bidding. Mrs Garrison was no match for the Nottingham businessman, Ernest Jardine, who won the day. He later negotiated the re-sale of the ancient ruins to the Church of England.

That summer the Cup was inspected by various other people of note. Among these were Annie Besant (elected that year President of the Theosophical Society) and the authority on the western mystical and occult tradition A. E. Waite.

Mrs Besant "gave it as her opinion that the Cup was very strongly magnetized. Also that there were those on the other side who were keenly interested in Its fate and who were working to bring about through It certain combinations of people and circumstances". She also advised that the Cup should be kept in its present hands and anticipated very curious and important developments.

Wellesley visited Waite at his London office, not long after seeing Mrs Besant. The story was given due consideration, but Waite wrote later that he could accept no link between the glass vessel and the Grail of legend. But from his own impression of the meeting, Wellesley reported that Waite had "never felt so impressed as when he saw the Cup". The older man's experience over the years with some of the more dubious devotees of the esoteric orders under his supervision had taught him the wisdom of caution. Certainly, he was impressed, but in no way convinced. During the same period as all the Cup activity at Glastonbury and Bristol, Waite had been exploring the mystical and sacramental contexts of the Grail story, delivering his views in a succession of articles for *The Occult Review*. Compiled together these formed the substance of his book, *The Hidden Church of the Holy Graal* (1909). For him the Grail was primarily a spiritual and symbolic object; he was not the sort of person to be easily persuaded by claims for its material existence. But aside from the Grail question he did accept that it was "possible that under other aspects the Glastonbury relic may be of great interest.., and importance". He was not dismissive:

> "At that very early period of the Church when the vessels of altar were of glass, it is quite possible that such an object may have served as a paten and there are other explanations in view which, although they make the sacramental connexion more doubtful, have a cogency within their own lines; but I leave the development of these in the hands of Mr Tudor Pole, as he has the first right to speak of them and will, I believe, do so when he has completed the course of his investigations."

Archdeacon Wilberforce, on the other hand, went along all the way with the idea that it *was* the Holy Grail that had been found at Glastonbury.

Albert Basil Orme Wilberforce was born on 15 February, 1841, the son of Bishop Samuel Wilberforce, and grandson of William Wilberforce, campaigner in the British Parliament for the abolition of slavery and the slave trade. His mother had died from fever less than a month after his birth, a circumstance attributed to the fact that the town drain passed directly beneath the ecclesiastical family home.

He was rigorous in some matters and infinitely flexible and liberal in others. He campaigned vigorously for the temperance lobby, had no respect at all for the medical profession and was totally opposed to vivisection. His openness in matters of religion drew criticism. He was condemned for allowing an unbaptized Hindu to address his congregation from the pulpit. He also administered the sacrament of anointing the sick with oil - something quite out of keeping with current Church of England practices.

Much of his spiritual direction had come from outside the Church. He used to attend the annual conferences held at Broadlands in Hampshire (later the home of Earl Mountbatten), which had been started by American Quakers and welcomed all-comers. Here

ARCHDEACON BASIL WILBERFORCE

Wilberforce met James Williamson Farquhar, who had by turns been a Presbyterian, a Swedenborgian, a Spiritualist - and had even lectured on behalf of atheism! Farquhar's *Gospel of Divine Humanity* had a profound influence on Wilberforce.

The Archdeacon was also a dedicated attender of spiritualist seances. For him, communication with the departed seemed a perfectly normal and proper thing to do, in no way in conflict with his ministry. Something of his metaphysical position is shown in this extract of his revision of the Creed:

> "...The Holy Spirit is the Lord, the Life-giver and the Sustainer of the Universe; the Inspirer of art, science, literature, prophesy, inspiration, holiness, prayer. Though limitless, dateless and universal, He is revealed as discoverable and accessible in the Holy Catholic Church. He is the invisible bond between souls that are sundered. He assures of pardon; convinces of the non-reality of death; and of the endless continuity of the individual life. Amen."

Politically Wilberforce was a Liberal and supported Gladstone, who in turn repaid the churchman by appointing him to the Canonry of Westminster - but with the proviso that he did not preach abstinence from alcohol from the pulpit of Westminster Abbey.

However much an individual and an innovator, he could not have been closer to the heart of the establishment of the nation. He performed his State duties meticulously, carrying the Imperial Crown at the coronation of Edward VII in 1902 (and later the Queen's Crown at the coronation of George V in 1910).

A notable feature of the congregation at his Church of St. John the Evangelist, Smith Square, was that women outnumbered men by ten to one. It was observed that "women somehow felt safe with him", pouring out their troubles "into his patient ears, secure not only of genuine sympathy, but also of sensible advice".

His biographer wrote:

> "He had known in his life the guiding influence of a woman's love, and his sense of what he owed to it affected his view of everything that pertained to womankind. Conspicuously it made him an eager advocate of female suffrage; it led him to rely on woman's help in all works of moral reclamation; and it inclined him to a lenient judgement on woman's faults, even when the suffragettes tried to destroy St. John's Church."

The marriage of Basil and Charlotte Wilberforce was a remarkable spiritual and emotional entity. As Gladstone observed: "So nearly did the union of thought, heart and action both fulfil the ideal and bring duality to the borders of identity."

The kindly, genial man who received Wellesley at 20 Deans Yard was genuinely concerned to hear everything his younger visitor had to tell him - as might be expected of someone whose character was said to encompass 'a blending of boisterous fun and animal spirits with a deep and absorbing sense of the seriousness of religion'.

The house that Wellesley entered for the first time on 23 June was exceptionally well-appointed in every way. The Wilberforces had effected many striking alterations and renovations since their arrival in 1894. These included the restoration of some fourteenth century frescoes discovered in a stone walled chamber below the level of Deans Yard. As entertainers Basil and Charlotte were second-to-none among the social élite of the capital city.

Wellesley gave Wilberforce a full account of the Cup and his own understanding of it. While he was there he was introduced to two other visitors of note: the American author Mark Twain (Samuel Clemens) and the physicist and psychical researcher, Sir William Crookes.

Clemens was in the middle of a visit to Britain, hastening through a tight schedule of appointments, private and official. The day before he had been a guest at the King's Garden Party at Windsor Castle, and was elated to have been driven away with other dignitaries through streets of cheering crowds. Wilberforce was an old friend. They both shared an interest in the figure of Joan of Arc, the Archdeacon being particularly fond of Mark Twain's curiously titled *Personal Recollections of Joan of Arc* (his comedy-spoof *A Connecticut Yankee at King Arthur's Court* might have been more apposite to this occasion).

Wellesley was taken into Wilberforce's library and was introduced to Samuel Clemens, who later described him as "a plain-looking man, suggesting in dress and appearance the English tradesman'. He was then shown an object which the Archdeacon pronounced as being "The Holy Grail". Clemens would normally have been quick to ridicule any such pretensions, but the fact that the sapphire blue bowl was so different from its traditional representations made him less sceptical:

"I am glad I have lived to see that half-hour - that astonishing half-hour. In its way it stands alone in my life's experience. In the belief of two persons present this was the very vessel which was brought by night and secretly delivered to Nicodemus, nearly nineteen centuries ago, after the Creator of the Universe had delivered up his life on the cross for the redemption of the human race; the very cup which the stainless Sir Galahad has sought with knightly devotion in far fields of peril and adventure in Arthur's time, fourteen hundred years ago; the same cup which princely knights of other bygone ages had laid down their lives in long and patient efforts to find, and had passed from life disappointed - and here it was at last, dug up by a grain-broker at no cost of blood or travel, and apparently no purity required of him other than the average purity of the twentieth century dealer in cereal futures; not even a stately name required - no Sir Galahad, no Sir Bors de Ganis, no Sir Lancelot of the Lake - nothing but a mere Mr Pole."

The other visitor, Crookes, was there in order to see the Cup. The discoverer of the element thallium and cathode rays, he also had the distinction of being the first person to live in a house lit by electricity, having made the bulbs himself. Wilberforce had brought him in because of his knowledge of the properties of glass. He had been president of the Society for Psychical Research for four years from 1896.

Wellesley agreed to let him have the Cup for a week so as to make a more careful examination of it. Crookes' report came up with some useful details about the way the Cup might have been made; not being an antiquarian, he made no comment on its age or origin:

"The Cup is a saucer-shaped vessel 136mm outside diameter and 23mm deep at the centre. It is about 7mm thick, but varies slightly in places. The curvature is roughly spherical, i.e., a segment of a sphere 56mm would fall within the thickness of the glass. It is formed of two surfaces, each from two to four millimetres thick and separated by fragments of silver leaf.

Each surface is built up of squares of glass mosaic having on them a beautiful design like a double Maltese cross. The obverse is made up of 25 to 30 such squares arranged in 7 rows, 4, 5 and 6 pieces in the centre rows and a less number in the top and bottom rows; the reverse not so many.

From the appearance of the ground work, it appears as if the mosaics originally were about 24mm square and 4mm thick, the great distortion of all but the centre ones being caused by subsequent fusion and moulding into shape. Each mosaic square has been sliced off a compound bar of glass made somewhat as follows:

A thick rod of green glass is taken as a centre, and round it are packed four triangular lumps of reddish-brown glass, with the blunt points inwards, so that the cross-section will be like a Maltese cross. Lozenge-shaped pieces of the same reddish-brown are then packed between the arms, so as to form in section a double Maltese cross. Thinner rods of green glass are now packed outside each of the eight points of the cross and the whole mass is heated in a furnace to the softening point and then dipped into a bath of clear colourless glass of a little lower fusing point. When well cemented together by the clear glass the whole lump is roughly fashioned to a rectangular shape and then drawn to a bar about 24mm square. While still hot, but hard, it is cut into slices about 4mm thick by sudden blows with a hatchet-shaped tool. It is seen that each slice will thus form a mosaic having on it an ornamental, double Maltese cross set in a square of clear glass. These square mosaics are then fitted together and at red (softening) heat squeezed into contact.

In the Cup the joints can be traced by streaks of air bubbles, showing that the main rod of composite glass had been allowed to cool and condense moisture, or has become soiled on the surface. This interferes with the perfect union between two pieces of glass. An examination of the different mosaics where they have not been too much distorted by fusion, shows that they have been cut from the same compound rod, for it is possible to trace little peculiarities in the formation of the pattern through each piece. For instance, taking the four lozenge-shaped pieces between the four arms of the cross it is seen that each has a definite character. One is more pointed at each end, another is pointed at one end and more round at the other, while another has a small flaw at the outer end. These peculiarities run through all the mosaics, and prove that they have all been cut from the same compound rod. From careful examination, I think the workman made an oblong sheet of mosaic glass large enough to form the obverse and reverse of the Cup. When in a soft plastic state one half was laid on a convex mould of baked clay, silver leaf was then put between, and the rest of the half of mosaic turned over and squeezed down, the whole being returned to the furnace from time to time until all parts were melted together.

But on the reverse the soft glass naturally ran down to the sides, and it was forced or plastered back towards the centre, some of the mosaics hereby being distorted almost out of recognition. The obverse concave surface being supported by the clay mould would not suffer such distortion. When still soft an iron rod with a lump of glass on it, technically called 'punty', was stuck to the centre of the reverse side to act as a temporary handle, and the vessel was trimmed at the edges with shears (these shear marks can now be seen). It was subjected quickly to a good heat to glaze the obverse surface and the cut edges and the temporary

THE CUP OR BOWL
(by kind permission of the Chalice Well Trust)

handle of glass removed by a drop of water and the vessel was cooled and annealed. The rough piece remaining is then ground off.

A careful scrutiny of the reverse side shows that the 'punty mark' has been ground off in the middle. The pattern does not go through, the mosaics on the obverse do not correspond in fashion with those on the reverse. The obverse side shows by certain circular markings on it that the mould in which it has been pressed had probably been turned on a potter's wheel, for circular markings on the mould are reproduced on the glazed surface. The reverse side must originally have been different thicknesses in different places, and after removing the 'punty mark', the whole has been roughly ground to bring it approximately to the same curvature as the obverse.

Another explanation of what I call the 'punty mark' may be suggested. The original vessel might have had an ornamental stem or foot. In Murray's Dictionary, under the heading 'Cup' it is said that "the larger and more ornamental form (e.g. a wine cup or chalice) may have a stem or foot". The stem might have been broken off by accident and the remaining fragment ground away, so as to preserve the upper portion as a shallow cup.

I have now described the mode in which I imagine the Cup may have been fashioned. The modes of glass working detailed are such as are in use in most large glass houses at the present day and do not differ materially from what we know were the methods of work in much earlier days. The workman who fashioned the Cup was an artist whose ideas were far in advance of the somewhat crude appliances at his disposal."

On 28 June Janet went up to London to collect the Cup. Wilberforce told her that he had decided to convene a special meeting of scholars and religious leaders at his home on 20 July. Wellesley would be able to give an address and the Cup viewed and discussed by all present. The event should be kept private.

The news caused much anticipation and not a little apprehension within the group at Bristol. Publicity for the Cup could cause difficulty. As on other occasions when the vessel was 'public' they would observe an unbroken vigil of silent prayer in the Oratory.

So on Saturday, 20 July, the various invited dignitaries foregathered at Deans Yard quite unsure of what to expect. Crookes was there along with the United States Ambassador, the Duke of Newcastle, Sir John Evans, Canon Duckworth, the Rev. R. J. Campbell, Lord Halifax and Dr Ginsberg of the British Museum - altogether some forty people. Deeply absorbed in the proceedings was Alice Buckton, a writer and educationalist destined to play a major role in the Avalonian life of Glastonbury.

The presentation of the event had been thoroughly prepared. The Cup was displayed in its glass-fronted casket on a table in front of the guests. Wellesley was introduced and invited to explain how he came by the vessel and his beliefs about it. He went through everything - his quest to find a holy relic at Glastonbury; his vision of Bride's Well; Goodchild's role and the recovery of the Cup and subsequent events.

It was a novel occasion for all present; whatever else they may have thought, it was in no sense boring. The scientists attending were sufficiently impressed to recommend further investigation.

It was too much to expect things to be kept quiet for long. Somehow the news of the event leaked out. By Friday, 26 July, the Daily Express was carrying a long article which attempted to cover everything that had transpired at the meeting. The headline proclaimed: Mystery of a Relic; Finder Believes it to be the Holy Grail; Two Visions; Great Scientists Puzzled; Discovered at Glastonbury.

There were many errors, but the general drift of the Cup story was there as given by Wellesley Tudor Pole the previous Saturday, as the opening paragraphs show:

"A small circle of eminent leaders of religious thought, antiquaries and scientists are at present discussing with the deepest interest, the discovery in remarkable circumstances of a glass vessel of beautiful workmanship and supposed great antiquity, in a spot near Glastonbury Abbey.

The discovery was made by the sister of Mr Wellesley Tudor Pole, of Bristol, and two other ladies, as a result of a suggestion by Mr Tudor Pole that they should go and search in a place which he had seen, either in his mind's eye or in what seems to have been a waking dream'.

Mr Tudor Pole has submitted the vessel to various experts, who are unable to assign a date for its origin. It may be 2,500 years old. At any rate, it has been pronounced within the last few days to be pre-Venetian.

One of the strangest features concerning it is that it was placed in a spot near Glastonbury nearly nine years ago by Dr Goodchild, of Bath, a man of much antiquarian knowledge, also as the result of what is described as a 'trance', and Dr Goodchild entertains the belief, consequent upon his strange experiences, that it is the cup which the Saviour used at the Last Supper, and which, according to the Glastonbury Legend, was brought to Britain after the Crucifixion.

Mr Tudor Pole communicated his story to an eminent dignitary of the Church of England in London with whom he is acquainted, and at this gentleman's request attended a meeting at the house of the dignitary in London on Saturday last, and narrated all the circumstances concerning the discovery."

The 'first-hand' quality of the text suggests that the writer must have been present at the meeting:

"Mr Pole is the managing director of a large grain business at Bristol. He is about thirty years of age [actually he was twenty-three!], a man of keen intelligence, with clean-cut features and dark, deep-set eyes. He confesses that he is to some extent 'clairvoyant' or 'clairaudient', although he has not devoted much time to the study of the occult.

While Mr Pole holds that there is not sufficient ground for believing that the object of his discovery is of the sacred nature attributed to it by Dr Goodchild, he is firmly convinced that it is a 'holy relic', and has now installed it in a room in his house, which has been set apart for it. The room is draped in white. The vessel reposes in a casket on a table, and lighted candles are kept in the room.

It will be seen that the whole treatment of the 'cup' is of a mystical nature. The story which Mr Pole told to his distinguished audience on Saturday last was of the most extraordinary kind, and although it cannot be said that it was accepted as a statement of hard fact, the gentlemen and ladies present found no reason to entertain the slightest suspicion of the good faith of the narrator."

The details of the events described in the rest of this long report have been given more accurately elsewhere. A commentary in another column of the paper is much more interesting and reveals some surprising insights into current attitudes to the 'unknown':

"The astounding story, told at length in another column, of the finding of an alleged 'holy relic' at Glastonbury Abbey has a particular value in showing once again the immense and widespread interest felt in things supernatural and mystic. This is a utilitarian age, an age of steam and commerce and speculation. But it is, at the same time, an age of almost disquieting mystery. The phonograph and the wireless telegram are things far more mysterious, actually perhaps far less explicable, than the mysteries framed and believed in past ages. The more man discovers, the less he feels he knows, and the less is he inclined to adopt an attitude of absolute denial in face of any assertion of any proposition, however improbable it may seem. A Bristol gentleman discovers a mysterious vessel at Glastonbury. Twenty years ago he would have been merely laughed out. Today, eminent men, among them divines and scientists, solemnly meet to discuss his story and to endeavour to discover what the vessel may be.

It is good for the world to have really learned that 'there are more things in heaven and earth than dreamt of in our philosophy'. The science of the middle Victorian era was cock-sure in its materialism. It smiled loftily at the idea of miracles, it sneered at the existence of the mystic and the unseen. But wisdom did not begin and end with the disciples of Darwin and Huxley. Life can never be understood if one limits its possibilities to that which can be perceived by the senses. Certainly the more modern interest in the mystic has led to much folly and made easy much fraud. But in so far as we are moving away from a purely materialistic explanation of the universe, we are moving in the right direction. There is no reason why we should leave our common sense behind us, or that we should shut our eyes and rejoice in being duped. But knowledge, after all, is only one part of wisdom. We express no opinion as to what the Glastonbury find maybe, but it does seem to us both interesting and, in one sense, admirable that the finding of an alleged 'holy relic' should stir the interest of a body of eminent men of widely differing opinions and culture."

We might add, interesting and admirable too that the 'holy relic' should stir a gentleman of the press to come up with such a piece of inspired copy.

In the days that followed its publication, the *Daily Express* article was reproduced in provincial papers all over the country. There was much excitement and yet more commentaries appeared in print - not least in the home territory of the story.

The Bristol Evening News reported that their representative "had had a conversation on Friday morning with Mr Tudor Pole, the Bristolian whose discovery has disturbed scientific circles and caused a wide-spread sensation". The report goes on to speculate whether the Cup is the 'Great Sapphire' mentioned in an inventory taken at Glastonbury in the time of Henry the Eighth. The effect of the sudden publicity is also discussed:

"The discovery was made some time ago, and so far the secret has been carefully guarded. It was not the wish of those who knew of the discovery that the fact should have been made public yet awhile, but the researchers have had time to get to work, and may be trusted to have made enough progress not to allow outer influences to make any difference. As Mr Tudor Pole said, the matter has become of the very highest interest; and it may well be that the present publicity may be the means of assistance rather than hindrance."

The press was after everyone. A journalist from the Western Daily Press called on Dr Goodchild at Bath - primarily to check on the claims made about the Cup:

"Dr Goodchild's own opinion is that, while the vessel may not be the actual one used at the Last Supper, it is one carried by the Saviour in the belt which all teachers wore, and used by him, either personally or by his disciples. Dr Goodchild pointed out that a great many experts were at present engaged in the interesting work of solving the mystery, and in due time a full and ample account of the whole discovery would be given... Dr Goodchild concluded with adding that Sir William Crookes was engaged in the pursuit of investigation, and going most minutely into the various theories, Sir William was absolutely convinced of its antiquity, of its unusual merit, and of its special character."

As it turned out, Sir William was rather less than convinced when he responded to an enquiry from a *Daily News* reporter with impeccable scientific reservation: "I must not say anything at all about it. Up to the present I have not had sufficient examination to enable me to come to any decision upon the matter."

When Wilberforce was approached he refused to discuss the matter at all.

Thomas Pole thought he was having a quiet weekend in Glastonbury when he was cornered by a reporter from the *Central Somerset Gazette:*

"Asked for his opinion with regard to the supposed antiquity and sacred nature of the vessel, Mr Pole said that when told of the matter by his son he was inclined to be sceptical and rather leaned to the belief that the cup was of Italian workmanship of recent date. Later on, however, proceeded Mr Pole, my son gave me a full account of his personal experiences - of which you have doubtless read in connection with the find, and also some other remarkable coincidences. These caused me to think seriously of the affair, and eventually my opinion changed, and I no longer had any doubt, but became fully convinced that the cup was not only of great antiquity, but that it had been used for some very sacred purpose... The whole affair, went on Mr Pole, is a most extraordinary one, and there can be little wonder that it is regarded with a certain amount of unbelief... But there is no doubt that no collusion between Dr Goodchild and my son took place."

An interview with Abbot Aidan Gasquet appeared in the *Daily Express:*

"I certainly think it is an ancient piece of work, but what its history is can only be guessed. It is a very curious piece of glass. I know nothing like it, and none of the antiquaries to whom I showed it could tell me anything like it.

But I can only say that there is no historical evidence in support of the story that is told of it. There are two weak points in the chain at least.

First of all, there is no evidence that, either at the dissolution of the Monastery of Glastonbury, or for the centuries before any claim was ever made, that the Holy Grail reposed at Glastonbury. Secondly, there is no evidence that, if it was ever at Glastonbury, it was ever taken to Bordighera, or anywhere else in Italy.

They say it was brought to England by Joseph of Arimathea. There is no historical evidence of that. There is only the legend... The only point of view from which I am interested in the vessel is the antiquarian point of view."

All this talk of the Grail and the Cup of the Last Supper was worrying Dr Goodchild. He decided to write to the editor of the *Daily Express* about this and the errors in their report:

Dear Sir

There are certain errors of fact in the *Express* account of the 'Cup' which I should be glad if you allow me to correct. I had met Mr Tudor Pole and corresponded with him on various occasions since his first visit to Glastonbury in the early part of 1904. Prior to this I had only met him *once.* The 'Cup' however, formed no part of our conversations, and between 1900 and September, 1906, I did not myself believe it was at Glastonbury.

The story of my purchase of the 'Cup' is fairly correct, but the price paid was about £3, and not £6, as reported. In my experience at Paris in 1897, not 1896,1 was *not* told that this was *'the Cup carried by Jesus the Christ'.* I was directed to take it to Bride's Hill, Glastonbury, a place which I had never visited. The concluding phrase of my directions runs:

'Later, a young girl will make a pure offering of herself at the spot where you laid down the 'Cup', and this shall be a sign to you.'

This 'sign' was given by Miss Tudor Pole last summer, but I did not at the time know to what it referred, nor did I connect it directly with the 'Cup'.

The 'Cup' was *not* sent to me by my father, but brought to me by my sister some time after my father's death.

The place of deposit is neither a 'well nor a spring', but a sluice, locally a 'clyce', under a thorn by the river Brue, and I have visited it annually since 1898, except in 1905. In 1900 the clyce had obviously to a great extent been cleaned out. In 1902 I was accompanied by a friend who had had the entire spot most elaborately described to her when a child by an old clergyman then residing in Bath. She herself had made no previous visit to the Thorn.

In 1899 the late William Sharp published *The Divine Adventure*, which contains his own vision of the Thorn. On August 1st, 1904, he paid his first visit to Glastonbury in company with myself. In the clyce we found a small token left there by Miss Tudor Pole, and returned it next day with such tokens of thanks as we deemed suitable.

On September 2nd, last year, friends of Miss Pole's saw the 'Cup' and left it beneath the Thorn. On the 25th they called on me and informed me, much to my surprise, of what they had seen. On the 29th, Mr Pole and his sister called upon the same matter, and I gave them a full outline of all the facts within my knowledge, warning them at the same time that my story was one which they could not expect any sane person to accept unless it had full and ample corroboration elsewhere. It says no little for Miss Tudor Pole's entire faith in her brother's visions that two days later she went by herself to Glastonbury, and on a chill, rainy, October day waded into deep and peculiarly unpleasant mud, found at once the object of her search with her feet, and carried it home with her.

One last note; I have *no* reason for supposing that the 'Cup' was ever at Glastonbury before I myself took it there, nor have I any reason for connecting it directly with the Joseph of Arimathea legend.

Yours very sincerely
J. A. Goodchild

Goodchild had already written to the Clifton group before the Deans Yard meeting to stress that in his Paris instructions the word 'cup' was always used - never 'grail'. It had now become a point of some difficulty. The impression is given that in his view Wellesley and his friends had become too much 'carried away' with the Grail idea, preventing others from taking the matter seriously or apprehending its true purpose. He saw the whole operation as a ritual enactment of the reawakening of the slumbering mysteries of the Celtic West through the placing of the Cup of Christ in the sacred well near Bride's Hill, the site of an ancient shrine dedicated to the cult High Queen of Ireland. The Joseph of Arimathea story had no bearing on his thesis, neither did the Arthurian material to any great extent.

Meanwhile Wilberforce was proposing another meeting for some time in the following winter, limited to a handful of carefully vetted 'experts'. Before this he and his wife paid a visit to the Oratory at Royal York Crescent. We know it was on 6 November, but there seems to be no record of their reactions.

The second Deans Yard meeting did in fact take place on 27 January, 1908. It was a discouraging affair; Dr Ginsberg, Mr Reed and Mr Cobb were present. Ginsberg gave out the 'results of his investigations' and the proceedings closed with the general consensus that the Cup was 'fairly modern'.

By this stage Wilberforce may have been having doubts about his own precipitate enthusiasm for the Glastonbury 'Grail'. His hoped-for news blackout of the first meeting had failed and he was likely to have trouble with his superiors in the Church even though the press report had studiously avoided naming him. Something of the Archdeacon's dilemma is revealed in a private memorandum written by his godson, the late Col. H. M. Farmar, in 1939.

Col. Farmar and his wife were married by Archdeacon Wilberforce on 31 July, 1907. Not long afterwards they were invited by Mrs Wilberforce to lunch at Deans Yard. There was another guest, a Mr Daly, who had missed the meeting on 20 July owing to an acting commitment in Dublin. They found themselves listening to Wilberforce telling Daly all about the Cup. The now familiar story was fully explained. Additionally, they heard that the churchman had turned down a request from Wellesley to place the vessel for a period of time in St. John's, Westminster. He had advised him that it ought to remain in his own keeping.

After an absence abroad, Col. Farmar saw Mrs Wilberforce again and asked her if there had been any developments regarding the Cup. She replied that the Archdeacon did not wish to answer any questions on that subject; it had led to some complications, and for the while he should not be worried.

Meanwhile the Bristol group were not put off by Dr Ginsberg's unhelpful verdict - after all, others had deliberated differently. But one thing is clear: from that time on they were careful to play down any suggestion of a link between their Cup and the Holy Grail. There is a note in their diary which attempts a revision of their position:

> "The word 'Grail', when it occurs in this record, must not be taken to mean the Holy Grail of medieval legend, which was the inner vision of the Soul - the Mystic Cup no mortal eye can see. It refers in this connection to the vessel found at Glastonbury, believed to be the Cup of the Master Jesus."

The lesson here ought to be that if you do not want people to think you have found the Holy Grail, it is sensible to call it something else. It took the likes of Goodchild and A. E. Waite to persuade them to think more deeply on the symbolic aspect of the image, which in their initial enthusiasm they applied too literally to their find. It might also have saved Archdeacon Wilberforce a measure of embarrassment.

An understanding of the allegorical status of the Grail matured in Wellesley to allow him to write in such terms to Rosamond Lehmann in the last years of his life:

> "Half a century ago, in the Women's Quarter at Glastonbury, from the depths of the Well of St. Bride, a Cup was brought out into the light of day. This vessel is the symbol of the heavenly and eternal Grail, the Chalice of Christ, the Promise of the Future."

CHAPTER EIGHT

Builders of Joy

THE PEOPLE OF GLASTONBURY were somewhat bemused by the national publicity about something of which they had previously been quite unaware. Not least, farmer James Mapstone, of Northload Bridge, was very put out to learn that someone had found an object on the land he owned at Beckery and had gone off with it without his permission. He decided to make his own investigation of the well to see if anything else was there. He and some friends recovered various trivial items of little monetary value, including a George III twopenny piece, two mother-of-pearl ornaments, two glass bangles and a solitaire. Over many years these had been placed there by people seeking spiritual help from the holy well. Ignorant of the practice, a local reporter sought to dramatize the situation by suggesting they might have been the proceeds of a robbery.

Back in Bristol there was a lot to contend with as enquiries flooded in from all quarters, among them many from people who had been at the Deans Yard meeting. Most wanted to find out more about their activities; others had more bizarre intentions. The eccentric Ralph de Tunstall Sneyd* turned up to ask if he could take away a chip of the Cup to place in his own eclectic Buddhist, Druidic, Christian, and Arthurian Oratory of the Order of the Holy Grail set up in a converted stable block at his home at Onecote, near Leek, in Staffordshire. He was given a polite, but firm, refusal. There were also further communications from psychic sources

The day after Wilberforce's meeting, Miss Helena Humphries received a clairvoyant vision of an ancient manuscript, which if recovered would help to fill in the story of the origin of the Cup. Quite independently, a South African medium, Miss Leslie Moore, sent a telegram to Wellesley on that same day, asking him to meet her in

---

*I had no idea that Steve Sneyd, who used to contribute poems to *Torc* magazine, was a kinsman of this gentleman. Thanks to Steve for correcting the erroneous description of him which I had copied from the pilgrims' diary in the first edition of this book.

London as soon as possible.

Wellesley lost no time at all and travelled to London to meet her and her friend, Miss Hooey, the next day. They discussed matters at some length. Leslie Moore explained that she had had clear psychic indications that the finding of the Cup was an event she had been waiting for. She was sure that there were further revelations to come, and that they should keep in touch.

Two days later, Miss Moore, apparently by that time in France, received some more communications which seemed to indicate very positively that certain ancient documents relating to the Cup could be found at Constantinople, buried beneath a marble slab near the Seraglio palace. After a further meeting Wellesley was sufficiently impressed to make preparations for a journey to Constantinople to find out. A sealed packet of the psychic communications was sent to Archdeacon Wilberforce should any future verification be needed.

Wellesley left for Constantinople on 21 August, 1907, after a day-long vigil of prayer for his mission had been observed in the Clifton Oratory. The political situation in Turkey at that time was precarious, and the area where Wellesley hoped to carry out his investigation was vulnerable. He identified the spot he believed had been described by Miss Moore, close to the Harem gardens and within the palace precincts. Armed guards were everywhere, making access too risky.

During this time, the Bristol group was giving all the spiritual support it could. Miss Moore wrote to them saying that their prayers were assisting Wellesley in his difficult task. Dr Goodchild joined the devotees at the Oratory, calling upon various saints to intercede on Wellesley's behalf.

Saints or no saints, any close investigation of the Constantinople site was impossible. Wellesley decided to return to England, leaving an Englishman called Bryant to keep a watch over things after his departure. Bryant enlisted the help of several local people who could be trusted to seek out ways of inspecting the site without attracting attention. Wellesley arrived back in England on 16 September, somewhat disappointed but still hopeful of success at another time.

The Royal York Crescent Oratory was busy with even more visitors. Alice Buckton came on 20 September, staying some while and visiting Glastonbury twice (see Chapter 10). She was also introduced to Dr Goodchild for the first time. The Wilberforces came on 6 November.

More messages and words of advice kept arriving from Miss Moore. It was claimed that the 'spies' in Constantinople should not have been trusted and even Bryant was being bribed by agents of the Church of Rome to pass to them any ancient manuscripts that came into his possession. Wellesley was warned about the danger of going to Constantinople again.

What was so special about these supposed records? According to the communications, they comprised some sayings of John of Patmos, author of the Book of Revelation (who could neither read nor write), dictated to Polycarp. These writings - possibly inscribed on mica plates - were believed to contain references that would throw light on the early history of the Cup and also lay to rest some age-old questions of alleged inconsistencies within the four Gospels. They were believed to have been taken to Rome and later removed to their present location on the site of the library of the Emperor Constantine.

Wellesley left once again for Constantinople on 19 December. Mindful of the warnings given, he was evidently in disguise. Years later, he was happy to amuse people with the story of his ineptitude in carrying this off effectively. Apparently the false beard he was wearing fell into his soup while travelling on the Orient Express in full view of the other passengers. On arrival, one of Bryant's 'spies', who had managed to get within sight of the stone slab, showed him a drawing he had made of the markings on its upper surface. Wellesley was surprised and encouraged that these seemed identical with those described by Miss Moore in her own vision of the stone. However, the trip was not otherwise any more satisfactory, although Wellesley reported that Bryant had been 'quite reliable' as an assistant.

He returned to Bristol early in January, feeling there was good reason to suppose the documents had already been removed from the site. Not long after this Bryant wrote that he was keeping up his efforts to get near the stone, but had consistently met with difficulties.

The whole matter of these alleged buried records became something of a life-long quest and challenge for Wellesley and yet was never resolved. Many years later his friend, Sir David Russell, financed archeological excavations at the site which still yielded no evidence for the supposed documents. It became as perplexing as the search for the identity and origin of the Cup itself, and something which, in the end, Wellesley had to confess was one of his life's failures.

It will be remembered that Thomas and Kate Pole were keen supporters of the idea of 'garden cities'. They were, in fact, members of the Garden City Association, started in 1899 by Sir Ebenezer Howard. Born in the City of London in 1850, Howard was a practical idealist and a tireless campaigner for his beliefs. His younger years were spent work-ing as an office secretary, but included a spell farming in America. He was preoccupied with social questions and was determined to do something about the squalid conditions generated by the industrial revolution. He saw that town-living brought many advantages socially, but that human beings became psychologically impoverished if they had no contact with nature or the rural economy. In the garden city everything would be brought together. He shared and discussed many of his ideas with Sir Patrick Geddes (one-time Edinburgh associate of William Sharp and the first publisher of the Fiona Macleod books of WS). Geddes, though, tended to be more interested in curing the problems of major cities, but still employed a similar 'organic' analysis of human and environmental imperatives in his solutions. For both it was not just a matter of architecture - it had to make economic sense too.

It was Howard's stated intention "to build by private enterprise per-vaded by public spirit an entirely new town, industrial, residential, and agricultural". Inevitably there would be an abundance of green spaces and industry would be placed away from residential areas. Ideas were not enough; to convince the world at large, Howard knew that he had to make his dream become a reality in at least one living and functioning example. In 1903 his Association purchased 3,818 acres of land for £155,587 at Letchworth, in Hertfordshire. By 1905 the place was sufficiently developed for Howard and his wife to take up residence there. Early in 1908, the Poles visited the town with a view to making a move there from Bristol. They were met at the railway station by one of Ebenezer Howard's co-workers, the Rev. John Bruce Wallace - a point to be later of some significance for the older daughter of the family, Mary. They selected a site and before long they were living in their newly-completed home, Tudor Cottage, Field Lane, Letchworth.

Wellesley was now the only member of the family left in Bristol, although Kitty often came to stay (she continued to visit Glastonbury from time to time as well).

Dr Goodchild still kept himself in the foreground of events. When he was away during the winter he wrote regularly to Christine, Janet and Kitty - a little less often to Wellesley. What concerned him most was that these young people should become fully briefed in what he perceived to be the purpose of the Cup, its role at the beginnings of Christianity and its place in the coming age. He emphasized again and again that only women could be the channels of whatever inspiration the Cup might bring into the world. On a more mundane level men could discuss and investigate questions of history and documentation relating to it, but they would never have knowledge of its secrets. At that time he regarded Kitty as the rightful keeper of the Cup. His concern was to ensure that his young friends were properly aware of this and did not proceed in any direction which did not give due regard to that fact. As an early note to Wellesley advised:

> "...Take things as they come, and act as far as possible in accordance with your sister's ideas. She will not want [for] needful guidance from the other side, nor will any real mistake be made by her, whether she keep, lend, give, hide or exhibit, or even destroy the Cup; whilst any seeming disadvantage which may come to her - and I don't think there will be much of this - will merely be a part of her needful training. Personally I have always found Patience to be my best guide and that too much planning and thought for the morrow merely leads to continual disappointment."

It will be remembered that the second Deans Yard meeting brought forth some disappointing conclusions from the scientists and anti-quarians present. As these were merely 'male' opinions, Goodchild was not unduly worried by them. He wrote to Janet:

> "...I have written to WTP as to the experts' finding, as you can hardly argue on these heads yourselves. A *man* could not authenticate the Cup, but doubtless you three will."

At this point it might be helpful to think back to the time when Goodchild first saw the Cup in the tailor's shop in Bordighera. He purchased it with another vessel described as a 'platter'. The material in the two was not identical: the interlining mosaic in the Cup was silver in colour; we can presume (from what Goodchild suggests elsewhere) that the mosaic in the platter was gold. It might seem odd that he did not keep them both. However, he remained faithful to his psychic instructions and sent the platter off 'to a member of the Garibaldi family' (according to A. E. Waite, 'a son of Garibaldi').

In symbolic terms, silver is usually understood to be feminine and identified with the moon; gold is masculine and identified with the sun. The reason why the Cup was the object of so much attention and the Platter was not, was that the feminine aspect had been eclipsed in both religion and society and needed to be reinstated. Goodchild was not preaching absolute matriarchy so much as redressing the balance and reawakening all that was represented by spiritual womanhood. The Cup was an object to be cared for by *women*. Granted, men had their place, but their attributes were better disclosed within the sacred mysteries associated with the Platter.

Speaking of the use of the Platter and the Cup in the ritual of the first Christian assembly at the House of Pudens in Rome he said:

> "It is possible, indeed probable, that those who held the one held the other, but the teaching in the Mysteries of the Cup would be even more occult than those of the Platter, the chief directions of which were for men only."

Elsewhere he wrote:

> "I may be wrong, but it seems to me that the one thing needed is the clear *Witness of Christ Himself* in some authentic document. For instance, such a 'saying' as, 'The Gold in my Platter wasteth not; neither is the Silver within my Cup tarnished', would be a clear reference, and if in addition there were words in which Jesus spoke of the design of the Cup as typifying the manner of his death, the allusion could hardly be questioned. [Goodchild is referring to the cruciform design of the mosaic motifs within the glass of the Cup.]"

Goodchild had evolved a complex theory about the nature of the first Christian meeting-place in Rome, believing he had substantial evidence for linking it with Glastonbury. It will be remembered that the doctor was in Rome just after the time of his first communication with 'Fiona Macleod'. He had visited the Church of St. Pudenziana, on the site of the House of Pudens.

The link with Glastonbury came through the person of Claudia, born in Britain and possibly educated at the women's seminary at Beckery, who had married Pudens, a Roman senator. The fact of their marriage and the role played by their home in the life of the first Roman Christians is attested by various writers, among them the pagan commentator Martial, a close friend of Pudens, in his *Epigrams*. He commends her for her 'illustrious birth', beauty and great learning, especially in Greek and Latin literature, expressly stating that she was British. Goodchild believed that Claudia may have been introduced as a child to the Christian teaching which had arrived at Glastonbury immediately after the crucifixion. She could have been initiated into both the Celtic and Christian mysteries. More than that, she was the leader of the Roman Church before St. Peter or St. Paul had anything to do with it. The crux of this theory rests on the identification of certain figures grouped around Christ on a mosaic in the apse of the Church of Pudenziana.

It would be radical enough to suggest that the Church of Rome was founded by someone other than St. Peter - even more so if that person was a woman. Goodchild contended that the principal female standing figure in the mosaic was Claudia. Inscribed behind her is the name BRYXAI (BRUCHA or Mother). She would have been regarded as Mother, not only of her children, but of those Christians who were gathered under her roof. There is a passage in the Second Epistle of St. John, which Goodchild believed was addressed to Claudia, the Church-Mother. The Epistle begins:

> "The elder unto the elect lady and her children, whom I love in the truth; and not I only, but also they that have known the truth."

It is not a proof - and this passage has been the subject of some debate - but there is no question that it could apply well to the situation at the House of Pudens. Far less equivocal is the close of the Second Epistle of St. Paul to Timothy in which he extends his good wishes from those who were also with him in Rome:

> "Do thy diligence to come before winter. Eubulus greeteth thee, and Pudens, and Linus, and Claudia, and all the brethren."

Among the different aspects of the case that Goodchild presented to his 'young ladies' in Bristol was the question of the lineage of this Claudia (or Gwladys, to give her her British name), and the arrival of Christianity at Glastonbury. He wrote explaining this:

> "Claudia [was the] daughter of Caractacus, son of Bran the Blessed, son of Llyr the Italian - so named for his having been educated at Rome with the Imperial Princes under Augustus. The immediate predecessors of Llyr are differently given in Welsh genealogies, but it is evident that the family claimed descent from the semi-mythical Welsh ancestors, Anwyn Tro, Hu Mor and Prydain. These are, I believe, merely corrupted from the Irish Royal Ancestors, Angus 'of the Brugh', grandson of Hu-ab-RA, whilst Prydain probably conceals the name, not of the father of Angus, but of his mother...
>
> Gildas gives AD 38 as the authoritative date of the first arrival of a

Christian teacher in Britain. All British authorities point to Bran as the first Christian Prince in Britain and associate him with ILTUTUS (or 'ILID the Israelite, to be distinguished from his later namesake 'Iltutus the Knight', who, if I remember rightly, was a friend and contemporary of Gildas).

Iltutus appears to have been located at Glastonbury from the first, and was certainly later identified with Joseph of Arimathea (there is *no evidence* at present that this identification was not a late one. More than 20 years later than AD 38, Iltutus is found accompanying Claudia's elder sister Eugenia (Eygen), when she founds the church at Llantwit, and he is then distinctly stated to have left his church at Glaston for the occasion. There are also local legends which point to his having been with Bran at Branscombe, near Seaton, in his later years.

The interesting fact here, upon which certain theories may be formed, is that a Christian teacher arrived in Britain when Claudia was two years of age, appears to have been well received and established at Glaston under the Silurian Royal Family, and would have been in contact with, and probably instructor to, the chief ancient seminary for young ladies in Britain.

It is not merely possible, but I think probable, that the daughters of Caractacus were not merely educated at Beckery, but baptized in the waters of the Brue, and attended the services of the ⊕ TITULUS AD GLASTONIAM, though this, of course, would be a very late form as applied to the Church of Iltutus, which may *possibly*, if not probably, have been recognized as the ⊕ TITULUS-TERMINIS, or 'Boundary-Church' of this earliest Christendom, whose message Claudia was to bring to Rome."

The placing of Ilid the Israelite as the bringer of Christianity to Britain, and not Joseph of Arimathea, says much for Goodchild's preparedness to take an independent line regardless of popular assumptions and traditions. But he does not wholly dismiss the possibility of Joseph having been at Glastonbury:

"…Twelfth century and later documents regarding J of A should be disregarded, except as furnishing possible clues in names, etc., but the traditions of J of A about the mouth of the Rhone, as to his presence in that district on his journeyings between Palestine and Britain, are not to be disregarded, as they coincide in a curious way with the Pilton legend, and existing remains in the churches of the Saintes Maries, of St. Martha of Jerusalem, etc., prove that the tradition there must be a good deal earlier than the 12th Cent., and carry it back to the ninth. At the same time it is quite evident that the Saxon Church did not claim any authority from Joseph, and if their earlier British predecessors did, they kept the thing jealously to themselves."

As we shall see, Goodchild made further investigations in the church at Rome, and encouraged the others to do likewise.

The other great subject that absorbed his interest at that time was gematria - the means by which every word or group of words is given a numerical value according to the sum of the numbers assigned to its component letters. Different words and phrases might have the same value, implying that they share a special power and quality transcending their more obvious meaning. The system was applicable to different alphabets (and even a function in the evolution of those alphabets in past times). In Hebrew it was more obvious as the letters are used for numerals in any case. The rules for Greek and Roman letters followed more or less identical sequences. In Latin this was: (units) A=1 to I=9; (tens) J=10 to R=90; (hundreds) S=100 to Z=800. For example:

BOOK =2+60+60+20 =142;

LOSTSHEEP = 30+60+100+200+100+8 +5+5+70 =578;

TORHILL = 200+60+90+8+9+30+30 =427, etc.

(These are random examples with [possibly?] no special meaning in their number-values.)

The best-known work on gematria was *The Canon* by William Stirling, first published anonymously in 1897. Goodchild was familiar with this study, but critical of some of the author's claims. It is almost certain that the doctor's own interest in the subject came from his association with William Sharp. How Sharp got started we do not know, perhaps simply from reading Stirling. He may have had access to the large quantity of gematric papers that had been given to his friend, W.B. Yeats, by members of the Stirling family soon after the latter's suicide in a London hotel. In 1903, this pile of MSS was offered to A. E. Waite, who returned it to Yeats with the observation that it would be no serious loss to the world if it were never published. It is possible that Yeats then gave this material to Sharp; at some stage, he, or Elizabeth Sharp, could have passed it on to Goodchild.

As to the question of numbers and the Bible, the obvious example that most people think of is the number of the Great Beast, 666, in the Book of Revelation. Understandably, when Janet first enquired of Goodchild about gematria, it was on this point. He replied:

March 5, 1910

My dear Janet

In my hurry last night I forgot to answer your questions about '666' etc. The earliest tables of numbers we have at present are the Names and Numbers of the early Sumerian Gods in Babylonia, on tablets copied from earlier ones of 6 or 7,000 years back. The Egyptians also named and numbered their Gods and Kings from the earliest known period. Our own alphabet is what is known as the Western Alphabet, and the forms of the letters are many of them practically the same as those found on pots used for trade purposes in the Mediterranean before the historical period. They are found on predynastic pots in Egypt, and are found on similar pots in Asia Minor, Spain, etc.. The Latin Alphabet is the same as our own, except that W (= 500) is wanting and is supplied by + (= 500), or UT 'as' PLUS +, etc.. The Irish attached the same numerical values to their letters as they have in the Latin, but for some reason dropped several letters after they had adopted Christianity, or only used them for special purposes.

As to the number 666, many interpretations have been put on it, ancient and modern, but there are two which would certainly not have escaped the writer of the Apocalypse. One is that it is made up of those Latin letters used as vulgar numerals, and capable in that form of producing certain imperfect results which hindered the true knowledge of the Divine Name DCLXVI = 666. 666 is a special number, being the Pyramid of 36, and also the Number of a Magic Square dedicated to the Sun. In Hebrew also there are certain titles of Christ to which probably John objected as being used to restrict His Rule by Latin calculations on His Name. ישׁוֹעֲנצרי 'Jesus of Nazareth' and שמי ישׁו 'The Name Jesus' are upon that Number. In English, JESUS' MARK and ROMAN RULE keep this in remembrance. The strongest substantives we have on the Number confirm this in the words BUSINESS and TRESPASS.

Greetings from
Yours J A Goodchild

There was one number that Goodchild held up above all others. In a letter quoted earlier he states that "the Oratory at Clifton is the one Church in which the Name and Number of the Master are exhibited and taught *openly*". The calculation of this number was on the Hebrew form of the name ישׁוֹעֲנָצְרִי מֶלֶךְהַיְּהוּדִים יֵשׁוּעַנָצְרִי (meaning Jesus of Nazareth, King of the Jews, Jesus of Nazareth), giving the Divine Number 1642.

Any other combinations of words which also yielded this number, Goodchild regarded as being similarly holy, whether Hebrew, Greek, Latin, English or Gaelic. Sometimes two languages were juxtaposed, as in (Latin) JESUS CHRISTUS (=1325) and either (Greek) O AΔAMAΣ (=317) (Adam) or NEANIAΣ (=317) (Young Man). Inevitably we are back with the Divine Number 1642 (1325 + 317). Any words giving the holy number were indicated in Goodchild's writings with the sign ⊕. (This is why this sign is shown twice in the earlier quotation about Iltutus.)

Goodchild seemed to have the knack of instantly spotting anything that might yield a significant number. He was not without humour in this, and was once quite unashamed to offer the following in the course of a very long letter about the Pudentine mosaic: "...These do not appear in the photos from which I am working (a good set by ⊕ ANDERSON, BRITISH PHOTOGRAPHER, ROME)..." Yes, these thirty-one letters *do* add up to 1642!

How the doctor arrived at his knowledge the 'Number of the Master' is unclear. He put some store on the witness of the Campo di Fiori Medal, a coin-like item in the Ashmolean Museum, Oxford, of uncertain date, said to depict a profile of the head of Christ. His starting point may have been the fact that the Hebrew inscription on one face added up to 1325, and on the other to 317. These are the same values as those just shown for Jesus Christus + O AΔAMAΣ .

In the summer of 1909, Christine and Janet Allen were making plans for an extended absence abroad. There were some serious implications for the work of the Triad here. On 29 July they met to discuss their question and decided for the time being to dissolve their operations together. Goodchild was ready to help the two sisters with useful hints for their investigations at Rome:

September 6th, 1909, Bath

My dear Miss Allen

I have made a set of notes for your Roman trip which may prove of use. Parts of them you will not yourself be able to follow, but they are intended for the use of any archeologist or other person seriously interested. Many will not be interested, but a few will know them to be of prime importance, and will be friendly or hostile, according as they

love Light or Darkness. Any scrap of information regarding the Pudentine house, and those who lived in [it], may be of unexpected
importance. I did not see the fragments of the Baths of Novatus [a son
of Claudia and Pudens], and other ruins attached. You and your sister
should do so. Also please go quite into the Apse, and have a good look at
the Dove, and see whether there is any sign on or above it. I was only in
the Church for a few minutes in 1899, and knew nothing of the mosaic
then, except what I saw at first glance... I also send York medals of Helena
and Constantine, who removed the seat of the Empire from Rome to
Constantinople, leaving the Pope virtual master of the former city. The
importance of the fact that this was done by a Christian Emperor of
British descent on the mother's side, is, I think, worthy of much more
consideration than it has received recently, and dovetails with a rather
large theory which I have formed. JOY be with you on your journey in
the name of ישוע

Yours, etc.,
J. A. Goodchild

Janet, in particular, became very absorbed in the vision offered by
Goodchild of the ancient Celtic/Roman Church. The Roman trip
served to set her on a spiritual path to which she remained abidingly
faithful, before all other concerns, to the end of her life. Her heart had
been enriched by the part she played in the recovery of the Cup and the
prayerful pilgrimages to the holy sites of Glastonbury; her keen mind
was now enthused with the challenge of unravelling the complexities of
history to reveal even more of the wholly radical theories of the doctor
on these matters.

If Claudia had been initiated at Glastonbury into both the Irish
(Celtic) and Christian teachings, then she would have carried within
her the knowledge of herself as a representative of Bride, the High
Queen of Heaven in the West, finding herself placed by providence
(through the capture of her father Caractacus by the Roman army)
in Rome to fulfil the highest honour of offering herself, and, in a sense,
the Church, as the 'Bride of Christ'. The mosaic in the Church of
St. Pudenziana depicted, so Dr Goodchild believed, Claudia enrobed
as the Bride of Christ, and Christ depicted as her Bridegroom. All
this notwithstanding her earthly status as the dutiful wife of Senator
Pudens, who was also shown in the mosaic, together with their sons and
daughters and St. Peter and St. Paul.

In 1910, the doctor himself made a visit to the site of the church of

Claudia and Pudens, relaying his observations back to his friends in Bristol. The Triad had come back together by then, after Janet and Christine's return to England in May, even though Kitty was sometimes at Letchworth. The public aspect of the work of the Oratory had been brought to a close meanwhile owing to the difficulties it imposed on normal life.

On 5 October 1910, Goodchild wrote to Janet from Rome:

"I had an excellent journey - 'as thy day is, etc.' has always proved true in my case. We arrived fairly to time, and when I had had a wash and a cup of coffee, I strolled round to Santa Pudenziana ⊕ which I found in charge of a small boy. I got there at about 9am (8am English time), and my landing on that month was very good, for I had obviously the best light of the whole day by which to see the Mosaic, the sun shining through the windows of the front upon the pavement before the altar, which reflected it upwards. It was strangely different in its general effect to my former memory of it in another light, and I have various corrections to make in what I have previously written or told you. First, as to the 'Dove'. There is no mark as far as I could see directly above the centre of the Cross. Nor could I see any sign of the Lamb mentioned in the pamphlet which I gave you last year, but hidden in the darkened space behind the arch is what at first sight one would take for a pair of dark outstretched wings (of the Spirit above the Waters - this sign is well-known in the farthest East). They would suggest those of a Seabird rather than those of a Dove, and it is to be remembered that the word Columbis meant originally a Seabird rather than a Dove, as the sign of the Spirit. I fancy my mark was intended to give that suggestion, but I could discern no sign of a body or head, and I believe that this highest sign in the Mosaic is that of the Fish, who are in the far sea, and which, amongst other things, Christ fed the multitude. This sign is well-known in the farthest East in connection with the teaching of the Dove, and you will find on almost all Chinese and Indian Fish, especially if they are cut flat (for the flat fish looks upwards whilst the fat fish looks about him), the sign of the two doves, which the flat fish sees and follows if he would rise above the Waters into fuller height. It is curious that the only thing that I bought as a sign in London and brought out, was a rather choice little Japanese enamel vase, with two small fishes painted upon it.

Secondly, the Mosaic has been rather carefully retouched in places since I saw it last. The special marks of the Bridegroom and Bride upon the robes of Christ and Claudia have been either obliterated or made much more difficult of recognition. I could no longer read the word

'Bruchai', or the beginning of HIC PA(ULUS) though armed with a glass, which I was not in 1899. Perhaps the most curious lapse of my own memory which I noted this morning was that the Mantle of Brucha is Golden (the Bridegroom's colour, the Robe of the Sun, and not Green), the undergarment at throat and sleeve being Sapphire, the same colours as Christ's in this Mosaic. I was probably misled by the constant translation of the word VAIS as 'Green' by Sharp and all modern Celts, but it also means Glassy, Crystalline, Shining, Brilliant, etc., and it may be noted that the Flag of the Macleods, the 'Green Banner of Bride' *is* Golden-Yellow.

But enough for today, for I am tired. I noted, however, a little modern leaflet from St. John's Gospel on the wall by one of the altars, in which the words 'VERBUM CARNE FACTUM EST' = 1842 (The Word is made Flesh) were printed in capitals, and so drew my attention. It is obvious that the mere deduction of the last letter T, will give the true Number $\oplus$, and the translation would be 'Thou art the Word made Flesh'

Yours
J. A. Goodchild

PS
By the way, Santa Pudenziana does not look to the East, but to the North-West. I expect if its bearings were taken they are on Britain, possibly, if very accurate, on Glastonbury or Salisbury. This is a mere suggestion for a competent architect, or sailor, to look at if it interests him."

The doctor seems in a muddle on some points. However, he went into the church again four days later, that time during the afternoon, which gave a different light, making clear some things he had been unable to see during the morning but concealing others:

"...the Dove, which I had failed to see on Friday, was quite distinct. It appeared merely a dark fish-shaped mass then. Yesterday it was a delicate silvery-grey, with a row of white markings on each wing. I remember now that it is just what I saw 11 years back, and had endeavoured to recall in vain....

I think I have got at the original meaning of the word VAIS, as attached to Brucha's mantle, by the aid of old Cormac, who translates VASSAL as 'Noble', and gives the illustration of Christ VASSA FIL,

'HE is over them'. i.e. 'Supreme'. In the Mosaic, this supreme garment of Christ as Bridegroom is Golden throughout, save for two bands of sapphire blue. Brucha, as his Bride, also wears these two colours."

On October 17 he wrote again:

My dear Janet

Thanks for yours, just received, and I am certain that I have had much help from you and the others, since I arrived here. For one thing, I must correct all that I wrote on my arrival, for I have what I immediately want in the help of a young nursery governess in the hotel, who is looking for a place, and speaks Italian well, whilst she is much interested in Santa Pudenziana ⊕. I have been there twice with her, and learnt a good deal by her aid.

Firstly, both the Dove and the Lamb, are said to be still on the wall, but have been completely concealed by the baldachino and reredos for about half a century, so these two symbols are hidden...

I had hoped to find specimens of *silver* mosaic, which would at once answer the objections of the experts to the JESUS CUP, and prove many things. It is possible that such a sign may exist elsewhere in Rome, but it would be more valuable and more convincing if found here than elsewhere, and prove that those who knew the teaching of the Golden Mosaic Platter, knew that of the Silver Mosaic Cup also.

Albercius, Bishop of Hieropolis, who was at Rome in the 2nd century, and I think saw this Mosaic, has a phrase in which he speaks of Mary as catching the Great Fish from the Spring, and giving it to Christians as their food, which looks as though 'those who held the Gleaming Token', had instructed him in the form ⊕ MARIA PISCATRIX CHRISTI, 'Mary, Fisher of Christ'.

Goodchild has a good deal to say on the subject of the allegorical means of teaching in the first centuries of Christianity. The 'higher' teachings were those of the Sea and the Waters. Christ, as the greatest mystery, swam as a 'Fish' in the Great Deep. Brucha, in her royal descent from the office of High Queen, was also understood as the 'Sea Queen', nurturing fellow Christians, possibly as 'fish' swimming in her waters. The emblem of the Fish in the underground early Roman Church is well-known.

The doctor made two or three more visits to the church, but with the departure of the 'nursery governess' was less inclined to go. He wrote several times to Janet, and indicated more than once that he was suffering from health problems, 'a form of indigestion' which had attacked him before. In one letter he excused his "bad scrawl, but I am lying down, and a little heavy from an opiate which I had to take this morning".

On the question of the High Queen, there are some interesting considerations in a letter written to Janet in December from Bordighera:

...I have been working hard the last week at various old puzzles relating to the Mother-Church at Glaston, and not without success so far as obtaining some very interesting historical hints which will one day, I hope, be of use. I am sending them as I write them to my brother, but later, when they are more intelligible and consecutive, I hope to let you and your sister have them. Meanwhile, I am pretty clear of this, that from the establishment of that Church before the middle of the 1st century, a woman, always a Princess of the Royal Blood, was its Supreme Head and Nursing Mother, until she laid down her authority about the middle of the 6th century at an Irish Church Congress held under the presidency of Comgal of Bangor.

St. Bevan 'Benignus' appears to have returned with her, and acted as chief teacher up to the time of his death in 568.

Histories of Glaston will tell you that 3 British Abbots succeeded to the Rule of the place before the Saxons came in, and give you their names in Saxon letters. In Celtic these read:

1. Worgraet. 'Ruin, destruction of what is venerable.'
2. Lademund. 'Slovenly Teaching'.
3. Bregoreid. 'False Rule.'

Wrecker, Lazybones and Liar would be fair English equivalents, and I doubt whether these last British teachers called themselves by them, though they probably fairly imply the state of things between the Mother's resignation and the new Saxon Rule instituted by the Abbess Bugge and St. Aldhelm.

I hope that Miss Armytage may find help at Santa Pudenziana, and help others to know that Church as the Mother Church of Rome. Meanwhile,

JOY be with you both,
Yours etc. J. A. Goodchild"

The ever-questing Goodchild would seize on anything that might suggest some lingering memory of Claudia, the hostess of the Apostles in Rome, in the byways of the land of her birth. He is persuasive in his reasoning that hymns written by the Church-Mother in Rome and sent to Britain may have survived in their usage down through many centuries:

> "Martial, the friend of Pudens, boasts that copies of his poems were sent to Britain. This would probably be through his British friends in Rome; perhaps through Claudia Rufina herself; at any rate, copies of her own hymns would be sent by her to her sister, and other relatives. Now the Welsh tradition is distinct that at Glaston, Amesbury and Llantwit, a choral service was kept up during the 24 hours. What was sung during these hours? Not improbably a set of hymns written for the purpose by Claudia. This hint may help towards the identification of this first hymnal. My only ground for saying that this hymnal was still preserved at St. Alban's in the 13th century, is Morgan's assertion, for which he does not quote his authority. Another possible hint towards the identification of a single hymn by the Church-Mother is given by the very curious old Irish hymn which is given (I think by O'Curry) as that which was sung by St. Ibar and his companions, the Irish representatives of the old British Church, when leaving Ireland for Little Ireland after the controversy with St. Patrick. This is ascribed to St. Bridget, but is certainly not by Bridget of Kildare. A phrase in it in which the writer expresses her earnest desire that the 'Apostles of Christ should be guests in her house, when she would give them the best entertainment in her power', suggests that this hymn may be a translation of some Latin hymn by Bri-Bruach [Claudia], or even merely an Irish variant of one written in her own native tongue. If so, the above aspiration to entertain the Apostles was realised in the case of Peter, Paul (and John), and possibly of others."

There are other letters written by Goodchild which give more insights into his rather original theories, perhaps deserving of publication elsewhere. The ones quoted here cover most of the main points and can suggest lines of further research. In the years 1909-1912 he wrote far more to the Allen sisters, and particularly to Janet. He was evidently on sociable terms with the family: "Remember me very kindly to your mother", he once wrote to her.

The activities at Glastonbury of a certain Bristol architect were attracting his attention at around this time. This was Frederick Bligh Bond, who was excavating among the debris of the Abbey ruins for artefacts and traces of lost foundations. Goodchild made a special point of keeping in touch with these investigations as a matter of his own interest. In his turn, Bond would sometimes seek the doctor's opinion, aware of his wide knowledge and grasp of religious history.

Recognizing that Bond was not in sympathy with the claims made about the Cup, Goodchild directed any discussion about that and related issues exclusively to the group at Clifton. However, as he got to know Bond better he was prepared to divulge more to him. By 1913 he seems to have been encouraging the latter to investigate the possibilities of gematria more deeply.

After 1909 the Clifton Oratory was no longer freely open to all-comers. However, many still arrived from near and far by appointment. The place was now effectively a guest house but occasional meetings and lectures enabled a body of sympathizers to continue to keep in touch with its aspirations.

On 18 June 1910, Wellesley met someone who was to usher in a curious episode in his life, and who claimed to be his kinsman in the Tudor line of descent. Neville Gauntlett Tudor Meakin was associated with one of the magical sub-groups or 'Temples' that had emanated from the Hermetic Order of the Golden Dawn, a fraternity founded by a group of Rosicrucian Freemasons in 1888. Members were ritually raised through different grades of initiation, gaining secret knowledge on the way, and hopefully some kind of illumination at the end of it all. Meakin was a member of the Stella Matutina Temple, presided over by Dr Robert Felkin. Another active offshoot of the HOGD at that time was A. E. Waite's Independent and Rectified Rite. In 1907 the two had reached an uneasy accommodation by signing a Concordat which clarified their respective responsibilities and defined the margins of their areas of agreement and independence.

Within these Temples it was usual to take a Latin personal motto. Meakin was known as *Ex Oriente Lux*, Felkin was *Finem Respice*, and Waite *Sacramentum Regis*. Innocuous enough compared with W. B. Yeats' *Demon est Deus Inversus*!

Quite separately from his membership of Stella Matutina, Meakin had another responsibility: he was Grand Master of the Order of the Table Round. This privilege was associated with the claim that he was the fortieth descendant of King Arthur. The Tudor name is the key here, as the line of succession evidently came through the family of the Welsh patriot Owen Tudor, founder of the Royal House of Tudor through his grandson Henry VII, and claimed as an ancestor by the Tudor Poles. (In 1963 WTP wrote to Rosamond Lehmann, "My forebear Owen, enraged at the conquest of Wales, enticed King Henry's widow [Katharine] to his bed in revenge, ultimately marrying her and starting the Tudor dynasty". To this day, each generation of the Pole family has a Katharine within it and now everyone has the name Tudor.)

The Meakin claim is not wholly secure. Although he tries to affirm that the line of descent from father to son is unbroken 'from the time of King Arthur', it is admitted that there was once a lapse of more than three hundred years until the office was restored to (possibly) Meakin's grandfather.

There are further complications about Meakin himself. He was the stepson of a Rev. Meakin. When Neville was twenty-one, his stepfather told him that his real name was Tudor, and gave him some family papers which showed he was the rightful heir to the Grand Mastership of the OTR.

The grades of initiation within this Order were: Page, Novice, Knight, possibly some side-grades, and above these, Mage. When Meakin met Wellesley there were three Knights: Meakin, his stepfather, and a half-brother in America called Plantagenet. Dr Felkin had also been received into the Order and was ultimately raised to the level of Senior Magus.

Meakin was unmarried and suffering from tuberculosis when he was introduced to Felkin and his wife by a mutual friend in 1909. He was not old, only thirty-nine, but concerned to ensure the continuity of the Order in the event of his death from the illness. Felkin had all the necessary qualifications, save that he was not of the blood-line of King Arthur (the line was even said to have pre-dated Arthur, and, according to WTP, passed through Joseph of Arimathea, and before him, the Royal lines of Israel and Assyria). Finding Wellesley was the fulfilment of all Meakin's best hopes: here was a person who understood Owen Tudor to be a forebear and who had lately found a 'Grail' - even if not *the* Grail. Another possibility for their interest in getting him initiated might have been that he was seen to be too much of a maverick figure on the scene and that it was part of a strategy of containment.

Wellesley had chanced upon making this contact at a time when the Bristol group had come together again after the Allen sisters' wanderings abroad. They were planning a venture to reawaken the ancient spiritual shrines of the West. Wellesley explained to Meakin his vision of the three spiritual centres of the British Isles. These were Avalon, Iona and 'the Western Isle', this last place as yet unnamed. If these three locations were of the 'heart', then the three capital cities, London, Edinburgh and Dublin, were as a triangle of the 'brain' of their respective nations. Neville Meakin was enthused to incorporate this concept into his Arthurian scheme within the OTR.

The first place the Triad planned to activate was Iona. On 24 June they made a preliminary pilgrimage to Glastonbury to prepare themselves. They went to the usual spots. While there, Christine had yet another of her curious visions. She 'saw' an old man in a white robe with a 'key pattern' on it. He held his fingers in front of him in the form of a triangle and then 'seemed gathered up into the trees'.

On 26 June the three arrived on Iona. Over a period of several days they trekked around with the Cup, visiting all the sacred places, where they stopped to meditate and pray for their revival. Wellesley came up on 1 August. At a service in Priors Chapel he experienced a vision 'of a great crowd of people from another world', apparently greatly agitated and disturbed by something. They returned together to Bristol, impressed that an opening had been made for new spiritual life on the enchanted Scottish island.

Neville Meakin came to the Oratory on 19 September and stayed in the guest house. The next day he is said to have 'experienced his own vision of the Cup' (recorded in some notes which have since unfortunately been lost).

At some point after that, it is likely that Meakin began instructing Wellesley in the lower grades of the Order of the Table Round. It led, according to Wellesley's account, to an invitation for him to receive 'the final family degrees' on 5 October 1912, thus ensuring a revival of the near-defunct Order. Curiously, a vein of tragedy had run through many generations of the Table Round family. Meakin had prophesised the breaking of this spell when the OTR was re-formed in the twentieth century. He was not quite quick enough. On the eve of the proposed initiation Meakin died, so it is said, 'in the arms of Dr Felkin'.

On the following Tuesday, in the aftermath of this calamity, A. E. Waite met Felkin to discuss the situation. His notes of this meeting concur with Wellesley's account, but it is clear that Felkin wanted to keep WTP's identity from Waite. The supposed 'relation of EOL in Scotland' may be a deliberate evasion on the part of Felkin. If there really was such a person, then Meakin had unreasonably kept WTP in the dark about it. This seems unlikely. In Waite's following account, Meakin is referred to as EOL and Felkin as FR (Denis Felkin is presumably Felkin's son):

"It has been stated to me definitely that the whole order has lapsed into the hands of FR by the death of EOL, and that he can do what he likes. One would suppose therefore that he is the forty-first Grand Master, but he intimated that he did not wish, or probably did not wish, to be, or to remain, such.

In this case the office would involve a relation of EOL in Scotland who is either page or knight - I am rather confused on this point. In the event of FR's death, this person has a claim on the papers of the Order, now deposited at the Bank, or about to be. He is instructed to communicate with me - as if I were some kind of executor.

Had EOL lived, on that Saturday which actually followed his death, he was to have made Denis Felkin a page and also another whose name was not disclosed to me. On the Tuesday thereafter he was, I think, to have knighted the kinsman mentioned above. I asked the name of this kinsman, seeing that he has my name, but was told that he - FR - could not disclose this. Part and parcel of this mystery which always prevails. This notwithstanding, his idea is that I should be appointed Senior Magus."

In September 1916 (just two months before he enlisted for military service), Wellesley wrote, regarding the OTR, that "I am consulting A. E. Waite about the hidden tradition on Sunday, as he has seen some records". This suggests that it *was* WTP who had been instructed to contact Waite regarding the papers of the Order, and tends to identify him with the unnamed person 'from Scotland' in Waite's notes. It was too late for any recovery of the succession. Perhaps WTP knew this - Waite could have told him. Felkin had visited New Zealand with his wife in 1912, soon after the death of Meakin, taking all the signs, symbols and rituals of the Order with him. Here he established at Havelock North two secret schools: Whare Ra for spiritual wisdom (Golden Dawn) and a school of Christian chivalry. Although he soon returned to England, it seems that for a while Felkin himself became the Grand Master of the OTR. He resigned in 1914 and a new appointment to the office was made in New Zealand. Very soon this person left for war service and yet another succeeded him. The Felkins returned to New Zealand permanently in 1916. The schools of initiation Felkin had founded there were continued by his wife and daughter after his death in 1926. Wellesley, for his part, no longer gave the matter any further serious consideration.

Waite's own notes of 13 August 1916 confirm that he had been in touch with WTP at around this time, having just received some notes from him "on the symbolism of Avalon, Iona and the Western Isle". Waite was curious about this latter, as ever unnamed, and speculated that it might be "one of the Isles of Arran". In truth, it had yet to be identified. It was not until many years later that it was revealed to be

Devenish Island, at the southern end of lower Loch Erne, a large inland lake in Co. Fermanagh, Ulster. Wellesley believed it was an even older centre than Avalon or Iona. In the sixth century it had been the home of St. Molaise. The ruins of his monastery remain, and the 81ft high round tower is still complete, and is noted for the outstanding quality of the masons' work. There is also a 7ft high sculptured cross of a type unique in Ireland.

Why did Wellesley take so long to reveal the identity of this island? Perhaps it was because he found it such a spiritually 'difficult' place. He described it as "overrun by hostile elementals", and "unlike Avalon and Iona, not ripe for re-illuming". Even in later years the place still defeated him, and he complained that well-meaning exorcists had caused the premature release of negative energies, making necessary the "arduous and dangerous task of reconfining them. The problem of the 'Western Isle' was never wholly resolved. There were even thoughts of appointing another of the islets in the Lough to fulfil the Irish representation in the trinity with Avalon and Iona.

Spiritual leaders from other countries and cultures were among the guests continuing to arrive at 16 Royal York Crescent. On 10 September 1910, two distinguished Indian visitors were at the Oratory. Professor L. T. Vaswani and the Rev. Promotho Sen were keen to find ways of building greater brotherhood between East and West and to work towards a greater unity of all religious aspirations. The professor was especially interested in the Holy Grail legends and found seeing the Cup a profoundly moving experience. He was impressed with the feeling of great holiness within the Oratory itself. In a talk given two days later he spoke of his desire to see the Cup become the focus of a new mystical awareness shared between people of differing religious allegiance. Once back in London he wrote to say how much he missed the atmosphere of the upper room at Clifton. Even Dr Goodchild had to pass comment in his own inimitable way, writing from Italy: "I am very glad indeed to hear about Vaswani. Vaswani's Evidence ⊕ = Powerful Evidences ⊕."

That November found Wellesley visiting Egypt. While there he delivered a consignment of gifts to Abdu'l Baha Abbas, leader of the Baha'i faith, from some of his friends and followers in England - the introduction having come through Archdeacon Wilberforce.

Abdu'l Baha was the son of the seer and prophet Baha'u'llah, who had founded the Baha'i movement in 1863 as a development of the teachings of his forerunner, Bab. Like John the Baptist, Bab foretold the coming of a great prophet who would bring fresh illumination to the world.

WELLESLEY TUDOR POLE

The founder was born at Nur in Iran in 1819. He taught, not a new religion, but the initiation of a force to unify existing belief-systems, pointing to the divine origin of every faith. He gave his followers a vision of a noble destiny for the human race, built on love in recognition of the oneness of the Creator with His creation. Baha'is renounce the use of force or violence of any kind. In 1908 the family of Baha'u'llah were finally released after forty years' confinement in Turkish jails, during which period the leader himself had died in captivity in 1892.

The friendship Wellesley shared with Abdu'l Baha was important in the spiritual direction of his own life. The healing power he felt in his presence together with his remarkable displays of authentic prophesy confirmed to Wellesley that he was indeed a world teacher for the coming age. One extraordinary thing that happened when the two were together was that when their interpreter had to take a break (neither spoke the other's language), each found himself quite able to understand everything the other was saying. This ability ceased when the interpreter returned.

Everything the Baha'i faith taught came very close to Wellesley's own spiritual standpoint, but he was never able to abandon his view that Christ held a unique position above all other teachers. What he did gain from his contact with Abdu'l Baha was a more positive sense of his own destiny and a point of departure from the theorizing of Dr Goodchild with regard to the Cup. Not that the doctor was wrong, but his own tasks were unfolding in a special way which suggested that certain matters were best left in the hands of the women of the Cup.

On 23 September 1911 Abdu'l Baha was at the Clifton Oratory. He held the Cup in his hands for a long time, saying nothing. He blessed it and handed it back. He made another visit early in 1913.

Wellesley met the Iranian prophet at other times over many years. The most significant encounter was towards the end of the war in 1918. Abdu'l Baha and his followers had settled in Haifa, Palestine. The occupying Turks had threatened to kill the Baha'i leader and his family if the British attempted to move in on the city. Wellesley was able to get a message, cutting through all the red tape, direct to the War Cabinet in London. It explained who the leader was and the threat to his life. When the army finally moved in they were briefed to immediately place a protective guard on Abdu'l Baha's home, ensuring his safety until the situation was fully under control. This decisive action, which almost certainly saved the old man from death, assured Wellesley a revered place in the canon of Baha'i history. Many years later he expressed his sadness that the movement had crystallized into a new religion of hierarchies and temples.

The active campaign for women's suffrage arrived on the political scene close to the time when the finders of the Cup were embarking on their mission to reinstate all that woman represented within the realm of the spirit.

The ideas behind the movement to achieve democratic rights for women had been circulating for some time. A progressive barrister, Dr Richard Pankhurst, and his wife Emmeline, had abandoned their support for the Liberal Party after seeing Gladstone fail to include women's suffrage in the 1884 Reform Act. They placed their allegiance with the Fabian Society and the Independent Labour Party instead. Dr Pankhurst died in 1898. In 1903, Emmeline and one of her remarkable daughters, Christabel, started the Women's Social and Political Union. In 1905, Christabel was arrested with another activist, Annie Kenney, after staging a protest by unfurling their banner at a Liberal election meeting held in Manchester to endorse the candidacy of Winston Churchill. The short prison sentence imposed on them caused a national scandal and pushed the WSPU into a more militant phase. Soon after this, Christabel, by then a qualified lawyer, moved to London, while Annie Kenney, a mill-hand and trade-union activist from Oldham, established a campaign base in the West Country.

Annie Kenney gained many converts to the cause through her wit and impressive oratory. She went everywhere - including Glastonbury on 24 February 1909, where the meeting was characterized with jeers and the usual barracking of the 'get back home and do the washing-up' variety.

Janet and Christine Allen's older sister Mary was one of the many young west-country women who joined the ranks of the suffragettes after hearing just one of Annie Kenney's highly-charged performances. Her father's reaction was predictable - and unreasonable. "Either you give up this suffragette nonsense absolutely and for good - or you leave this house!", he told her. Allen girls never meekly give in; she left.

News of Mary's career with the suffragettes was a source of much wonder, and often anxiety, among her sisters. There were lines of communication open which could by-pass their father. More than that, although he did not know it, his wife was occasionally spirited away, under some pretext or other, to meet their daughter in London.

The WSPU favoured any kind of direct action provided there was no risk of injury to any other person. Mary went and offered herself to Mrs Pankhurst in whatever capacity she thought best: "I had sacrificed much. She asked me to sacrifice more. She wanted volunteers, not to lead a splendid forlorn hope - but to go to prison."

Before long, Mary was arrested with some others trying to break through a police cordon to take a petition to Parliament. They were given a month in jail. It was a grim regime - mostly bread and water, and they were forbidden to speak. Mary's delicate constitution was brought low by it; but she bore up, got released and prepared herself for more law-breaking.

The next thing the family in Bristol heard was that Mary had been charged for criminal damage to a window at the Home Office. She was sentenced to another month in jail. This time she went on hunger strike, demanding 'political prisoner' status. She took neither food nor drink and was only saved by the timing of her release. She was very soon sentenced again to a further month in custody. She again refused to eat and found herself in the prison hospital being held down and force-fed through the nose with one and a half pints of milk and a beaten egg. It only made her sick. It was an ordeal that was repeated until she was given an early release on account of her weak physical condition.

On seeing her, Mrs Pankhurst forbade her to risk further arrest. She was limited to public speaking and organizing others for militant action before the movement was dissolved with the advent of war in 1914. But the cause was won: after the war women had the vote.

What had all this to do with the Cup group at Bristol? Reasonably, it cannot be supposed that members of the Allen family went about their business in isolation. Mary was aware of what Janet and Christine had been up to. She understood something of their devotion to the spiritual elevation of womanhood and knew both Wellesley and Kitty. But that atmosphere was not her natural *métier*. She was intensely practical with a flair for organizing people - and, above all, she was older, and, like Mary Tudor Pole, removed from direct involvement with the younger Glastonbury pilgrims for that reason alone. Similarly, Christine and Janet were supportive of their sister's campaign of action within the WSPU; Christine even joined Mary's Woman Police Volunteers a few years later.

It should be noted that Annie Kenney *did* go to see the Cup at the Oratory. She called in with the Bristol-born Treasurer of the WSPU, Emmeline Pethick-Lawrence, on 5 November 1910, apparently while WTP was away visiting Abdu'l Baha in Egypt.

In 1921 Annie Kenney married - and settled for a quieter life in Letchworth.

CHAPTER NINE

Diaspora

O N SUNNY DAYS the broad sweep of Royal York Crescent shines brilliantly out of the south-facing slope of the higher ground of Clifton. A short walk away Brunel's suspension bridge spans the rocky Avon Gorge. The residents of the Crescent are blessed with a stunning view across the Cumberland Basin to the edge of the Mendips at Dundry (the Druids' Hill?), with its church tower on the skyline.

Bristol, proud of its gems of Georgian architecture, is careful to forget how they got there. Sea-faring merchants built them on the profits of the slave-trade and the plantation produce of the West Indies. Large families with their own servants once enjoyed the prestige of living in the quasi-Mediterranean splendour of the Crescent. Now mostly split into flats and bedsits, the occupiers might be unaware of the irony they are perpetrating or what ghosts are being laid if the rhythms of soul and reggae ever spill out of open windows on warm summer evenings.

Apart from a few excursions, this was where the Cup reposed for nearly seven years from 1906. If we are prepared to believe that the power and attributes of the Grail as a universal symbol were transmitted through this vessel, then perhaps some consideration should also be given to what its home represented.

The Cup was seen as a focus for women's spirituality, there to make good something missing at the heart of the religious and secular life of the world. Royal York Crescent was raised on the proceeds of its opposite: the rampaging male spirit in its cruellest aspect. That the one should have sheltered the other is either a piece of gross cosmic hypocrisy or it bears witness to a process of healing and renewal.

If this seems far-fetched, take note that it was the grandson of the slavery abolitionist William Wilberforce who brought the Cup to the attention of the wider public in London. A hidden agenda? Maybe, for even Cup-finder Christine eventually found herself in Africa, providing large numbers of the poor of Cape Town with a square meal a day for thirty years at minimal cost.

If anything was evident from the later period of those few years at the Clifton Oratory, it was that the Cup had become an agent of reconciliation. Visitors were coming from other lands and cultures. The link with Bride may have suggested certain Celtic associations, but as the 'Jesus Cup' from the Holy Land, the mission of the vessel was for the *universal* good.

Both the keepers of the Cup and many visitors declared that its purpose was to make a bridge between East and West. With such an auspicious destiny, we might wonder if any sign might have been given at the Bristol location beforehand. It was - the information came from a lady who was a visitor to the Oratory. The diary compiled by Janet and Christine records her experience:

> "In June 1906, at the time of the great religious revival in Wales, when many curious lights were being seen in the sky, she was passing along the Crescent and noticed a curiously bright star shining over the house which was then empty and where the Cup is now kept.
>
> It was of such extraordinary nature that she drew the attention of several friends to it, but only one other could see it with her.
>
> When she heard that the Cup was in an Oratory at 16 Royal York Crescent, she remembered her vision and found it was indeed the same house."

There has never been anything like the same degree of public reverence for the Cup since those days at the Clifton Oratory. Its advent there may have been announced with lights in the sky and visions; its departure came about through more mundane pressures.

The first of Thomas and Kate Pole's children to marry was Mary, the oldest. A dedicated vegetarian, she shared the spirit of the Glastonbury adventurers from afar, going there on her own pilgrimages at other times and with other friends.

In February 1911, Mary Tudor Pole married the Rev. J. Bruce Wallace, an Ulster-born Congregational minister who, as a friend of Ebenezer Howard, had discussed with him the founding of Letchworth Garden City and had seen many of his own ideas incorporated in it. He had lived there since 1905 after some years in mission work among the dockers of the East End of London. He preached in the Brotherhood Hall and lectured on more general 'new thought' topics in that most eccentric of buildings, 'The Cloisters', so named because its open-sided classrooms were completely exposed to the ravages of the outside elements. It was originally designated 'an adult school for Theosophical Meditation' and has latterly passed into the hands of the Freemasons.

At fifty-six, Wallace was a good deal older than Mary, who was thirty-four when they were married at the church of St. Mary Redcliffe, Bristol. They settled in a little house in Letchworth which was presented to them by some of the Rev. Bruce Wallace's friends and students.

1911 was also the year in which Thomas Allen died. That October, in a move apparently precipitated by this event, Christine Allen went off rather suddenly to live in Edinburgh, thereby breaking the unity of the Triad. The following March Christine met Janet and Kitty in London and announced that she was engaged to the Scottish painter John Duncan. The Triad made a statement of 'separating in complete harmony', leaving the Cup in the safekeeping of the two remaining members.

Meanwhile, Wellesley had become engaged to Florence Snelling, daughter of a surveyor from Sidcup, Kent, who had met him when on a visit to the Oratory. Very caring and capable, Florence had become so ill doing settlement work in deplorable conditions among the London poor that it had cost her a lung.

There had been talk that Christine might have wished to marry Wellesley. Whatever the truth of that, WTP would have been well aware that they both possessed very strong, definite, and highly incompatible temperaments.

On 27 April 1912, Christine married John Duncan. Now this is a curious thing, for Duncan had been, with William Sharp, a leading member of Sir Patrick Geddes' University Settlement group in Edinburgh in the 1890s. Christine's daughter, Mrs Bunty Martin, believes it was more or less an 'arranged marriage', set up by Christine's mother, Margaret Allen. Without doubting this, one must suspect that Dr Goodchild could have had a hand in making some sort of introduction here. His friend Sharp was once involved in Geddes' work and Duncan had been the professor's principal artist within the programme of the group. The potential links are too strong to be easily dismissed. It was again a marriage with a big age difference: Duncan had been born in 1866, Christine in 1885.

On the face of things, it is easy to see how much John Duncan and Christine would have had in common. The ethos of the Clifton group had sprung from their perception of the Celtic mysteries, especially all that was identified with the figure of Bride, or Brigid. Duncan was the artist *par excellence* of the Celtic revival, deeply steeped in the lore of the Western Isles and of Erin. He could speak the Gaelic tongue and had the gift of second sight. His friend, the Scottish poet and biographer of Aleister Crowley, Charles Richard Cammell, wrote of Duncan in his *The Heart of Scotland* (1956):

"He loved poetry, and my poetry he loved sincerely from his first knowledge of it; and he loved me, and my wife and little son.* He was himself a poet, as well as a painter: he has read me verses of his own making, the measures of which had a sweet faery-haunted music, like, yet unlike, the fay-poetry of William Sharp what time the discarnate spirit of 'Fiona Macleod' possessed him. Duncan had known Sharp well and had travelled with him in his latter days in the Western Highlands and Hebrides. He often talked to me of Sharp and 'Fiona'. He told me that he himself had seen the people of the *Sidh* (pronounced *Shee*) with his own eyes. He told me and my wife that he could teach us how to see these faery-folk; that you never see them in front of you, but sidelong through the corners of your eyes, that is, with the *oblique* glance, to which one finds allusions in the old legends. Duncan had painted more than one of the *Sidh* from memory; so vividly had they impressed themselves on his mind. These pictures were beautiful, and they were curious: I recollect one especially - a profile with the forehead and nose forming a single line, as with the ancient Greek Ideal of the beautiful; but the line was not the same as in the Hellenic type, it was subtly curved, slightly aquiline. The eyes, too, were singular - large and long, with pointed corners to the lids, which gave them an appearance distinctly unhuman."

In his mid-forties when he married, Duncan already had a distinguished career behind him. His murals adorned the walls of the Edinburgh University Hall, in the Halls of Residence on the Mound, in Geddes' house in Ramsay Gardens, as well as houses in his native Dundee. At the age of thirty-six he had been appointed Associate Professor of the Teaching of Art in the University of Chicago. Cammell compares him with Blake:

"Celtic as was Duncan's vision, his sense of beauty and approach to art reveal with what admirable judgement he had absorbed the teachings of

---

*This is Cammell's son Donald, an infant artistic prodigy doted on by John Duncan. After studying at the Royal Academy Donald worked for a while as a portrait painter until his career took a different turn into film directing. He is best remembered for his psychedelic psychodrama *Performance* (1970), which featured Mick Jagger, James Fox and Anita Pallenberg. He died in his Hollywood home in April 1996, 45 minutes after shooting himself in the head.

the early Italian masters whom he had studied in their native land. William Blake he approached by affinity rather than by influence; and the spiritual affinity was strong. Perhaps Duncan is closer spiritually to Blake, as an artist, than any other painter of whatever nation. Not that his vision corresponded with Blake's. The more authentic the vision, the more intensely is it individual. Blake's visions were Biblical, Duncan's were of Faery; but their visions were seen with equal lucidity and were translated into visible art with the same surety and simplicity. Like Blake, Duncan loved to draw the pure outlines of his visions, with little or no modelling. He was at once a strong and delicate draughtsman; and his sense of beauty was exquisite. Doubtless the cult of the Beautiful, of which we were both lifelong devotees, did much to precipitate and intensify our friendship."

Barely four months after Christine, on 17 August, Wellesley married Florence Snelling, and 16 Royal York Crescent became their marital home. Kitty seems to have still stayed there at times and we are told that Janet was working 'separately, quietly in touch' with her. She was also quietly in touch with Dr Goodchild, for of all of them, she was the most taken up with his ideas and followed closely any new developments. He would send her papers and drawings which explained his theories about Glastonbury, Rome or Celtic matters.

In 1913 Kitty and Janet saw a lot of each other, going on several pilgrimages to Glastonbury. They felt a need to settle the question of the third pilgrimage shrine in Ireland. While on a visit to Glastonbury in March, they were taken over Tor House at Chalice Well by Alice Buckton 'who had just bought it'. They prayed at the Catholic altar, which was still there, 'for the coming of the Kingdom of Peace and Joy'.

In May Janet brought Miss Winifred Ada Bax to stay at the Clifton Guest House. Miss Bax was particularly interested in the connections between Ireland and 'Little Ireland' at Beckery, Glastonbury. Janet returned to London, where she was then living, while Kitty and Winifred Bax went off to explore Ireland without coming to any definite conclusions about the elusive third centre.

On 28 June 1913, Kitty left for Letchworth with the Cup. It was decided to keep the Oratory simply as a 'silent room' in the Guest House. Everyone seemed to agree that this was the right thing to do. Their work as a group at Bristol had run its course.

Sometimes psychics came forward who claimed to have received 'messages' relating to the Cup. One such was Miss Gerda Fröbel, from Sweden. Wellesley was sufficiently impressed with the genuine character

KITTY TUDOR POLE

of some automatic writing she had received at Tintern Abbey, that he wired both Kitty and Janet to go to Clifton to meet her with the Cup. She was even allowed to take the vessel away with her for six days, returning it to Janet in London. No startling revelations seem to have come from this episode.

Goodchild observed these changes philosophically, and wrote to Janet: "The Oratory has no doubt done the work for which it was designed, but there was little Light there when I saw it last, as on one or two previous occasions, though on others I was much helped there."

He had been spending time at Glastonbury, looking into the possibility of 'cult-stones' being found there. He had advanced the rather wild notion that Egyptian hieroglyphs might be inscribed on them. Bligh Bond was drawn into this quest, and reported their investigations in the *Proceedings of the Somerset Archeological and Natural History Society* for 1913.

Dr Goodchild divided his time between Bath and his brother's vicarage at Berwick St. John, in Wiltshire. How far the Rev. William Goodchild subscribed to the doctor's more unorthodox views is hard to judge. We do know that Dr G. sent him numerous papers in which he set down the reasoning behind his belief in the connection between Glastonbury and the early Church in Rome via Claudia. On the face of it, it is difficult to imagine him accepting the thesis that a woman could have been in effective leadership of the first Christians in Rome, let alone the suggestion that she was also an initiate of the 'women's mysteries' and a graduate of the 'college' at Beckery. For in spite of all his undoubted good works, the villagers knew the incumbent of Berwick St. John as an uncompromising misogynist. The young men of the community were favoured with generous personal bursaries to support their further education; the women were ignored. When couples were picked up from the station, the parson allowed the men to sit up alongside him while the women were ordered to get in the back of the carriage. On the other hand these attitudes were not at all unusual at that time. Elsewhere in his own writings, he is quite open about admitting that in the seventh century small abbeys or mission stations, housing both monks and nuns together, "...were always under the direction of an abbess – usually a royal princess – and women on all occasions took precedence." (W. Goodchild, *Christian Wessex 634-734* – unpublished lecture notes).

1914

The major event of the following winter was the death of Dr Goodchild at his hotel in Bath. There was a small notice in the local papers but no mention of any funeral. In fact, his body was taken to Berwick

St. John where he was honoured and interred according to the rites of the Church of England with all the due respect and affection his brother obviously felt for him. His plain marble tomb with no headstone is just to the right of the entrance to the churchyard. A Celtic cross is carved on its upper surface. The inscription on the side reads: *In loving memory of John Arthur Goodchild, surgeon, formerly of Bordighera, Italy. Born February 26 1851; Died February 16 1914.*

With Goodchild gone, the advent of the Great War set the final seal on the activities of the now far-flung Glastonbury pilgrim-group. The Cup was in Letchworth; Wellesley was, for the while, excused from military service as his company was marketing essential foodstuffs and supplying the army; a number of babies had arrived: Christine had given birth to a daughter in Edinburgh in November1913; Florence had a daughter in Bristol in February 1914; in Letchworth, Mary Bruce Wallace also had a daughter in July 1914.

On another front, Mary Allen had left the suffragettes and had decided to try to form a voluntary women's police force with Margaret Damer Dawson, a humanitarian and animal welfare activist based in London. They were given the blessing of the Commissioner of the Metropolitan Police, Sir Edward Henry, to go ahead, provided they took no pay and kept well out of the way of the men.

The Women Police Volunteers officially began in September 1914. Their purpose seems from the outset to have been to protect or rescue women and girls from the clutches of undesirable men. There was not, at that stage, any intention to replicate the normal function of the all-male police force as if gender was of no issue. They existed to act on behalf of women in areas where men would be inept - or not even interested to proceed. By 1917 their operations had been so successful that Mary was awarded the OBE.

The cause of the war had become paramount in the life of the nation. Back in Bristol, Wellesley had become uneasy about his exemption, and in November 1916 joined up with the Royal Marines. It meant leaving his family - in May 1915 Florence had had another child, a son - and relinquishing his directorship of Chamberlain Pole and Co. for good, selling his position on to his successor. By September 1917 he had gained his commission and was posted to the Cheshire Regiment with rank of Second Lieutenant. He arrived in Egypt at the end of November, and in a short time was seeing active service on the Palestine front.

On the moonlit night of 2 December 1917, WTP was in command of a force of Devon Yeomanry a few miles north-west of Jerusalem.

They were surprised by a large brigade of Turkish snipers and completely overrun. Hardly anyone was spared; even the wounded were finished off by the Turks and thrown into nearby wells to contaminate the water. WTP was caught by a bullet from a man hiding up a fig-tree. It entered near his right shoulder, passed right through him and out of his left side. For a long time he lay there, losing blood, protected by the body of his sergeant, who had been killed while trying to help him and had fallen on top of him. He was aware of the presence of a 'guide', instructing him to remain still until a 'rescue plan' could be effected. He was eventually able to crawl to a cave where he found fresh water. Luckily he was discovered and taken in a basket on the back of a pack-animal for many hours until he was safe behind British lines. From there he was despatched to the Nazieh Military Hospital in Cairo, where, despite his near-death condition, he was reprimanded by the Matron because he had arrived without toiletries, blankets or a servant!

The surgeon in charge of him was astonished that he could have suffered such an injury without any vital organ being damaged. From his hospital ward, Wellesley had cause to reflect on a conversation he had had with a fellow officer the night before he was wounded. The other man had told him that he was sure he himself would not survive the war. He told Wellesley that there would be a greater and more tragic conflict in the future and that when that time came he, and others like him, would be waiting to help from the Other Side: "Give us a chance to pull our weight. You will still have 'time' available as your servant. Lend us a moment of it each day and through your silence give us our opportunity. The power of silence is greater than you know. When those tragic days arrive do not forget us."

The man died the next day. From the seed of this encounter came the inspiration for the 'Silent Minute' which WTP inaugurated during the Second World War.

By mid-December, the British army under General Allenby had taken Jerusalem. As soon as he was well enough to take a desk job, WTP was appointed by the General to work in his Headquarters in Cairo in the department of the Occupied Enemy Territory Administration. He retained this position for over a year, and by January 1919 had become its Deputy Assistant General with the rank of Major.

It was among his tasks to issue official permits for those wishing to enter Palestine. It will be remembered that this was the period shortly after the Balfour Declaration, which gave official sanction to the aspirations of the Jewish diaspora to establish a homeland in Palestine. The first Zionist missions had to apply for their permits through WTP.

During this period in Egypt, Wellesley explored the hinterland of the Nile Delta, experiencing numerous incidents of a paranormal nature. These are described in detail in his semi-autobiographical testimony, *The Silent Road.*

Anyone might be forgiven for wondering that all the reports of 'things seen' that fill many of the pages of WTP's books might be nothing more than the product of an overactive imagination. But there were never such doubts in the minds of people who knew him; everyone was impressed with his sincerity and integrity. He was, after all, in most respects a thoroughly 'ordinary' man, conservative by nature (and politically), and a skilled manager of his worldwide business interests. Perhaps an example of how the reality of his powers could be found acceptable to even the most unlikely of dispositions would be appropriate here.

Israel Sieff (later Lord Sieff) was as worldly a man as one is ever likely to meet. He was one of a breed of rich socialist-capitalists who were genuinely concerned to use their considerable influence to improve the lot of working people. He had been in the same class at Manchester Grammar School as Simon Marks, of the family who owned the chain stores, Marks and Spencer. They became lifelong friends. Israel married Simon's sister, Rebecca, and became a guiding light in the fortunes of the firm. They were members of the quite considerable Jewish community in Manchester which suddenly found itself host to an impassioned, visionary orator, Dr Chaim Weizmann, stirring them to support him in his campaign for a Jewish homeland in Palestine. The Russian-born lecturer in chemistry at Manchester University found a willing disciple in Israel Sieff, who effectively became his personal assistant and secretary.

After the signing of the Balfour Declaration in 1917 the Zionist Commission sent a party to Palestine to prepare the way. Israel was a member of this delegation which had to pass through WTP's office in Cairo. He recorded this experience in his *Memoirs:*

"My first impression of the Middle East was a rather weird one, and as a result of it I have never regarded 'The Mysterious East' as merely a romantic cliché. On my second day in Cairo I was told to take an official letter to a Major Tudor Pole, whose responsibility was the administration of conquered enemy territory. When I entered his office, he rose from his desk, and before I had time to utter a word, he said: 'You are bringing me a letter. It instructs me to...' And in a beautifully modulated voice he summarised the letter's contents. I did not know what was in the letter, so I handed him the envelope. He opened it and read the note. 'Quite so,' he said, and handed the letter back to me to read. He had got it pat. I did not know what to make of this: perhaps it was a common knack in the Middle East Command. We proceeded on our business. As I was leaving he said, 'Come down to the river sometime and see my boat'.

A few weeks later I went down to the river, where he had the kind of small launch to be seen on the Thames in summer, decked and furnished with a couple of berths. 'Delighted you have come,' he said, with his usual courtesy. 'I hope you won't mind if I have to break off for a spell around eight-thirty. I shall be in France. If I seem distrait, do not worry; just sit there quietly, I shall soon be back.' I hardly knew whether to take him seriously, but sat down, took a drink, and behaved as if I were accustomed to being welcomed with such information. We had a pleasant and interesting conversation for an hour or so, but at eight fifteen he turned down the lamp, an oil lamp, I remember, and lay back slowly against his cushions. His face became pale and his breathing deeper. He was obviously in, or pretending to be in, a trance. I sat there quietly and rather frightened. Fifteen minutes later he sat up, quite composed, and turned up the lamp. 'I've been to France,' he said, in a grave but otherwise normal voice. 'It's the Somme. The Germans have broken through, we're having a terrible time of it, there are frightful casualties.' His clairvoyance was beyond dispute. The Germans had blown a huge hole in the British lines and in a matter of days had pushed through many miles. We resumed our conversation and shortly after I left."

Sieff kept in touch with WTP and they met from time to time after the war. One day WTP told Sieff that he was sorry to have to warn him to expect a tragedy in his life. Someone he knew and loved was going to die. Two weeks later WTP telephoned him from Algeria: 'Israel I must tell you that your sorrow is about to fall on you'. The next morning his eighteen-year-old son, Daniel, was found hanging from a cord in his bedroom. It was the day he should have left England to spend the summer at the Hebrew University in Jerusalem. On the floor lay a book that had caused much hilarity at a family dinner party the night before, *Pleasures of the Torture Chamber.*

Daniel was destined for a brilliant career as a biologist. Some time later Weizmann, whose son, Michael, had grown up with Daniel, proposed to the Sieffs that a scientific institute should be built in Palestine as a memorial to their son. All contributed to the cost, and the Daniel Sieff Research Institute was built at Rehovoth, some fifteen miles south-east of Tel Aviv. It opened in April 1935. Weizmann, of course, went on to become the first President of the State of Israel in 1948.

We might well feel uneasy about the fatalistic way this tragedy was allowed to unfold in spite of warnings and premonitions of doom. Did it help to tell the man that something unpleasant was going to happen? Perhaps it was up to Sieff to do something after being forewarned, but he did not. Do some deaths *have* to occur? Was it somehow all tied up with the hidden forces that attend the making of history? The Sieff family was indeed close to the making of history: the State of Israel plays no minor role in the precarious equilibrium of international affairs to this day. But more than anything, it is the impression WTP's demonstration of psychic perception made on Israel Sieff that is of significance here. He never forgot it.

By 1915 Christine and John Duncan had had two daughters, Christine Margaret and Vivian Mairi. Christine, quite unable to stick around at home simply being a good housewife, was ready to seize any chance to get out and do something in the outside world once the children were old enough. She and Janet had watched the progress of their suffragette sister's career with interest. Many young women found in Mary Allen's Police Volunteers the sort of opportunity that had been unavailable to them before the advent of the franchise campaign. The issue of women's roles in society now had a high profile, notwithstanding the distraction of the war in Europe. Even Christine joined the Women Police Volunteers in Edinburgh. After a period of training she found herself assigned to the task of rescuing young women caught up in organized prostitution, commonly known as 'white-slavery'. The former officiator at the mystical celebrations in the Bristol Oratory was now snooping round the back alleys of the less salubrious corners of Scotland's capital city resplendent in a smart navy-blue suit, long greatcoat and high black leather boots.

The Duncan's well-appointed Edinburgh home was more than adequate to accommodate the countless visitors who called in on account of both John and Christine's work in their chosen fields. Another of Christine's tasks within the police was to care for the welfare of women released from prison. It was a rich and interesting time for her two daughters, as Christine ('Bunty') recalls: "My sister and I had a wonderful upbringing as our house was full of mother's criminals, who came to tea, and my father's students (he lectured at the Art School). He had Chinese students, men from Nigeria, Indians, and all sorts of exciting people. He was friendly with W.B. Yeats, who I remember used to tell us fairy-stories before we went to bed."

With the death of Margaret Damer Dawson shortly after the war, Mary became Commandant of the Women Police Service, as it was then known. A period of difficulties followed. A succession of Metropolitan Police Commissioners did all they could to undermine their work. Moreover, largely out of the experience gained from observing the usefulness of Mary's volunteers, an official body of policewomen was set up, with the very limited function of intervening when men and women were found lying together in public parks. The upshot was that Mary now found herself in court, accused of 'impersonating (the 'official') police officers'. To meet the requirements of the law, the uniform was subsequently modified and the WPS changed to the Women's Auxiliary Service. Ironically, Mary's women were officially appointed to advise and train policewomen outside London, both in the provinces and overseas.

Mary was never out of her uniform, an extraordinary vision no-one could forget, including Bunty: "I first met her in Edinburgh in the early 20s and thought she was a man. She had a monocle and was always dressed in uniform, jackboots and all."

In 1922 she was invited to Cologne to establish a training programme for German policewomen. The British troops which had occupied the country after its defeat in the Great War were being withdrawn. Mary was satisfied to see the native trainees stepping in to fulfil invaluable service in the years that followed. When the Nazis came to power in 1933, this service was disbanded.

Unfortunately, the uniforms, discipline and organization of this new dispensation were everything Mary had always dreamed of: she came to *admire* them. How far she subscribed to other policies of the Nazis is hard to know. In her *Lady in Blue,* she chiefly commends Hitler for ridding the nation of its Communists. The nearest hint of racism in her eulogy for the Führer comes in the statement: "I recognize in him an enduring friend of England, and a blood-brother of the ordinary decent people of Europe, whatever their nationalities, who want peace for their trade and safety for their children."

In 1934, Mary was in Germany again, this time at the invitation of the new government. At the risk of seeming too charitable, we might allow that she was swept along more by the theatrical phenomena of the events she witnessed than the ideas they were trying to promote:

"I was fortunate to reach Germany in time to be present at the enormous meeting following the Reichstag burning, when Herr Hitler explained his policy in full for the first time, not only to thousands of waiting Germans, but to a breathless and uneasy world.

For two and a half hours I sat absolutely entranced beside the Chancellor's charming sister, listening to the great Dictator. When he sat down at last, I looked at my watch thinking he had been speaking about half an hour! My German is elementary, yet this man's hypnotic gestures, his passionate, forceful voice and his visionary eyes held me spellbound. He is one of the greatest orators who have ever lived...

I felt afraid that, with all this extraordinary activity going on, there might be no time for the interview with Herr Hitler that had been arranged for me. I need not have been apprehensive, for at the close of what must have been to the Chancellor a day of superhuman mental and physical strain, I was told that he would see me at midnight.

He sent his representative, Dr Ernst Hanpfstaengel, to the Kaiserhof Hotel to fetch me, and together we crossed the square, covered in snow and wrapped in midnight silence which our muffled footsteps did not break. We entered a large house in the Wilhelmstrasse.

A few moments in the lift, a short walk through anterooms piled high with flowers, and I was in the presence of one of Europe's most remarkable men. He rose, made the famous Nazi salute, shook hands, and asked me to be seated.

In private, he is a charming man, courteous, quiet, patient. But the steadfast eyes and the unflinching mouth do not let one forget that sincerity and fixity of purpose which have carried this 'little corporal' from political refugee to virtual leader of one of the greatest nations of the modern world."

Hitler went on to explain why he had had to disband the Women Police of Prussia. The units "were not of his political persuasion, and it was impossible to retain officials who did not subscribe to the United Nazi front". He was, however, much interested in Mary's "arguments in favour of Nazi policewomen, and said that General Goering had provisionally agreed to enrol a hundred policewomen in Berlin under his own charge".

In fact a meeting with the General followed. He explained to her the conditions in Germany immediately prior to the Nazi regime. Two revolutions had clashed, nationalism and internationalism - loyalty against disorder; National Socialism against Communism. "He believed that the Communist plan was to spread from Russia, first to Germany, then to France, then to England, and he found ample proof that these suspicions were correct."

It is hardly surprising that, with such sentiments expressed in print, Mary came within a hair's breadth of internment at the outbreak of the war with Germany in 1939. Perhaps she later revised her views. Her family considers it was only the German police which drew her praises, not the Nazis themselves. Biased? Of course. But they knew her and cherished her as a human spirit. Love can forgive all. But it may be longer before the world, or the Almighty, sees fit to offer any such absolution to the little man with the moustache.

John and Christine Duncan inhabited a very different world - or they did for a while. Theirs was a Celtic world of faerie. They did not live it day in and day out together; not in the way of the native people of the Western Isles, thrown on to each other's resources all of their waking hours by the hard necessities of existence. John was often away. He was sometimes abroad, possibly America, where he had long-standing connections. What they did understand together was the meaning of the story of Bride, the Celtic Isis, and all that was conveyed in the tale of her being borne by angels across land and sea to Jerusalem to be the Foster-Mother of Christ. They knew it as it had been expounded theoretically by Goodchild and poetically by Fiona Macleod. It was the theme of one of John Duncan's best-known and best-loved paintings.

Summer was a family time. Each year John, Christine and the two little girls took a large house on Iona, Traigh Mor, for the holiday period. John would paint. The children explored and got to know so much about the island's history and flora and fauna that they were able to conduct American tourists to interesting places. Their satisfied 'clients' often sent them gifts of books and such when they returned home.

For reasons unclear, or unsaid, this seemingly ideal and idyllic life came to an end.

In the autumn of 1926, Christine decided that she no longer wanted to play the role of being John Duncan's wife. She sent the two children, then aged eleven and thirteen, to her sister Elsie in Belgium. She wanted to go *somewhere* but did not know exactly where. She took a map of the world and a pin. Shutting her eyes, she brought the pin down until it stuck in the paper. She hoped it might be somewhere where she could make good use of herself. When she looked, she discovered the place of her future destiny: Cape Town, South Africa. She borrowed fifty pounds from another sister, Dolly, a Christian Science practitioner who lived in Surrey, collected the children and set sail for Cape Town.

Luckily, Christine got a job as soon as they had arrived as Secretary

ST. BRIDE BEING CARRIED BY ANGELS TO THE HOLY LAND
TO BE THE FOSTER-MOTHER OF CHRIST.
Painting by John Duncan

of the Child Welfare Society. She found a flat, and life for them in their new-found land progressed from there.

Even Bunty Martin is unsure why her mother made this drastic move: "She was a very forceful character and always spoke her mind, regardless of other people's feelings. It is difficult to know what propelled her to leave my father. He was a difficult man in some ways and spent a lot of the time away painting."

One of the unusual features of the population of Cape Town is the presence of a sizeable community of people of mixed race - that is, compared to most other towns and cities in South Africa. Their ancestry might be any combination of European, African, Asian or Malay. In the local terminology, these people are simply referred to as 'Coloureds'. Many of them are very poor. Before 1966 they were largely centred in an area above Cape Town proper called District Six. After that year it ceased to exist, bulldozed flat, apart from the occasional lone mosque, to fulfil the requirements of the apartheid laws.

The plight of these people, disadvantaged by circumstances beyond their control, touched the conscience of some members of the white population more openly than others. In 1935, Christine resolved, with two other women, Miss Doris Syfret and Mrs Nesta Crosse-Jones, to launch a scheme to provide good nourishing food for the poor of Cape Town at affordable prices. Premises were secured in Canterbury Street, on the edge of District Six, and the work began. Remarkably, even miraculously, this enterprise, known as the Service Dining Rooms, has proceeded from strength to strength over the years and is still flourishing. Local firms send in surplus goods, benefactors and philanthropists offer donations, and a staff of enthusiastic volunteers provides thousands of bowls of soup, meals and drinks throughout the year for a minute charge of a few cents, a levy that has never been increased over fifty years. Like the mythical grail, or cauldron, there seems to be a never-ending supply. Appropriately, true to the tradition of the legend, and the Glastonbury happenings of thirty years before, three women were again in attendance at its inception.

Christine returned to England several times after leaving. She spent some time in Glastonbury as the first warden at the Chalice Well after the Chalice Well Trust under WTP had purchased the property in 1959. Helpers at the Well remember Christine camping out in a more-or-less gutted and roofless Little St. Michael's cottage in those first months while essential work was carried out. People called her 'Sandy'. She was by then a widow, having married a Colonel Sandeman (Indian Army, retired) after her divorce from John Duncan. On a visit there in 1964, she was called away to attend to her sister Mary, then gravely ill. She looked after her until she died.

In 1972, she wrote to Barbara Crump in Glastonbury from her bed in a South African nursing home, concerning new developments:

> "You will be surprised to get a letter from SA, but a friend sent me your magazine *TORC* and I am deeply interested - not that we might think alike, but I am so happy that the young are making some effort towards reviving a spiritual life in Glastonbury. I worked with W. T. Pole in the very beginning, collecting the money to buy Chalice Well and when it was bought was in charge. In those days we did so much: rebuilt the house; made a lovely garden; had lectures, interesting people staying - and then the excavation on the Tor. There was a resident Trustee and he was a marvel at planning things. The whole place began to come alive. I left after the last excavation as it seemed better to have a man and wife in charge."

Christine Sandeman (née Allen) died of cancer a year after this letter was written, still with Glastonbury in her thoughts and still eager to hear of everything that was going on there. *Torc* was a local 'alternative' magazine published between 1971-75. Barbara Crump was a retired horticulturist who held 'New Age' meetings at her home at Butleigh Wootton and was friendly with the young 'hippie' newcomers to Glastonbury. She herself died a few years later.

As to religion, Christine was something of a restless spirit, being for a while an Anglican, and then, in South Africa, a Christian Scientist. At the end she was involved with a more obscure (probably 'esoteric') group. She kept this very much to herself and resented any interference. In a former life, she believed she had been one of the daughters of Akhenaton, the heretic king of Ancient Egypt. The great work of her later years was on behalf of the people who came every day to the Service Dining Rooms. In 1976, her daughter Bunty took over the running of it, and in 1990 received a Rotary Merit Award in recognition of her services. She retired from this work at the end of 1992.

Bunty's sister Vivian returned to Scotland when she was eighteen to study medicine. She married a fellow student from New Zealand. Both qualified as doctors. They moved to Cyprus were they chose to devote their lives to the arts rather than take up careers in medicine. Vivian died there in 1988.

John Duncan remained in Edinburgh, painting and teaching. He was also widely respected as an authority on ancient lore and literature. He kept his attachment for Iona and the other isles, visiting and exploring there whenever he could. One of his major commissions was for the great stained-glass window of the Children's Chapel in Paisley Abbey. The three central panels represent Christ blessing four children, with the legend: 'Of such is the Kingdom of Heaven'. Donald, the son of C. R. Cammell, was the model for the youngest of these. The model for the figure of the Madonna riding on a donkey was Lewis Spence's youngest daughter, Madge. The window was dedicated in July 1937.

Towards the end of his life, John Duncan became partially paralysed after suffering a stroke. Unable to paint or write, he had his bed moved into his studio where he could lie surrounded by his own beautiful works. After more than a year in this condition, he died in November 1945.

Just before the war of 1914, Janet and Kitty tried to reform the Triad with a new third member, Winifred Ada Bax. However, any plans they might have entertained were brought to a halt by the national crisis.

By then, Janet was living in London to be near her mother who had moved there from Bristol. Goodchild had gone, but Janet kept faith with his ideas and would do so through all the years to come. The doctor's vision of the church in the house of Pudens in Rome drew her compellingly. There, if only for a while, Claudia, the embodiment of Bride of the Celts, enjoyed a successful marriage with Christ in His Church. Now, nearly two thousand years later, she came to believe that she herself had taken on the mantle of Bride. It was more than just a matter of ideas and theories: she was *involved;* she and her sister had found the Cup of the Master Jesus in Bride's Well. Their own activities at the Oratory had very much honoured the spirit of Bride - perhaps more than the spirit of Christ. Now that was all over and there seemed little chance of its revival. Janet looked back once again to the source at Rome. There was only one spiritual institution that could provide any real link with that source: the Church of Rome itself. Any discrepancy between Goodchild's viewpoint and its own story of its origins could be passed over. An alternative scenario, privately cherished, gave no offence to the Mystical Body of Christ.

We do not know exactly when Janet started to attend Catholic church services. She may have had some direction from her cousin, Dom Aelred Carlyle, Abbot of Caldey, who had converted to Rome in 1913. However, soon after the end of the Great War he had left to work as a parish priest in Canada. But we do know that she was received into

SISTER BRIGID ALLEN AT STANBROOK ABBEY.

the Catholic Church on 10 January 1920, at Westminster Cathedral. Eight days later, she was confirmed by Bishop Butt, taking the names Margaret Brigid.

It soon transpired that this was only the first step on a larger journey. On 21 November 1921, she entered the enclosed community at Stanbrook Abbey, Worcestershire, as a Novice. The House Chronicle of the time recorded that she received the name of Sister Brigid, "after the Irish saint of that name for whom she has great devotion. She is a convert, and about 40, and has always been very delicate, but a most sincere disposition, full of zeal." She was clothed in the Benedictine habit on 1 June 1922.

She made her Solemn Perpetual vows on 24 June 1926. The occasion was noted in the Chronicle: "Sr. Brigid Allen made her Solemn Profession in the hands of Abbot President Kelly. A number of monks came from Belmont Abbey [Hereford]. Mrs Green Armytage and Miss Benson were the Matrons, as Sr. Brigid has no Catholic relations. Most of her family were present, although they declared they would never see her again... Sr. Brigid sang her part very well, and went through it all very bravely, for she is not strong... Commandant Mary Allen, DBC, sister of Sr. Brigid, was here. She is head of the Women Police in England, and with the late Commandant M. Damer Dawson, started the Women Police Service in 1914..."

This was the point of no return. But there is no indication that Sr. Brigid ever harboured any misgivings about her vocation in the years that followed.

It will be seen that quite a long time is allowed before the postulant takes her final vows. There is a progression through several stages of profession to test the commitment of the candidate and to give room for any change of heart. The clothing ceremony of 1922 might have had more significance for Sr. Brigid than even the Solemn Profession four years later. For in this, the postulant is clothed as the *Bride of Christ*, dressed in white, with a train and a veil.

There is a question here: To what degree did Sr. Brigid see herself as re-living the mystical union of Bride (or Brigid) of the Celts with the Saviour of Mankind? As far as can be judged, quite a bit.

Outwardly, within the community at Stanbrook, there is no reason to suppose that Sr. Brigid stood out from the others in any special way. She was, as much as all of them, thoroughly a Christian, a *lover* of Christ. Not many years ago there were still some elderly nuns at the Abbey who could remember her. Describing her as "very zealous and fervent", it was considered that she had a rather romantic disposition and was known to be very enthusiastic about Glastonbury and the Holy Grail. Perhaps she never took these discussions beyond a certain point. What is certain is that she brought with her into Stanbrook all her papers and letters from Dr Goodchild. In the time allowed for private study, she followed up his various references, corroborating them with some of her own. Most of the sources were from ecclesiastical commentators, so she was well-placed to obtain documents and books from other religious houses. Her friends, Mr and Mrs Robert Green Armytage, made her gifts of old books and manuscripts which have passed into the collection in the library at the Abbey.

As for the other members of the Glastonbury group, she kept in regular touch by letter. Kitty sometimes went to see her, but in those days visitors were confined to speaking through a grille. Of course, she never left the monastic buildings. The last time had been before she took her final vows, calling on all her relatives and friends, including Christine in Edinburgh.

Kitty was able to follow Sr. Brigid's researches with interest, understanding her devotion to Dr Goodchild's line of enquiry. She was also attentive to her brother, Wellesley's, different approach - far more directed by his own psychic perceptions, and apparently less interested in the question of Claudia or the role of women in the coming age.

Possibly seeing her sister take such a momentous step in 1926, may have prompted Christine to uproot herself from Edinburgh five months later. She sensed the end of an era and, even if perversely, resolved to make a new start in South Africa.

Sr. Brigid never held any major office within the Abbey. For some years she was Zelatrix to the Novices (Assistant Novice Mistress). Her advancement was probably curtailed by her very delicate state of health. Sometime around 1941, the onset of spinal cancer put an end to her capacity to do any physical work in the community. In August 1944 she sent out to Kitty a folio of notes that summarized her verification over the years of all Goodchild's sources. She confirmed that there was no inaccuracy or exaggeration.

Sr. Brigid Allen died on 4 December 1945.

The coming of the Great War brought changes to the life of the families at Letchworth. Mary and her husband decided to move to Northern Ireland in 1915, with their one-year-old daughter, Monica. A cousin had recently died, making available the old family home in the countryside about three miles outside the town of Limavady, halfway between Derry city and Coleraine. The house was very isolated.

Water was drawn from a well, paraffin was used for lighting and cooking. There were peat fires for warmth in winter.

The Rev. Wallace had many years before been the minister at Clifton Park Congregational Church, Belfast. He was a very idealistic, 'open-minded' man, a believer in universal equality and non-violence. His ideas were not shared by many of his congregation, who often took a narrow sectarian view of the world around them. He once preached on the text 'Walk in Love' on the Sunday before the Orange marches on the 12 July. Seven prominent families left his congregation in protest.

Mary was very lonely in her new home. Her husband spent a lot of time in his study, preparing a magazine he published called *Brotherhood*. Her parents were concerned enough to let Tudor Cottage to Belgian refugees, and to go across to Ireland to be nearby. Kitty, and the Cup, went too.

They bought a caravan, parked in a field by the river at Dungiven, eight miles from the Wallace home. Kitty slept in a house nearby on the edge of the village. That summer (1916) they also spent a few weeks at Castlerock. With the onset of winter, they rented a cottage at Portstewart, on the coast, where they remained until 1921. Kate, a practical woman who had been brought up in a family short of money, was good at making the most out of very little. She bought second-hand furniture, made curtains, and covered wooden boxes with material, padding the tops with hay. A man with a strong enough horse brought the caravan across the mountains from Dungiven and parked it in the garden. It became Kitty's 'den', where she slept and regularly practised her violin. The Cup was kept in its wooden casket under the bed.

Mary and her little daughter often used to visit the cottage at Portstewart, arriving by train from Limavady. It was here that she had a psychic experience while walking on the lonely shoreline. For the first time she heard the voice of a late friend, always simply referred to as 'AB'. She hurried back to tell her parents the news. From then on, Mary received regular communications from this same source. These were later published in two volumes and since combined as *The Thinning of the Veil*. It now made sense of their exile to the lonely wild places of Ireland. Here there was the calm and quiet helpful for 'inner' contacts to make their approach.

A few years after the first contact at Portstewart, Monica remembers witnessing communications taking place in their cottage sitting room:

"I was occasionally allowed (if I promised to be very still and quiet) to 'sit in' while my mother was receiving 'messages' in the evenings. It must have been winter, as there was a glowing peat fire, and my father would sit at a small table, with a green-shaded oil lamp, writing in shorthand as my mother spoke. She kept her hand over her eyes, and spoke very slowly, with a pause between each word. She said they came 'like drops of water into a pool', and as she heard each one she said it aloud, never letting her mind think of the *meaning*. Thus she was often quite astonished, and almost disbelieving, when my father had read out what had come through."

Often these communications took place in front of Thomas, Kate and Kitty when they were all together. At other times it was when Wellesley was there, or his younger brother, Alex. There is reference to this in the Preface the Rev. Bruce Wallace wrote to the first book:

"Nor have I been the only convinced witness, and gainer by, my wife's psychic development. It was during a visit that she paid to her father, mother and sister, that her psychic sensitiveness first revealed itself. Since then, whenever they have visited us, or she them, they have joined with her in her daily meeting with heavenly visitants. Each of her two brothers has also been present on two or three occasions. In rare cases - just three times - with the consent of her Guides beyond the veil, friends outside the family circle have likewise been admitted. And all these relatives and friends have through her got communications that have been to them distinctly helpful and quite relevant to their respective difficulties and needs. The cumulative convincing effect of such experiences could, however, scarcely be conveyed to strangers...

Precious is intercourse with those on earth who are morally and spiritually ahead of us, still more so is fellowship with those 'ministering spirits' who, from higher planes, are seeking to help us into the Will of God, as instruments of righteousness and love unto Him. Such fellowship is what is to be hoped for from 'the thinning of the veil'."

Evidently Mary was given certain 'proofs' about her friend's identity which convinced her that the contact was genuine. The messages came not only from AB, but also a higher being known as 'The Teacher'. Mary gives a very definitive description of her experiences in the Introduction to her book:

"The voice seemed to speak not to my outer ear but my soul-ear, and I heard every intonation of it, suiting the nature of the thought, tender, grave, encouraging, hopeful, joyous: every human emotion that is true and beautiful seemed expressed in tones more musical than any outward voice can reach. The Teacher told me that before long I should also see him, without any effort on my part to develop clairvoyance. This promise was fulfilled a few months later. I was walking alone by the sea, when, in one sudden flash, I saw a tall figure beside me, clad in shining raiment that looked like moonlight, and with a face so wonderfully calm and beautiful that I could not forget it. I saw silver sandals upon the feet, and then the vision faded, but again I heard the now well-known voice...

It is not easy to describe the starry beauty of these radiant ones. The body looks like a rosy alabaster lamp through which the glory of the spirit shines forth, illuminating even the raiment, and creating a surrounding atmosphere - aura - more or less dazzling according (I imagine) to the degree of development of the indwelling soul. Thus I see the aura of the Teacher like white flame, very dazzling, whereas that of our friend is softer, and looks more like candle-light."

In the spring of 1921, Thomas, Kate and their daughter, Kitty, returned to Letchworth. On their departure, the Wallace family took over the Portstewart cottage.

Mention is made that Alex Tudor Pole called in on them at Limavady and Portstewart. Alex has been absent from our story so far owing to his long periods of work overseas. Very different from Wellesley, he was energetic, keen on games and passionately interested in engineering from his boyhood. There was not much common ground between them apart from the normal family bonds. The younger brother worked for a while on the vessels which laid the first cables under the sea for telephone and telegraph communications between continents. After a while he transferred to the Marconi company, directing the building and operating of radio stations all over the world. All the younger generation of the family knew of him was that he would occasionally appear from some exotic place laden with wonderful gifts for them.

He caught small-pox in Mexico city and almost died. His recovery was attributed to his healthy lifestyle: vegetarian, non-smoker, teetotaller. He was also very taken up with Theosophical occultism - something else that Wellesley could not easily share with him. WTP used to say that if he went too far into the atmosphere of other teachings, his own powers would diminish. Alex died in Mexico in the 1960s.

Like Kitty, Alex had not been registered as 'Tudor' Pole at birth, but in both cases the name was incorporated soon afterwards. Thomas and Kate eventually referred to themselves as Mr and Mrs Tudor Pole although neither of them originally had the name. It was genuinely a family name, on the side of Kate's mother. Thomas and Kate both died in 1926.

Kitty stayed on in Tudor Cottage at Letchworth, teaching the violin. She usually visited Mary, in Ireland, twice each year. She followed her own spiritual path, one of quiet and contemplation. In her later years she joined the Quakers, much in sympathy with the importance they attached to silence. When the war came in 1939, the Cup was again with her for safekeeping. After 1969 it was kept at Chalice Well. Kitty Tudor Pole died at Letchworth in 1986, in her 104th year. Like Wellesley, her ashes were scattered in the garden at Chalice Well.

The Rev. Bruce Wallace died in 1939. When the Second World War started, Mary and Monica Wallace decided to move to Galway, in the Republic, after they found their home hemmed in by Army and Air Force bases.

They were dismayed at the presumed superiority of the Protestant community. They found their natural sympathies were more with the 'traditional' Irish, the Catholics. As much for this reason, and a sense of association with the ancient past, Monica was eventually received into the Catholic faith.

Mary Bruce Wallace died in 1970. Although not a centenarian like her sister, she had reached the grand age of ninety-three. Both were life-long vegetarians. Since the publication of the first edition of this book, Monica has also died.

In the Birthday Honours List for 1919, Major Wellesley Tudor Pole was awarded the OBE for his war service. No longer attached to the family firm in Bristol, he set up his own business at 61 St. James's Street, London: W. Tudor Pole & Co. He exercised himself in diverse fields, whatever happened to come along, in fact. He dealt in tea with Eastern Europe and Russia; clothing with Holland; bricks for house-building in the UK; concrete and wooden poles in Shropshire - and many other commodities over the years.

His Russian contacts alerted him to the plight of refugees from the Bolshevik Revolution. There was at the time such an attack on the Orthodox Church by the regime in Russia that its very survival was in question. The exiles regarded the Moscow Patriarchate as a token puppet of the government with no freedom to act on its own behalf. A complicated situation arose when the Metropolitan Evlogy, the

Russian bishop in Paris, met with other bishops and formulated a new administration for the Russian Church in Exile at Karlovtzy (Sremski-Karlovci, Yugoslavia) in 1922. This administration was regarded as illegal and declared uncanonical by the Moscow Patriarchate. Evlogy himself broke away from it to form the Russian Exarchate in Europe in 1926. In 1930 the Moscow Patriarchate finally disowned him because he prayed for Christians under persecution in Russia. In 1931 he placed his parish under the oversight of the Ecumenical Patriarch of Constantinople. He was again temporarily reconciled to the Karlovtsy group in 1934.

One of Evlogy's primary tasks was to establish a theological seminary in Paris to meet the need for the training of priests for the community in exile. To help in this work, WTP founded the Appeal for the Russian Clergy Church Aid Fund in 1926. He remained its honorary treasurer until 1937. When he withdrew from this responsibility, Evlogy and other members of the academy wrote in thanks: "You have for eleven years ceaselessly and untiringly carried the heavy burden of leadership of those whom we must indeed call the truest and best friends of the Russian Church."

By 1921 Wellesley and Florence had had three children: Jean, Christopher and David. The family moved to a remarkable number of addresses: Brighton, Hove, Hampstead Garden Suburb, Hampton Court, various London flats, Thames Ditton, Holland Park and more.

Although there was in many ways a moral and ethical association between WTP's idealism and his business interests, he kept his psychic side separate from his professional and family life. For someone whose gifts were so unusual he was remarkably *ordinary* in all other respects. He never gave demonstrations of clairvoyance before his children. They really only became fully aware of the dimensions of his 'other world' in later life after sight of his books. They were carefully raised to appreciate the dignity of all faiths and denominations, just as he had been by his own parents. He was concerned, long before it was 'fashionable', for the future of the environment, of the need to produce food by organic methods, and, later, raised his voice against both the wartime and peacetime uses of nuclear energy.

In between the wars he looked after the Cup. From time to time his 'Quest Group' embarked on excavations or lines of enquiry in hope of getting nearer to solving the mystery of the origin of the vessel.

The war against Hitler's Germany brought a new challenge, and WTP was not lost for inspiration in this time of national need.

There can be a power in silence, something creative. William Sharp's enigmatic triad, written on the back of an envelope in Glastonbury Abbey, began: "From the silence of time, time's silence borrow..." Kitty Tudor Pole was drawn to the Quakers for the opportunity there for silence. When in Stanbrook Abbey, Janet (Sr. Brigid) Allen wrote a meditation on a saying of St. Augustine, "God cannot be expressed, God cannot be thought, He is." She opened with these words: "The possession of God is the silence of the heart. The thought of God is the silence of the mind. For silence is not an emptiness but a plenitude; it is not a cessation of thought, but the fullness of activity..." The fellow officer who died the following day, quoted earlier, told WTP: "You still have 'time' available as your servant. Lend us a moment of it each day and through your silence give us our opportunity."

It was to aid the fulfilment of this last pledge that WTP went right to the top, meeting Churchill in September 1940. He put forward his suggestion that the Silent Minute of prayer for peace already established within some groups should be made available to the whole nation through the broadcasting network. Hugh Carlton Greene, the Director of the BBC, was contacted, and he readily agreed to inaugurate a period of one minute's silence, to be marked by the first stroke of Big Ben striking nine o'clock each evening. This was first heard on 18 September 1940. It continued until the autumn of 1961. It was a source of strength and hope in the war years, not only in Britain, but anywhere in the world able to receive the Home Service broadcasts on the medium wave. By all accounts, certain Nazi officers considered it a demoralizing force which they had no power to stand up to.

We might also note that WTP's first book, published in 1960, was *The Silent Road*. The last sentence in his Foreword reads: "In the long run it is through silence, and not speech, that Revelation is received."

It was only when his books started to appear that the larger world had any knowledge of WTP and his experiences. *A Man Seen Afar* (1965) was written in collaboration with the novelist Rosamond Lehmann, whom he had helped and advised after the tragic death of her daughter. It is partly in dialogue form, and comprises for about two-thirds of the book, WTP's 'glimpses' of the life and times of Jesus. At the time he was the keeper of the Cup, and it must be supposed that it acted as a kind of focus for the information received. Man's relation with the Kingdoms of Nature is also discussed. There is an interesting account of WTP's conversation with a copper-beech tree on the Austro-Bavarian border!

Many years earlier a small account of WTP's 'communication' with a soldier killed in battle in the Great War was published as

Private Dowding (1917). It has been reprinted several times since then.

In *Writing on the Ground* (1968), the dialogue form is again employed, this time with the journalist Walter Lang putting questions and adding his own comments. Similar subjects are covered as in the other books, and there is a detailed account of WTP's association with Abdu'l Baha Abbas, leader of the Baha'is.

Posthumously, his many private letters to Rosamond Lehmann were published by her as *My Dear Alexias* (1979).

Additionally there were several smaller booklets by WTP, some of which are still available and occasionally reprinted.

The most satisfactory achievement of WTP's later years was his 'rescue' of the land and buildings at Chalice Well, Glastonbury, from an uncertain future. The proper legal establishment of The Chalice Well Trust has secured its continuity into the present century. The public is able to visit the gardens and the well (and take away the iron-laden waters) throughout the year. Members, known as 'Companions', subscribe to an annual fee, which allows for free access to the gardens and admits them to an annual 'Companions' Day' luncheon and lectures, held in a marquee in the grounds. There is a Guest House and resident wardens. The bookshop is as good a place as any to seek out the works of WTP and other literature on related topics.

Florence Tudor Pole saw none of these developments, for she died in 1951. WTP developed cancer in his last years. Often in pain, and becoming weaker, his mind remained as bright as ever to the end of this life's span, which came on 13 September 1968. It might seem curious, but he never actually lived in Glastonbury. His later years were spent with his housekeeper and her corgi dog 'Kipps' in the modest house at Hurstpierpoint, in Sussex, to which he and Florence had moved just before she died.

The Cup was kept in a tiny attic sanctuary at the top of the house. It too was having a quieter life. Since its recovery it had travelled to a surprisingly large number of places. Even before 1914 it had been taken to Palestine, Syria, Egypt and Turkey, as well as most of the countries of Europe, usually to recognized sacred centres of pilgrimage. Between the wars, its mission was directed towards what are known as 'Michael centres' in Britain and the continent.

It is a fact that nearly all our pagan hilltop sites have been re-dedicated in Christian times to the Archangel Michael, defeater of the powers of darkness. WTP perceived Michael as being at the forefront of a new impulse for the coming times. The awakening of his sacred shrines was a necessary and useful work towards this end.

He collaborated with Margaret Thornley in making pilgrimages to many such places. Mrs Thornley recorded a list of 151 Michael place names that she visited in Britain, Ireland and on the Continent on a silk ribbon that was sent, at her own request, to Queen Elizabeth, the Queen Mother. A facsimile exists, incorporated on the wooden prayer-wheel which Margaret Thornley presented to the Chalice Well Trust, and which, appropriately, is now displayed there in the archive room at Little St. Michael's cottage.

It will have been noted that the whole aspect of the Cup having a special significance for women's spirituality seems to have been discarded somewhere along the way. However, there is an interesting incident which has a bearing on this.

In 1965 WTP was invited to attend a meeting of the 'Cocked Hat Club' of distinguished archeologists and antiquarians at Wells. The Cup was passed round for their inspection. They came up with the familiar conclusion: it was unique, but seemed too well preserved to be ancient. While it was being passed round, WTP suddenly became aware of the figure of Janet Allen 'in convent garb' standing well up over the centre of the table holding a replica of the vessel. She was smiling; she and her garments had a radiant luminosity. She then seemed to be joined by the other two 'maidens' (Christine and Kitty), who made a circle with their hands held together, the Cup seemingly suspended between them. Before the vision faded, Janet looked towards the Cup, saying: "Evidently our mission still remains to be completed. May Christ and His Angels be with us in our task."

The Cup is now kept at Chalice Well at the discretion of the Trustees. In May 1997, I visited the Well with Christine (Sandeman) Allen's daughter, Bunty Martin, over on a visit from South Africa. She was able to hold the vessel, which her mother had helped to retrieve from Bride's Well, for several silent minutes in the peace of the Upper Room. It was the first time she had seen it.

As to the Cup itself, it is claimed that recent scientific testing has demonstrated that it is not ancient. While this may seem to undermine everything that has been done in its name, there is still a sense that on another level the ideas and actions it has fostered as a potent symbol remain as valid as before.

CHAPTER TEN

Eager Heart

THERE ARE STILL JUST A FEW PEOPLE living in Glastonbury who remember Alice Buckton from their childhood days. She died in 1944 after devoting the last thirty years of her life in cultural service to the local community and to the countless visitors who were drawn by the personality and charisma of this dedicated, if eccentric, builder of 'Jerusalem in England's green and pleasant land'. She was an energetic and pioneering spirit whose natural talents had an early opportunity to flourish brilliantly under the guidance of her equally gifted father.

George Bowdler Buckton was the model neo-renaissance man: chemist, entomologist, astronomer, artist, musician. For all his high professional standards, he never lost the sense of awe and enthusiasm for the marvels of the natural universe that had informed his early days. It enabled him more easily to share his knowledge with the local children who were eager visitors to his laboratory in the family home on the slopes of Hindhead, just outside Haslemere in Surrey. If there was an image of her early years that had impressed Alice the most, it was the look of wonderment on the faces of those children as George Buckton held forth on such mysteries as metamorphosis or eclipses of the sun and moon. Often they were rewarded with gifts of specimens or small instruments. The experience made Alice determined to campaign to make good the lack of rudimentary science and nature study in the school curriculum at that time.

Born in 1818 at Hornsea, George Buckton had had to endure throughout his lifetime the crippling effects of a severe accident to his legs at the age of five. It meant that he could neither attend public school nor go to university. Thrown very much on to his own resources, he became a good classical scholar and extensive reader. His favourite recreations were music and art. He was especially attracted to natural history, and soon became well-versed in many aspects of zoology and entomology. He had two excellent tutors in the Rev. Oliver Lodge and the Rev. Dr Meuse.

After the death of his father he built a circular observatory at their London home, making his own telescopes, grinding the lenses and specula himself. Somehow surmounting his disability, he entered The Royal College of Chemistry, first as a pupil, and before long as an assistant, delivering a succession of important papers on various newly-isolated chemical compounds. He disapproved of too much specialization and discreetly carried on his zoological research at the same time. He became a member of the Linnean Society in 1845 and had the opportunity to meet Huxley on its Council. His most important study was a four-volume *Monograph on British Aphids*.

In 1865 George Buckton married Mary Ann Odling, sister of his friend Professor William Odling, of Oxford. They purchased the estate of Weycombe, at Hindhead, where George had a stone-gabled house built to his own design. His beloved observatory was transported wholesale from London. Eight children were born and raised in these fine surroundings. Alice Mary Buckton arrived in 1867.

As soon as she was old enough, Alice was helping her father in small ways with his scientific work. As with her younger brothers and sisters, she was educated at home until the age of nine or ten. Among her tasks was the colouring-in of her father's careful drawings of his biological specimens. She even became skilled enough to work on plates used for publication.

There was quite a gathering of worthies on the hills around Haslemere in those days, among them the Irish-born physicist John Tyndall and the poet Tennyson, a familiar figure in Alice's early life, who lived at Aldworth House on Blackdown, to the south-east of the town. Many years later, in 1925, Alice returned to Aldworth to address a meeting of The Poetry Society, reading some of Tennyson's poems and recounting how she had once spent a whole day with him as a child, walking through the fields and 'sitting on his knee as he chanted his poems'.

After George Buckton's death in 1905, Tennyson's son Hallam wrote of him:

> "Truly a devoted spiritual, knightly nature, with a faith as clear as the height of the pure blue heaven. His views and my father's upon Life, Death and Immortality were very much alike. My father used to say, 'My most passionate and earnest desire is to have a fuller and clearer knowledge of God'."

We might note in passing that Hallam seems to have lifted some of the wording of this tribute straight from a line of the verse his father had dedicated to his mother on the occasion of her seventy-seventh birthday:

" ...To you that are seventy-seven
With a faith as clear as the heights of the June-blue heaven
And a fancy as summer-new
As the green of the bracken amid the gloom of the heather."

As to Alice, people used to find it curious that a scientist should have produced a daughter so taken up with the arts and creativity. It was a shallow view; there was as much of the artist in George Buckton as there was the scientist in Alice. As if to put them all in their place, she dedicated this poem to him in 1898:

TO MY FATHER

Though thou, and I, seem to the casual eye
To work alone, in divers tracks of thought!
Dear father, 'tis not so! nor moves here aught
Which is not child of thine! That mystery
Thou ponderest day by day - as holding naught
Unworthy! even in the weakest worm and fly -
The Holy Mind of Man to occupy
Exploring still, in terms exact and sought!
Has led me too! upon the patient way
Thou and thy daring peers have made so great!
Heir of your toil! to sing with changeful lay
Man's hidden yearnings towards his higher Fate,
That fills with hope and joy, God's upper air -
And, as of old! with thee to worship there.

It was an instinct in Alice to try to improve the lot of others in some way or other. As a young woman she went to help the poor of London by joining Octavia Hill's Southwark Women's University Settlement.

Octavia Hill was a Christian socialist for whom religion and social responsibility were inseparable. Her mother had been manager of the Ladies Cooperative Guild, an organization which tried to release the destitute from a dependence on charity by finding them work to do. Octavia distrusted all landlords, and persuaded her friend John Ruskin to buy property in Marylebone where poor people could live at a modest rent and have help with organizing their finances. She persuaded local authorities to plan for open spaces in cities and, with Sir Robert Hunter and Canon H. D. Rawnsley, helped to create the National Trust. Sir Robert lived very near the Bucktons at Haslemere, so it is easy to see how Alice might have got her introduction to Octavia.

Alice felt in sympathy with everything that Octavia did; she was the role model for her own work to improve the quality of life not only for the under-privileged, but everyone compelled to live in large cities.

On a visit to Germany, she felt quite at home moving around literary and intellectual circles, but was struck by the lack of progress there towards women's emancipation. "Germany dates before us in many matters", wrote Alice in 1898, "but in the women's movement she is doubtless far behind, especially in such questions as woman's equal worth with man as a human soul, her personal and political freedom, and her right over her own property." Alice's 'new woman' aspired to more than simply taking on male roles and modes of employment: there was a special place for her to do woman-like things. For Alice, woman held cosmic authority in her own right:

"If we go back to the early history of the race, we find types of divergence from the first. Man was the hunter, the winner, the bringer-in of spoil, making excursions *outward* into infinity. Woman was the adapter and user of all things, the translator into terms of life, the fosterer and nourisher, explorer of the capacities of things, making researches *inward* into infinity. *Both* infinities are the realm of the soul: one is more especially man's dominion, the other woman's; and who shall say which is greater?"

She saw woman pre-eminently as mother; but a motherhood not confined to the raising of her own children. It stood for a 'power to feed and nourish and support life', wherever and however that life required it. For her ideas on education, Alice looked to Frederich Froebel, the great German early-childhood theorist who died in 1851. But there was more to him than just child-development; Alice points to his concern for the lot of women too:

"His desire to better the conditions of the human race, 'to give men and women themselves', had led him to occupy himself first with school-children, then with infants, and lastly with women...

Are our women conscious and fit for their great power? He found them not *themselves*: one-sided, and short-sighted as to their greatest power, namely, their womanliness. He foresaw what modern psychologists have so plainly laid before us, that, married or unmarried, the normal woman (and the normal girl) has tendencies and powers in her which it is dangerous to neglect - dangerous to herself and the community. *It* will suffer, and *she* will suffer.

Froebel insists, as Tennyson has insisted in his ever-memorable *Princess*, that, 'woman is not undeveloped man, but diverse'; not lower, but equal, splendid, powerful."

Within this perspective, all questions of education, children and women are embraced together, men are conspicuously not part of the equation:

"In the child are represented the needs of the body, the intellect, the feelings, and the will. It is in the fostering and training of these that woman comes to her majority, to the power of the ewig weibliche that Goethe sang; which draws us upwards and onwards 'by the heart, and not by the head alone'."

While in Germany, Alice visited the Pestalozzi-Froebel Haus in Berlin which existed to implement Froebel's educational principles and to serve as a training centre for young women. It had been started twenty-five years earlier by Froebel's niece, Henriette Breyman. The practices evolved there were taken up worldwide and have long been the foundation of the British education system at the infant and junior level. The Principal and House-Mother of the Pestalozzi-Froebel Haus from its beginning was Annet Schepel.

In 1898, Alice Buckton was a member of the committee which set up an institute in Acacia Road, St. John's Wood, called the Sesame Child Garden and House for Home Life Training, modelled closely on the centre in Berlin. With little difficulty Alice persuaded Fraulein Schepel to detach herself from the Pestalozzi-Froebel Haus to fill the post of manager and advisor to the new London project. Annet was a skilled administrator and used to the problems of day-to-day management and budgeting. Although she was much older than Alice, they became bound in a companionship that lasted until Annet's death in Glastonbury in 1931. Alice's first book of poems, published by Elkin Matthews in 1901, was dedicated to "Annet, who proved to me that the human heart has neither age nor nationality and thereby made me free of the World".

By 1902 Sesame House had sixty-five students, among them two from Finland and four Parsees. Gardening, household management, cooking and dietary studies were included in the course as well as the

HORACE KNOWLES.

INSCRIBED TO ALL
WHO SEE AND
WORSHIP THE ONE
IN THE MANY

welfare of children. A link was established with Edgbaston Training College, Birmingham, and exchanges of students were arranged. In 1904 a 'People's Kindergarten' was opened in Birmingham by Julia Lloyd, a former pupil of the Pestalozzi Froebel Haus who had kept in touch with Alice and Annet and later visited them in Glastonbury. Thus 'modern' methods of education for the young in Britain had their beginnings.

In her work as a lecturer and examiner for the Froebel Society, Alice had many opportunities to put her ideas on nature study and creative play for the very young into practice. In the programme she devised for the study of the natural environment throughout the year and its place in the human economy, she stated that her aim was 'to give children experience of the great rhythmic processes of Nature; to encourage love of Life in all forms, and the sense of responsibility'. She was an advocate of all those twigs in water and sprouting beans in jam-jars that many of us remember from our early school days. How much of that might we owe to Alice Buckton?

Alice cared deeply about other people; all her poems, plays and lectures on education were dedicated to the enrichment of their lives. In her London years she forged ahead ceaselessly, exercising her considerable powers to the full. Several plays and collections of poems were published. The most famous of these, *Eager Heart, A Christmas Mystery Play,* appeared in 1904.

Unlike a lot of other people working for social change and recommending new ideas, Alice had never forsaken the Anglican Church of her upbringing. She certainly transcended the *status quo,* embracing a kind of mystical pantheism while keeping hold of the essential tenets of the faith. The small flyleaf dedication to *Eager Heart* summarizes her view perfectly: "Inscribed to all who see and worship the One in the Many".

The archaic language of the play ought not to obstruct an appreciation of its true worth: as a spiritually-charged thing of beauty with meanings on more than one level. The simple fairy-tale form of the story overlays a dialogue liberally garnished with gems of mystical insight into nature and destiny. Take the following:

> "...All beasts and birds
> I question of this mystery; yea, and would force
> The innermost secrets of the hollow earth,
> But find no comfort. Yet sometimes comes the sense
> Of a life beneath the changing show of things;
> A glorious life, hiding itself in these,
> Eluding still my grasp! Could I command

ALICE BUCKTON

That changeless substance once within my ken,
Then should I know the object of my thought,
And Light transfigure all our griefs for ever!"

The play is meant to be in the 'present time', but somehow not quite in the world as we know it. It is Christmas Eve.

At the centre is the young girl, Eager Heart, a pure spirit whose sisters, Eager Sense and Eager Fame, represent false values. They live in a town-cottage in very humble circumstances.

They discuss a prophesy of long ago that the Holy Family might appear in person one Christmas Eve. Eager Heart believes that the prophesy is about to be fulfilled that night and prepares her room with bread and wine to welcome the possible guests.

"O Heavenly Child,
The night is wild!
Come in to me, I pray!
Make of this heart -
This longing heart -
Thy Bethlehem to-day!"

Her worldly sisters mock her and go off to a banquet at the palace. Eager Heart, left on her own, hears a knock at the door. She finds a penniless couple with a child begging for shelter for the night. She lets them in reluctantly, fearing it will spoil any chance of the Holy Family visiting her. She tells her guests whom it is she is expecting. They tell her they have seen no one while travelling, only some shepherds. She decides to give them the bread, wine and water.

The scene changes to a frosty plain under the stars. Two shepherds lie near an old and a young man who are debating about the belief that Christ might visit people on Christmas Eve. The young man rejects it but the old man has more faith:

"He sojourns here or not at all,
As they with Eager Heart shall one day know,
Finding within their doors a silent Guest."

The shepherds are surprised to hear some distant singing. Eager Heart appears carrying a lamp and persuades them to follow her. They all do so, except the old man who says he has already seen the Lord pass by that night. Left alone, he dies:

> "…And bid me part, for I have seen
> On Thy sad Earth Thy sweet Face go!"

A King enters, not seeing the dead shepherd, perplexed about the mystery of the King of Heaven.

> "…I thirst to know
> If any rule be mightier than mine
> In this dim universe! I cannot sleep!
> Vast shadows haunt my dreams, portentous things
> Known to the Fates and to the solemn stars…"

A second King enters bearing a casket. He anguishes over the purpose of life and death. He holds up a translucent lump of myrrh:

> "…Behold, embalmed, a perfect creature, winged,
> Lovely as life, encrystalled here for aye!
> So would I hold the soul within my thought,
> Clear imaged, imperishable! This myrrh
> I carry with me for my burial!"

They see a third King coming bearing a lighted censer. He addresses them at some length:

> "…Our feet have lost the simple starward path
> Our fathers knew. Yet, on this sacred night
> Our ways have met, once more!
> No monarch He, - Type of our inmost dream
> And Moulder of the world, - but One whose soul,
> Measuring itself in heaven, and earth, and hell,
> Utters with every breath the great desire
> Of all that lives! Such only may I worship!"

They find the dead shepherd:

> "…Within this breast the Lord of hearts did make
> A resting place! Surely, ye blessed hills,
> In you the King must dwell, since here indeed
> His subjects be!"

They see a brilliant star and go off towards it. They come across the shepherds and Eager Heart, also following the star. It leads them to a town street - and what turns out to be Eager Heart's home. She insists there must be some mistake:

> "…A poor maid dwelleth here, of no great name.
> The star points other-where methinks, not here!"

She has to admit that this is her home, but points out that only some beggars are lodged there for the night. Her companions realize this could be the Holy Family and bid her open the door:

> "…And let the pomp and glory of the world
> Go in to worship; for the King is here!"

The family is revealed in just the same position as Eager Heart had left them, but now clothed in white and suffused with light.

The Kings each offer a gift: the first his crown; the second his myrrh; the third his censer. The shepherds follow. Each sings a song. The first shepherd sings of deliverance:

> "Sing we, sing we joyously!
> Here we see,
> Man may be
> Free from offerings of blood!
> Life of pain
> Is life of gain
> To the strong and high of mood!
> Sing we, sing we joyously!"

With an angelic choir glowing visibly through the background veil, the scene ends with everyone gathered round the Holy Family. Eager Heart's arms are outstretched towards the child. The last sixteen bars of Beethoven's Pastoral Symphony are meant to be heard at this point.

As they leave the house they come across Eager Fame and Eager Sense returning. They say that they have met someone who reported seeing two beggars bearing a child - and on the child's head he saw a living flame.

The Kings tell them that they have returned too late; only through a life of simplicity and honest work can they become fit to be visited by the Lord's family. But they take pity on them and allow them to join the others. There is more music and all leave:

"-Let us begone;
So the great Sun, the Keeper of our Day,
May find us at our doings, even in toil,
Singing with happy hearts the glad Noel!"

The Prologue who addressed the audience at the start of the play returns. His last lines bring the drama to a close:

"Nay, let us enter in, before we part,
And pray together here with Eager Heart,
That never, O thou Son of Man! may we
Weary of search, or miss of seeing Thee
In every human form, and human dress -
The Homeless Child of Peace and Righteousness!"

Finally, the audience stands to sing the hymn 'Veni Emmanuel'.

A Christmas play normally reveals little of the philosophical or metaphysical outlook of its author. But, ever the wise teacher, Alice Buckton conjures through the dialogue images of her perception of the path to spiritual fulfilment. It is radical, subtle, and even - in its way - revolutionary. The emphasis is on heart rather than mind; inner response rather than theological doctrine; intuition rather than intellect. The central character embodies this: the young girl as a 'type' of the soul (or intuitive feeling) is found in many fairy-tales. Correspondences with the Cinderella story may be no accident. The sentiments of Alice's campaign for the affirmation and liberation of the special powers within woman move significantly beneath the naive overlay of the story. The spiritual awakening of the *heart* is the key to the transformation of, first, the psyche, then society, and finally the whole world.

Alice acknowledged that some women were arising as intellectuals, equal with men on their own terms. She could commend this, but with reservations. It was not what was really wanted from women - and she was not lacking in intellectual fibre herself. As she said elsewhere, the requirement was for something deeper: '...Is not this task of all of us, individually, self-realization; and as conscious members one of another, the greater self-realization?'

Even the figure of Eager Heart in the play embodies aspects of this essentially female self-awareness. It is, of course, in the name itself.

Alice allows one of the characters to use the name unwittingly, before he comes to know of the existence of the person to whom it can apply:

> "The sign He gave of old is the sign of to-day!
> Follow it, lads! with Eager Heart and find."

and again:

> "They with Eager Heart shall one day know,
> Finding within their doors a silent Guest!"

These words are spoken by the Old Man, who, together with the Third King, is a source of the wisest counsel in the play. The silent Guest 'within their doors' is the indwelling spirit, the true Gnosis, the consciousness of Christ. This knowledge comes through the *heart* and not the rational mind.

The Third King is described as 'A young man with an earnest clean-shaven face, wearing the spiked circlet of Inspiration with jewels on the points'. He is a healer and reconciler who,

> "...roams from shore to shore!
> Offering incense at the woodland shrine
> Of every god and demon - joining hands
> With them that hate each other, and would tear
> Each other's altars down - not seeing, all,
> The one Form loved of every secret soul,
> That all do homage to - the Lord of Hearts!"

At the level of mystical realization all religious disputes melt away. We are back with the initial inscription, "... to all who see and worship the One in the Many".

Another radical aspect of the play for its times was in its portrayal of the Holy Family on the stage. It was not normally allowed; every play had to be passed by the Lord Chamberlain's Office, and any transgression met with swift prohibition. Somehow Alice Buckton got away with it. This was all very galling to Laurence Housman, the much-respected illustrator and writer who eventually settled in Glastonbury's neighbouring town of Street. He had already suffered the censoring of his play *Bethlehem* and was unable to have it properly performed. As he wrote:

> "To help me on my way, Miss Kingston made renewed application for a
> license; and was met with the old traditional answer that Holy Families
> could not be allowed on stage. But since the censoring of my play,

another play called *Eager Heart* has been given a license; and in that play also the Holy Family appeared. When this was pointed out to the Censor, he began by denying it; but the text of the play convicted him: inattentively he had given a passport to the Holy Family, because it had come upon the scene in peasant disguise. He then fell back for defence upon the fact that in *Eager Heart* the Holy Family did not speak. To that I nailed him; if I so arranged matters that in *Bethlehem* Our Lady should remain speechless, would he grant a license? He could do no better than to say yes."

Actually Joseph does speak in *Eager Heart*, but only through his disguise. The Lord Chamberlain sounds confused enough not to have noticed this.

Alice Buckton's play was widely performed and enthusiastically received. From then on her name was associated with *Eager Heart* just as Rutland Boughton later became identified with his musical setting of *The Immortal Hour*.

Alice was a back-to-the-simple-life kind of socialist, much in the style of her friend Edward Carpenter, whose epic poem *Towards Democracy* she much admired.

Carpenter, born 1844, had at one time been in holy orders with The Church of England and was a Fellow of his college at Cambridge. Like William Blake, he longed for the rebirth of the true England:

"I see a great land poised as in a dream -
Waiting for the word by which it may live again.
I see stretched the sleeping figure - waiting for the kiss and the reawakening.
I hear the bells pealing, and the crash of hammers, and see beautiful parks spread - as in a toy show.
I see a great land waiting for its own people to come and take possession of it.

Ah, England! Have I not seen, do I not see now, plain as day, through thy midst the genius of thy true life wandering - he who can indeed, who can alone save thee -
Seeking thy soul, thy real life, out of so much rubbish to disentangle?"

These lines from *Towards Democracy* are typical of Carpenter's extraordinary invocation: powerful, irregular, uneven - a vision of how things ought to be. An attainable vision even, but now further from realization than in its own time - though not impossibly so. Carpenter always returned to basic things, and never more than in his closing lines:

> "The wind blows east, the wind blows west, the old circle of days completes itself;
>
> But henceforth the least thing shall speak to you words of deliverance; the commonest shall please you best;
>
> And the fall of a leaf through the air and the greeting of one that passes on the road shall be more to you than the wisdom of all the books ever written - and of this book."

Carpenter was another of the great illuminators of the pathway of life for Alice. As a token of her empathy with his elemental faith in the spirit of nature and the dignity of human labour, she presented him with a hand-written copy of this poem of her own:

UPON A WELSH MOUNTAIN

> This is my holy day; and, foul or fine,
> Here is the shrine where I am pleased to be,
> High-perched above a valley's deep decline,
> O'er woodlands sloping to ~ silver sea!
> Here, amid mountain fern and mossy bed
> That spins from crag to crag its living lace,
> Where ladies bed-straw knots her delicate thread,
> And scarlet lichens gem my pillow case,
> I lie and dream, my one-week summer through,
> Loosing the shuttle forth to roam,
> And weave the Vision, old! yet ever new,
> That more to the dreamer is than food or home,
> Where toil no longer looks a tangled clue,
> But, the mighty texture of a Day to come!

Many years later she copied this same poem for Councillor Hucker on his election as the first Labour Party mayor of Glastonbury in November 1937.

After *Eager Heart* came another play, *Kings of Babylon,* published in 1906. Set in Babylon in the sixth century BC at the time of the Jewish captivity, it was performed the following year at the Haymarket Theatre in London, with a musical setting of one of the songs by Gustav Holst. In 1908 a collection of poems appeared entitled *Songs of Joy.*

When Archdeacon Wilberforce invited Alice to the meeting at

20 Deans Yard, Westminster, on 20 July 1907, to hear Wellesley Tudor Pole explain about his Glastonbury bowl, a new era dawned in her life. From that day on she turned towards Avalon: the Cup had cast its spell.

She set down her impressions of the Cup and its future in a letter to Wellesley of 8 August. He responded with a visit to her six days later. The more she heard the more she wanted to be a part of what was happening.

On 20 September Alice visited the Clifton Oratory for the first time. She was very impressed by what she found there and told them that she thought that "a great work was beginning". Understandably, she was very satisfied with the emphasis on woman's spirituality and the role of the Cup in the reinstatement of the feminine within the religion of the West. She felt the vessel should stay with its present keepers, but "would remain shrouded in mystery". It was her opinion that it would one day return to Glastonbury and that a community of women would grow up around it.

Alice stayed on in the area for some time. On 23 September the members of the Triad took her to Glastonbury to visit the holy places along their pilgrimage route. The next day Dr Goodchild came over to Clifton from Bath to meet Alice Buckton for the first time. They had much in common; his views on the place of women in the Celtic mysteries and their role in the coming times would have met with her ready approval.

A month later the Triad and Alice made yet another trip to Glastonbury, this time visiting the Abbey House, which Alice thought would be an ideal place in which to set up a women's community.

Her ambition to get something started at Glastonbury had to rest until 1912, when news came that the Catholic seminary at Chalice Well was up for sale. It was a large property and a considerable liability for anyone to undertake, even with the resourceful Annet Schepel to hand. Alice was uncertain about the wisdom of bidding at the coming auction. It took all the persuasive powers of her favourite prelate to convince her that it was the right thing to do: Archdeacon Wilberforce, apparently with his worries about the 'Glastonbury Grail' now behind him, was once more looking in an Avalonian direction.

As well as Alice Buckton, there were two other contenders at the sale: a manufacturer of woollen goods and a wealthy American lady. When the day came, the latter got held up by a mechanical breakdown of the train in which she was travelling. In spite of her frantic telegram messages demanding the postponement of the sale and offers of huge sums of money, the auctioneer insisted on keeping the proceedings to schedule. Alice, who had sold a great deal of her possessions to strengthen her chances of success, outbid the manufacturer and found herself the keeper of one of the holy places of Britain.

She lost no time in starting to get her plans going for a programme of dramatic productions aimed at encouraging a revival of interest in ancient lore and legend. She was not alone in this intention; the composer Rutland Boughton had lately arrived on the local scene with much the same thoughts in mind. In fact, he too had had his sights set on buying the Chalice Well property. His representative, Philip Oyler, had paid a visit to Glastonbury in order to get local people interested in their scheme for an English Bayreuth-style festival. At that stage, Alice, too, was approached, and it seems that she was prepared to throw her lot in with them. This would have meant the collective acquisition of Chalice Well. It would also have introduced a group of people into the ownership of the site who were not versed in its spiritual significance in the way that Alice was. This was at the time before the sale when the property had recently come on the market. It may have been behind the dilemma that Alice placed before Archdeacon Wilberforce. In the event she decided to go it alone, apparently causing some upset within the Boughton group. However, there was still some preparedness to work together in the early stages, even after Alice and Annet had taken up residence at Chalice Well. At a meeting in Wells on 5 June, 1913, Boughton, Reginald Buckley (his librettist) and Alice Buckton spoke on their respective plans for establishing a festival centre at Glastonbury. There was no evidence of any conflict of interest on this occasion.

One reason for the display of harmony between Alice Buckton and the others may have been the accommodation that they seem to have reached over who should do what in the proposed activities. Boughton and Buckley would be presenting larger, more ambitious productions involving both local people and professionals while Alice would be putting on smaller plays 'of a legendary character' at more regular intervals, using only residents from within the area.

Evidently, as time went on, Alice Buckton and Rutland Boughton came to dislike each other with some intensity. There was a difference in personality, but more contentious was the question of the relatively small pool of local talent - mostly children - which they both drew on.

With 1914 and the war looming it was surprising that anything got done at all. Alice and Annet had made the old monastery building fit to receive paying guests, with the priests' cells converted into bedrooms, each with a quotation from appropriate works of literature on its door. The chapel was available as a place of quiet and contemplation. A light

A GROUP OF YOUNG GLASTONBURY AND STREET FESTIVAL PLAYERS.
Chalice Well, circa 1920.

was kept burning at all times on the altar which had been at the centre of the Catholic Fathers' devotions.

The featureless walls of the seminary gave the corner of Well House Lane a rather forbidding look and the small windows of the priests' quarters suggested more the appearance of some kind of penitentiary. A high wall ran up the side of the lane. Behind this was the garden, much overgrown and wilder than today, and concealed at its upper end was the source of the famous holy well. Attached to the other side of the main building, and facing the main road to Shepton Mallet, was a rather more pleasing Georgian-style residence which had once been an inn. This was where Alice and Annet lived. It also housed the office from which their various projects were administered and a library. All these buildings were demolished in the 1970s.

One of the first productions by Alice Buckton's newly formed Guild of Glastonbury and Street Festival Players was a masque called *Beauty and the Beast*. Soon after this the Players performed Alice's 'pageant play' *The Coming of Bride* in the Glastonbury Assembly Rooms, at Chalice Well and at Crispin Hall in Street, in the summer of 1914. It tells of the life of St. Bride, her shipwreck as a child on the island of Iona, through various other events up to her final arrival at the Isle of Beckery near Glastonbury where she foretells the coming of Arthur, the brotherhood of the Round Table and the quest for the Holy Grail. Many other plays were presented over a period of many years by the dedicated members of the Guild, not only in Glastonbury and Street, but further afield in other towns and villages all over the West Country. Alice wrote that the work of the Players had been 'planned on the lines of the old religious Folk and Mystery Plays, with the aim of celebrating and making beautiful in various ways the Greater Festivals of the year, from Carol Singing to the Festival of the Mid-summer Bon-fire'.

It was hoped that the kind of educational work which had been so successful at Sesame House could be carried on in a smaller way at Chalice Well. Within a short time of their arrival a pamphlet was prepared advertising 'A College for the Training of Gentlewomen for Dedicated Work (Undenominational)'. The proposed daily programme read more like a monastic Rule. Among the activities listed were gardening, beekeeping, weaving, missal painting, services to the sick and poor, and the education of little children. The year would be divided into the four seasonal quarters, a college term in each, centring around the associated natural and religious festivals, but there is little evidence that any serious body of full-time students ever attended the Chalice Well 'College'.

Even if this scheme failed to materialize there was much else that fared better. The plays were an acknowledged success and various arts and crafts activities flourished under Alice's guidance. When Dion Fortune came to live in her wooden ex-army home on the lower slope of the Tor she found herself a very near neighbour of all this homespun creativity. She wrote of the "little group of craft workers who used the most primitive of traditional methods, dyeing the raw wool with dye-plants collected from the Somerset hedges and lichen scraped off the trees of old orchards; and spinning with the prehistoric spindle instead of the medieval wheel". She also described the skeins of wool hanging on the gnarled trees all around the orchard while the dye-pot boiled nearby over a fire of sticks.

It was not long before Alice met Frederick Bligh Bond and came to share his belief in 'The Watchers of Avalon' - the heavenly company of one-time monks whom they understood to be overseeing the spiritual rebirth of Glastonbury and England. Bond honoured Alice Buckton by placing her poem *Glastonbury* after the Preface in his *Gate of Remembrance:*

> "Grey among the meadows, solitary, bare:
> Thy walls dismantled, and thy rafters low,
> Naked to every wind and chilly air
> That steeps the neighbouring marsh, yet standest thou,
> Great cloistral monument of other days!
> Though marked by all the storms that beat thee through,
> A radiant Parable of heavenly ways
> That scarce thy lordly builders guess'd or knew!
> Vanishing image of great service done,
> Smiling to God under the open sky:
> Even in thy translation, stone by stone,
> Keeping thy spirit-grace and symmetry,
> Through ruined clerestory and broken rood
> Our chastened souls with tears ascend to God."

from *Songs of Joy* (1908)

Another token of Bond's appreciation came in the form of the iron-work cover which he designed for the Chalice Well itself, employing the interlocking circles of the *Vesica Piscis* symbol, representing the blending of the spheres of spirit and matter. The circumference of each circle passed through the centre of the other, and the two were contained within a greater circle. A symbolic spear bisected the whole design.

Alice drew into her Glastonbury view all she had derived from the Cup group at Clifton, the ideas of Goodchild and the psychic findings of Bligh Bond. There is a touch of all of them - even Fiona Macleod - in this astrological and mystical poem, *At the Well - the Rune of the Water-bearer*, published in 1918, and inscribed to "The Watchers in Avalon and to all who dare to turn the rim of the Golden Wheel":

> "Ye have supped from the Pools of Sorrow,
> Ye shall drink from the Wells of Joy!
> The Golden Wheel is turning,
> The heavenly spheres employ.
> And she who bears the Measure
> Shall stand in the Dawn of Day,
> Pouring the waters of comfort
> To the weary by the way.
> Haste, 0 bride and bridegroom,
> Behold the promised Sign!
> The hand that draws the Water
> Has filled the cup with Wine!"

In an article on Alice Buckton in *The Chalice Well Newsletter* (No. 2) for 1982, Rosemary Harris, who had retired to Glastonbury from Kent for the love of the place, recorded the comments of Mr Harry Carter, who lived just along the road from Chalice Well, in Chilkwell Street. His earliest recollection of Alice was of being asked, when a child in 1918, to join in the dancing around a maypole which had been set up in the orchard not far from the well. He remembered the open-air wattle theatre with pillars of straw and puddled clay. A bottle containing a message was buried beneath the foundations of the stage. At other times the chapel was used for performances. He described her in later life as:

> "...An untidy eccentric lady with a stooped figure, wispy hair and a very kind, lined face, wearing a baggy old skirt and black wrinkled stockings. She often wore a massive straw hat with a veil, or a black cloak green with age that was said to have belonged to the poet Tennyson... She helped everyone, every lame duck. She was surrounded by theatricals, singers and so on, who came to stay with her - she was always a soft touch! She seemed to have money when she first came to Glastonbury, but she had nothing by the time she left. She gave all she had."

These observations of Mr Carter expose the economic reality behind Alice Buckton's thirty-year sojourn at Chalice Well. She relied on the goodwill of others and refused to regard her theatre group in any commercial way, never charging for admission. Some small income came from the Guest House and from the crafts shop that she opened in the Market Place in Glastonbury - but the graph was ever creeping downwards. In 1922, undaunted by these economic constraints, Alice embarked on one of her most ambitious projects: a dramatized silent film of key points in the history of Glastonbury down the ages. This created a great stir in the town at the time, particularly as many local people were involved. A considerable effort was made, and the annual Tor Fair with its livestock and sideshows was included, together with a lavish parade through the town. The period costumes for the historical sketches were magnificent. It is therefore quite extraordinary to learn that, once completed, interest in this remarkable record faded after only a few public showings. Luckily it was recently discovered that Alice had had the good sense to lodge a copy with the British Film Institute where it had lain in obscurity, protected and undamaged for some 70 years. The film was recovered and made available for public showing. There was a capacity house for two presentations with supporting piano accompaniment at the Strode Theatre, Street in February 2004, with another opportunity to view it the following autumn. For a much fuller account of this film and other aspects of Alice's life and work, see *Beneath the Silent Tor* by Tracy Cutting (Appleseed Press 2004).

In 1931 Annet Schepel died. Alice was in her sixties and already becoming rather absent-minded. In her forays into Glastonbury for provisions, it became a matter of routine for the manager of the grocery store to follow her up the High Street and very kindly remind her that she ought to have paid for the bundles of goods she had appropriated. It is quite possible that she knew exactly what she was up to, but such was their affection that no local person would ever have pressed charges against her.

There were other rumours. One was that Holy Communion was being celebrated in the chapel at Chalice Well with Alice officiating and administering the Sacrament. Quite a possibility in view of her contact with the Clifton group from 1907 onwards, where all the services were taken by members of the 'triad' of young women. Another more prosaic fact was the finding of quantities of hard-to-come-by butter under her bed during the war. She claimed that it was merely there to 'keep it nice and soft'! She also kept odd hours, writing into the night in

ALICE BUCKTON WITH STAFF AND FRIENDS, CHALICE WELL MID-1920s.

Alice second left; next to her is Dudley Mills, bandyman; Annet Schepel wearing sheepskin; on the right Elsie Weller (assistant)

a wooden hut in the orchard and sleeping through the morning.

In the 1930s, the monastery building and Tor House were let out as a school for boys. Alice was able to move into the cottages adjoining the garden which she had somehow managed to purchase in the late 1920s. Today these are the only original buildings on the Chalice Well site, and are used for the wardens' quarters, meeting rooms, library and guesthouse.

Fortunately there was a loyal band of helpers who shared the various practical tasks and made sure that Alice was fed and properly cared for. For all that this might suggest, Alice still retained her intellectual powers and lost nothing of her spiritual insight. With war dominating the national life once again just as it had done after her arrival in Glastonbury, there was little to feel inspired about. But even though ill, Alice had the courage to see beyond the conflict and consider the future of Chalice Well. Plainly she knew that she would not see that time herself. Not long before her final illness she sent a letter to her supporters outlining her hopes. There is nothing about it of a mind in decline:

"My dear friends, herewith I am outlining my future plans for the usefulness of the Chalice Well Estate. We are nearing a time of fulfilment, which for a long while we have anticipated, and have never lost sight of since the years of stress (1913 onwards) with the outbreak of the last as well as the present wars. It has long been the hope of myself and my friends to secure this ancient property with its unique associations in a Trust - for the continuation of its international and educational service.

The time is now come when the whole working of the scheme should be able to take its definite place, especially in view of the near future and its great possibilities.

You have felt here an influence silently as well as explicitly, working for the healing of the nations. The names 'Isle of Avalon' and 'Chalice Well' are by-words in many lands today. The yearly record of visitors and of the Craft Schools included, has surprised those who have looked into our doings.

All men and women of goodwill and of every nationality are welcome here. The sacred legends about this place are said to be unequalled, dating back, according to Sir Flinders Petrie, at least to 200 BC, as the old well structure indicates, supplying still, and unfailing in its pure volume of chalybeate water, automatically supplying many thousands of gallons per day through the rock bottom of the well.

To this day experts are baffled (British Soc. etc.) and are not ready to assign the positive secret of the well. Its position coincides with the first

Hermit Huts built by Christians in the sheltered orchard.

During the late trying years, I have been able, through the goodness of two or three friends of like appreciations, to obtain a certain amount of security which would prevent, in the possible event of my decease at any time, the falling of this Estate into irresponsible and exploiting hands. The saving of the Tor from such a danger was entirely worked for and planned and successfully achieved through the groups at Chalice Well and their friends. [This refers to Alice's part in getting the National Trust to buy the Glastonbury Tor land.]

Today I must preserve this 'mother-centre', so to speak, so that in all the days to be, men and women will find refreshment here in the cottages as well as in the monastic buildings which I took over from the Roman Catholic Fathers with their entire approval. The working of the place is interdenominational and has been the scene of many festivals; Plays, Lectures and Concerts - including Summer Schools - Greek Plays (Baliol Plays), Holiday Camping and Conferences.

The Estate is mortgaged to the approximate sum of nearly four thousand pounds. The whole property, with the exception of my own cottage, is at present well let. All the buildings have not been closed for a single day since 1913, when our work first commenced. I am, so as to admit no effort on my part, arranging that what royalties come in from *Eager Heart* and other books and plays of mine shall be devoted to this end of permanently freeing the Estate from this burden of mortgages. I have already a well-advised group of friends (headed by names well-known to the public), knowing well our cherished plans. They will not only forthwith take over the management for me, but will consider when and in what way the future working of this charge may be implemented, so as to serve generously the needs of the coming time.

Will you help me to this end, and thus fulfil the dream of more than thirty years? It was more than a dream, that Archdeacon Basil Wilberforce came to insist on my coming here - a charge that I have borne gladly with everything that I possess."

The middle of the war was hardly a good time in which to hope to get people to give much practically or spiritually to such an idealistic endeavour. But Alice took the larger view. Remarkably her vision became realized - at least in part, though not as directly as she had imagined.

Throughout her life, and even up to the end, Alice was always writing. There exist today many scraps of poems and reworkings of poems that were never published, and some never even shown to anyone. She knew the sentient depths of her own soul and she had magnificent gifts and powers to convey these inner treasures to others. Her compassion is shown in the last lines of a poem 'Sanctuary in the Forest':

"Who slays a fleeing thing pays the bitter toll,
Who wins the chase, destroys his unborn soul!"

There were several variants of a poem written during the war inscribed to 'Faraday - the Discoverer of Electricity' and elsewhere subtitled 'The Night of a Blackout'. Science, art and devotion are one, as the last six lines show:

"If thou have tidings, in that listening Place,
Where the shuttle of the mind roves through Space
Re-charge our broken batteries this hour!
Re-harness them to heaven's high rhythmic power!
Re-store us to our starry Ancestry,
Who watched the Spindles of Eternity!"

In 1944, with her health failing, Alice left Chalice Well to be cared for by her friend Mrs Ethel Kenney at her home in Vicar's Close, Wells. She died some months later on Sunday, 10 December.

Her funeral at Wells cathedral the following Thursday included the Chorale from *Eager Heart*, 'Behold the King of the Earth', as an anthem.

She was cremated at Arnos Vale, Bristol, and her ashes brought back to Glastonbury and scattered on the slopes of the Tor.

A memorial service was held at St. John's, Glastonbury, conducted by the Rev. Lionel Smithett Lewis. Alice's favourite hymn 'The Strife is O'er', was sung, and after the Grace Mr Lionel Graves sang the setting by Gustav Holst of Alice's 'The Heart Worship'. The Rev. Lewis later described her in his parish magazine as a 'great soul, a great mind, a most remarkable personality'.

In her Will, made in August 1943, Alice had appointed Mrs Ethel Kenney and Mrs Ethel Ashford as her executors, and together with four other people nominated as Trustees of a new body to be called 'The Chalice Well Trust'. As stated before, Alice Buckton had grand visions of the place as an international centre of culture and healing. The Trustees found themselves unable even to find a way to sustain the material fabric of the property, let alone extend the activity there after Alice's death. They did at least have the Trust recorded with the Charity Commission, but felt obliged, in 1949, to sell the entire property to Cyril Hollingworth and Bernard Watts of Glaston Tor School for £2,315 on condition that the public could have access to the well. *1958* Nine years later Wellesley Tudor Pole, Ethel Ashford, Cynthia Legh, Legh Cornwall Legh (later Lord Grey), Arthur Saville, Clifford Hampton Watts and William Higgs bought the Chalice Well property, excluding the school, back from Hollingworth and Watts for £2,000. The Chalice Well Trust was reinstated the following year.

Since the first edition of this book in 1993, there has been a renewed interest in Alice in the Glastonbury area. On the afternoon of Saturday, 10 December, 1994, the exact day of the 50th anniversary of her death, the author and three readers presented a commemoration of her life and work in St. John's Church, Glastonbury. In addition to the recovery of the film already described and the book by Tracy Cutting, a number of events also took place at Chalice Well on her 60th anniversary in 2004.

CHAPTER ELEVEN

The Immortal Hour

IT MIGHT SEEM A STRANGE THING that the works of our British concert-music composers of the first half of this century have not found better favour among the advocates of the New Age and the rebirth of Albion. Everything there should invite their attention: music inspired by ancient legends, psychic experiences, tracts of our land-scape and even Madame Blavatsky's Eastern 'Masters'. Think of Arnold Bax's orchestral tone-poem *Tintagel*, Ralph Vaughan-Williams *Ninth Symphony* depicting the landscape between Salisbury and Stonehenge, John Ireland's Symphonic Rhapsody *Mai-Dun* (Maiden Castle in Dorset) or his *Legend for Piano and Orchestra,* written after having a vision of 'children from the past' dancing round him in silence as he ate his sandwiches on the Sussex Downs. Then there was Cyril Scott, 'bringing through' his compositions from the beyond while the spectre of the Master 'Koot Hoomi' hovered over his piano.

There has always been a problem with British music. It has never been given the same exposure in the concert hall as the tried and tested Germanic giants of the genre - Bach, Mozart, Beethoven, Wagner and the rest. Only in recent years has the dedication of such enthusiasts as the film-maker Ken Russell and the musicologists Christopher Palmer and Michael Hurd brought our native music out of the shadows and presented it in its true context and shown its worth and richness. But if all of this music has been in the gloom, in an even darker corner has stood the lone figure of Rutland Boughton.

Boughton is our Glastonbury composer. No, it was not his birth-place, but he did make his best dreams come true here - or nearly so.

Rutland was born on 23 January 1878 at Aylesbury, the county town of Buckinghamshire, one of the three surviving children of William Boughton, grocer, and Grace (née Bishop), school-mistress. He was exposed to music from his earliest years, both in church and at home, where his mother enjoyed playing the harmonium.

He *had* to compose. With no theoretical understanding at all, he got together a children's orchestra, including penny-whistles and home-made zithers. They even performed in public with Boughton conducting.

Given the family's circumstances, his pathway to gaining a proper musical training was somewhat irregular. Most other composers came from families sufficiently well-endowed with the means to meet the costs of tuition and boarding.

A London job with a kindly concert agent afforded him the chance of getting some lessons. By the age of twenty several of his compositions had been tried out on concert audiences. There was little acclaim from the critics. Eventually Sir Charles Stanford was sufficiently impressed to persuade Ferdinand Rothschild, the wealthy MP for Aylesbury, to pay for Rutland to attend the Royal College of Music. Here he learnt a lot in the way of technique and self-discipline but remained an outsider throughout. He left prematurely. His allowance had been used up and his parents were in financial difficulties. He managed to find work arranging and copying music and writing articles for magazines. The Welsh singer David Ffrangcon-Davies employed him as his accompanist, introducing some of Boughton's songs into his repertoire.

In 1903 he finished his first opera, *Eolf,* which foreshadowed the idiom of much of his later output. It even included an incidental appearance of King Arthur, but was never performed. That year he married Florence Hobley, the daughter of his next-door neighbour in London.

Boughton struggled on. A two year stint playing the harmonium in the pit orchestra at the Haymarket Theatre helped to keep the wolf from the door. At around this time he began to form his socialist ideas, much influenced by the writings of John Ruskin and William Morris. He believed in the Christian ethic, but not in the Church, which he judged hypocritical.

In 1905 the Boughtons left London for Birmingham where the composer Granville Bantock had offered Rutland the post of Teacher of Piano and Rudiments at the Midland Institute. At first they lived at Coventry in a house already shared by Rutland's mother, brother and sister. Before long they had moved to a village nearer to Birmingham.

Rutland found himself well-received into the musical life of the midland city, and many were caught in the spell of his extraordinary vitality and enthusiasm. It brought new opportunities for composition. As a natural consequence of his quest for an English 'voice', he turned to folksong for his thematic ideas.

The Birmingham Triennial Festival of 1909 saw a performance of

Boughton's choral Symphonic poem *Midnight,* taking words from Edward Carpenter's *Towards Democracy.* Like Alice Buckton, he had been much moved by Carpenter's vision of a society of equality and peace, and his mystical and poetic proclamation of the dawn of a socialist new world order. The work met with approval within the considerable socialist following in Birmingham. Predictably, there was another section of the population distinctly put off by such sentiments.

Boughton met Carpenter at the time when this bearded ex-academic was busying himself with the accoutrements of the 'simple life' in his cottage at Millthorpe, near Sheffield. The friendship came to an unfortunate end. Boughton had heard talk that Carpenter might be homosexual. When he questioned Carpenter about this he was dismayed to learn that it was true. It was something that he could not bring himself to accept; he was never able to know him on the same easy terms again. But his respect for Carpenter's ideas remained with him throughout his life.

With Bernard Shaw a friendship grew which lasted until the death of the great Irish playwright in 1950. Shaw was to become the most significant advocate of Boughton's artistic experiment at Glastonbury and a valiant supporter of his music.

It was not surprising that Boughton looked to the Arthurian legends as the most appropriate material for the music-dramas he was planning on the lines of the operas of Richard Wagner. He was at a loss as to a suitable libretto until he came across Reginald Buckley in 1907. This young journalist and poet shared Boughton's artistic vision. They pooled their ideas in a book, *Music Drama of the Future,* which included the first part of Buckley's Arthurian Cycle *Uther and Igraine* (later re-named *The Birth of Arthur*).

By 1910 Rutland and 'Flo' had had three children, the last named Arthur. But it was not an easy marriage; Flo was wasteful with money and indifferent to her husband's art. When he met a young art student called Christina Walshe, he was powerless to resist. She understood and shared his aspirations. He decided he could not do without her. After some measure of upheaval, Flo handed them the children and a legal separation was completed - but not a divorce. It was a scandal in those days. Rutland and Christina left for Berlin but returned to London after a few months where they both earned a small income as critics for daily papers.

Then suddenly Boughton was invited, through the aegis of Shaw, to take up an idyllic appointment in the countryside near Hindhead, in Surrey. An elderly friend of Shaw's, Frederick Jackson, owned a large estate, 'Tarn Moor', at Grayshott and needed someone to help him write down the songs he had composed. Soon, the whole family had moved into a cottage on the estate. It was an atmospheric place. Jackson had the idea of putting on weekend musical performances there, sometimes inside, sometimes outside, using different parts of the woods. Boughton was very taken with the way the quality of the sound produced by a group of singers changed mysteriously as they moved around. This strangeness somehow awoke again an earlier desire of his to make a setting of *The Immortal Hour* by Fiona Macleod.

Here in the countryside of the Surrey, Hampshire borders, a mood fell upon him almost as strong as the mood that fell on William Sharp when he was overtaken by Fiona. The music seemed to come to him from the trees themselves as he walked through the woods. Slowly the mystery and enchantment of *The Immortal Hour* became perfectly assimilated into its musical incarnation. A providential coincidence of time, place and personal circumstances had brought Rutland's sensitive, reflective nature to a hyper-real pitch of inspiration. Christina had prepared the way; she had brought him closer to the spirit of the Celtic world she loved, and to its great witness, Fiona Macleod.

It had been their intention to perform the new work at Grayshott - it was even advertized - but Boughton did not complete the orchestration in time.

Boughton and Buckley had a dream of establishing an annual festival in the countryside in association with a permanent group of artists who would also share the duties of running a collective farm. Buckley favoured Letchworth as a suitable venue for this project.

But someone else had other ideas. In 1912 they were approached by Mr Philip Oyler, who was running something described as a 'Nature School' in Hampshire. Oyler was a lover of Glastonbury and its traditions. He had read Boughton and Buckley's essays and was aware that they were working on a cycle of Arthurian music-dramas. He had made up his mind that the only possible place for the realization of their programme was at Glastonbury. He announced to them that he was going there to sound out local opinion and attract interest in the scheme. Among those who were drawn in were the Vicar, some musical people at Wells and Alice Buckton. He also discovered that the Chalice Well property was on the market, and 'took steps' to secure it for them.

Possibly on the recommendation of Alice Buckton, he went up to Bristol on 11 February 1913 and called on the Tudor Poles at the Oratory at Royal York Crescent. There he saw the Cup. It was recorded that the force of it "almost overpowered him". Some kind of psychic revelation came to him while he was there about its history. He declared that he felt that there was "'more than one set of documents relating to it".

However good Oyler might have been at seeing into the past, his prognostications about the future left something to be desired. His steps to secure Chalice Well had been ill-judged.* It transpired that Alice Buckton had stolen a march on them and secured the property for herself. It did not kill off the Glastonbury plan, but left them without a base to work from. Oyler lost interest from then on; Boughton and Buckley found themselves dealing with the people at Glastonbury on their own, with Miss Buckton a somewhat less-than-welcome associate.

A meeting was held of the potential benefactors. Those present promised to provide the necessary means if musicians of standing could support the scheme with favourable references. These were easily solicited from Sir Edward Elgar and Granville Bantock, each writing strongly in favour of the plan.

A public meeting was subsequently convened at Wells on 5 June 1913. Kitty Tudor Pole and Janet Allen attended and recorded that they had heard

> "...Mr Rutland Boughton and Mr Reginald Buckley speak of their ideas concerning a national Theatre which they wished to see established at Glastonbury. They also spoke of the production there of Mr Buckley's Arthurian play, which Mr. Boughton had set to music. Miss Buckton pleaded for support and sympathy in order that Glastonbury might become a centre at which sacred plays might be performed, more especially those concerned with the Arthurian Legends. Her ideal was that Glastonbury should become a second Oberammergau."

To which might have been added, 'or a second Bayreuth', if Boughton and Buckley's hopes were to be realized.

A planned performance of part of the *Birth of Arthur* at Glastonbury that summer met with an unexpected obstruction. Word had got around among members of the festival committee that Boughton was not legally married to the woman who purported to be his wife. Several, including the Vicar, were not prepared to compromise their moral principles to support anyone involved in such a sinful liaison. It was all

---

*Oyler then disappeared from the scene. In the 1920s he found satisfaction living the 'good life' in the rural Dordogne valley in France, last witness to a way of life unchanged from the middle ages. His account of this, *The Generous Earth: A Glimpse of a Vanished World*, has become something of a classic and is still available. His experiences led him to become a founder member of the Soil Association

very distressing, but undeterred, Boughton transferred the whole programme to Bournemouth, where a performance at the Winter Garden of *The Birth of Arthur*, before an audience largely of seaside holidaymakers, was the culmination of a three-week summer school directed by the dancer Margaret Morris.

Margaret Morris taught a 'natural movement' method, and based her system on the illustrations of dancers found on Greek vases and pots. She dismissed conventional ballet technique as a gross aberration.

It was deemed a success. After this hopeful start, a performance of some extracts of *The Birth of Arthur* was given at Crispin Hall, Street, that October.

By the end of 1913, Boughton had completed *The Immortal Hour*. An appeal was launched for further funds with the blessing of many of the greatest names in the land. But it was hardly the best time to try to start anything. Forebodings of trouble ahead were being felt long before the outbreak of the Great War in the summer of 1914. Surprisingly, their ambitions were undiminished. But among Boughton's *entourage* opinions were divided about continuing at Glastonbury. He wrote:

> "Further steps were taken during the ensuing winter to get the Glastonbury theatre going, though with but little financial result, and some of our people were in favour of removing the whole scheme to Letchworth, where more solid local support had been offered. Others of us, however, clung to the West of England as the real home of our legends, and the following summer [1914] we held a holiday school at Glastonbury itself, culminating in the production of my musical setting of Fiona Macleod's strange mystical drama, *The Immortal Hour*. This work seemed to be a success from the outset, and has, in fact, done more than anything so far to carry the Glastonbury ideas abroad. Since its first production it has been given by The Glastonbury Festival Players in London, Bristol, Bath, Bournemouth, and by the Birmingham Repertory Company in Mr Barry Jackson's beautiful little theatre. Again, though, it was the Bournemouth performance that did most for us. There for the first time we heard it with its proper orchestral colouring, and the performances in January, 1915, were attended by certain representatives of the London Press."

All the Glastonbury Festival performances were achieved with only a piano accompaniment. The funds were simply not available to support an orchestra. As it was, it was difficult enough to cover the existing expenses, which were generally met throughout the ten or so years of the festival by such local patrons as the Clark family, famous shoemakers of nearby Street. After an unsuccessful attempt by Boughton to get himself accepted for military service in 1916, he returned to continue to work for the festival, now supported by an allowance of two pounds a week from Roger Clark towards the living expenses of himself and his family.

To placate the moralistic lobby within the local population, Boughton seems to have arranged for himself and the family two different addresses in the town, one at 3 Bere Lane and the other at 'Bona Vista', Street Road. Only rented accommodation was used during their years in Glastonbury, and the above ploy was probably not literally observed for any length of time.

There was even evidence of a puritanical objection to the stage presentations themselves:

> "We also had to meet with a certain amount of jealousy from that section of the community which regards all positive happiness as tending to evil, and all beauty as an endowment of the devil; for it did undoubtedly happen that the young things who studied with us acquired a liveliness and a physical carriage that marked them out from their fellows, though we have every reason to believe that all the children who have been in the Festival School Classes and productions look back on that time with pleasure, and will in after-life regard it as having been of some permanent benefit to them. Therefore it has been rather trying to be met with refusals from parents who seek to save 'the eternal souls' of their young from the satanic influences of the arts in general, and of the Glastonbury Festival in particular. The fact that the junior side of the work met with so serious a check was due to nothing but the stupidity and selfishness of such parents and their advisers."

Bernard Shaw was a frequent visitor, and made sure the rest of the world heard all about what was going on in Glastonbury. He attended the Easter performances of 1916, liking everything he saw:

> "...There was far less to suffer and far less to excuse and allow for at Glastonbury than at the usual professional performances... In some vital respects it was a better performance than Sir Thomas Beecham could have afforded in London."

The venue for all the Glastonbury productions was the Assembly Rooms, a rather unedifying barn-like building built in the 19th century.

Approached through a passage-way between the shops on the south side of the High Street, it left much to be desired in the way of general ambience and practical amenities for the players. Crispin Hall, in Street, was far better in every way. Several performances were given there. But Street was not Glastonbury, and the residents of each town regarded the other with some disdain.

The Glastonbury Festival School was a year-round extension of the life of the festival, allowing for coaching in all aspects of music and drama and affording an opportunity to prepare the seasonal performances more adequately.

The accusation was sometimes made that Boughton had exploited the festivals simply to promote his own music. Plainly, his own works predominated in nearly every programme, but by no means exclusively. Among the other items offered were works by Purcell, Gluck, and the contemporary English composers Edgar Bainton and Clarence Raybould.

Christina Walshe put her artistic training to good effect designing scenery which went some way towards making up for the drab interior of the Assembly Rooms. She also found herself holding things together for the period after Boughton had been called up for military service in 1916. Ironically, when he had volunteered he had been rejected; now that he had been conscripted his, and Shaw's, protestations that he had more worthwhile things to be getting on with fell on deaf ears.

The festival activities were suspended while Boughton spent the war years as an army - and later, Flying Corps - bandmaster. Christina put on short plays at the Assembly Rooms, although part of *The Immortal Hour* was presented in September 1918, with Gwen Ffrangcon-Davies appearing for the first time as Etain. The daughter of Boughton's former employer had already taken the lead in a performance of the morality play *Everyman* at Glastonbury. Her great talent and beauty played no small part in making *The Immortal Hour* such a success. Likewise, Boughton's music-drama gave her the opening she needed to launch her distinguished career.

With the resumption of the festival programme in 1919 even more was offered. Hopeful professionals were coming forward to enjoy the prestige of associating themselves with the now famous Somerset event. In 1920 there were also nine chamber concerts of music by English composers. The chorus of the productions remained local, and amateur, but the leading-role players were usually brought in from outside.

The year 1919 brought with it good and bad tidings. The purchase of a large house with grounds on behalf of the Festival by a wealthy

HERBERT LANGLEY AS MERLIN AND GWEN FFRANGCON-DAVIES AS
IGRAINE IN *The Birth of Arthur.*

devotee promised to make good the lack of a centre for their work. 'Mount Avalon' answered all their needs; they even entertained dreams of building a theatre within the grounds. The only requirement was that the users of this facility should pay back the purchaser once funds allowed.

The unhappy event in that year was the premature death of Reginald Buckley. While Boughton had been prepared to take things as he found them and work on from there; Buckley had had a 'grand vision' of a British 'Bayreuth' which was never realized.

However, even after a hopeful start, the project at 'Mount Avalon' had to be abandoned. Insufficient money was coming in, despite an appeal.

The Festival activities were extending beyond Glastonbury, further afield to other towns and cities. This was just as well as Boughton was becoming very conscious of the opposition to him. The numbers of children attending the Festival School had been dropping off. The question of his 'adultery' would not go away. There was also gossip going around about his alleged assignations with other women. The fact is, it was not all his fault: they simply would not leave him alone. He was an engaging, dynamic artist - to some women quite irresistible.

Whatever the hearsay, the fact is that by 1920 there was another woman in his life. Kathleen Davis seems to have offered him a kind of stability that had been lacking in Christina. She was one of his pupils - a point not lost on the opposition. If things declined further at Glastonbury from then on, it was mostly a direct result of his personal life.

That year, 1920, the Vicar of Shapwick, a village a few miles west of Glastonbury, offered Boughton the use of 'Vicarage Cottage' in order to get away from everything and work in peace. Here he set to music *Alkestis,* a play by the ancient Greek dramatist, Euripides. He was more than a year there, involving himself in few outside distractions.

The grand festival of 1920 also included a performance of *The Immortal Hour.* It is surely this occasion which Dion Fortune describes in *Avalon of the Heart:*

"I had the unique privilege of seeing a performance of *The Immortal Hour,* which, timed to fit in with the exigencies of the local buses and trains, began at sunset. The first scene started with broad daylight shining in through the uncurtained windows of the Assembly Rooms. But as it progressed the dusk grew on, till only phantom figures could be seen moving on the stage and the hooting laughter of the shadowy horrors in the magic wood rang out in complete darkness, lit only by the

RUTLAND BOUGHTON

stars that shone strangely brilliant through the skylights of the hall. It was a thing never to be forgotten."

Thinking back to the correspondence between Dr Goodchild and Fiona Macleod in 1900 in which they discussed the original play, it might seem a curious thing that the work of the bard of Iona should have found its way, all on its own, to be re-born in this new form at Glastonbury, the place where the two of them had once shared the secret of the Cup of the New Age.

But there were greater things ahead for the music-drama. After a highly successful series of performances in Birmingham in 1921, Boughton was presented with a request that it should be tried out in London. He refused. Why he did so might seem strange. The answer lay with his temperament, his background and his political beliefs.

He was far happier at Glastonbury with its shabby building and the ordinary people whose lives he made richer through the opportunities he gave them to develop their ordinary talents to the full, than he could hope to be among the fashion conscious élite of the tainted citadel of capitalism that he deemed London to be. It was his turn to play the puritan; sending *The Immortal Hour* into such a den of thieves would be a form of prostitution.

In the end he had to give in to the pleadings of the performers who had served him so well. *The Immortal Hour* opened at The Regent Theatre, Kings Cross, on 13 October 1922.

Initially there was a poor response, but the promoters held out. Gradually attendances improved and it was noticed that some people were returning again and again, perhaps, in part, more entranced by the allure of Gwen Ffrangcon-Davies in the leading role. It was kept on for six months. The run of 216 consecutive performances broke all records for a serious English opera. The following winter saw a revival of a further 160 performances, with an additional thirty-six performances of Boughton's nativity play *Bethlehem*, first presented at Crispin Hall, Street, in 1915.

Even if Boughton felt that people went to *The Immortal Hour* for the wrong reasons, there is no question that its other-worldly charm played on their inner responses however much the depth of the story escaped them.

One of Dion Fortune's friends, Netta Fornario, who wrote esoteric tracts under the name of Mac Tyler, attended twenty-three performances before writing an 'interpretation' of its symbolism for the benefit of future audiences. Evidently her eavesdropping on conversations

FESTIVAL SCHOOL

GLASTONBURY

Festival of
Greek Drama

August—September, 1922.

PRESIDENT: SIR THOMAS BEECHAM, BART.
DIRECTOR: RUTLAND BOUGHTON.
HON. SEC.: J. W. BOSTOCK, Chalice Leaze, Glastonbury.
HON. TREAS.: ROGER CLARK, Street, Somerset.

GUARANTORS:

F. J. ALDRIDGE, M.D	MRS. E. F. HALE,
H. N. ALVES,	C. V. HEAPHY,
H. C. ANDERTON,	MISS M. S. JEFFERY,
P. L. BOWN,	W. J. KENNEDY,
J. W. BOSTOCK,	P. NAPIER MILES, J.P.,
ROGER CARTER,	W. NIXON,
JOHN B. CLARK, J.P.,	GEO. A. ROBINSON,
ROGER CLARK,	M. H. STEAD, J.P.
F. S. COLLIHOLE,	MISS A. K. SWAINE,
H. O. DICKIN,	R. N. TANNER,
F. DOWDNEY,	MRS. M. A. TUCKER,
GEORGE HOTEL CO., LTD.,	W. TULLY,
F. J. GILBERT,	C. WALTER,
J. A. GILBERT,	J. W. J. WILLCOX, M.D.
R. T. GOULD,	E. G. WRIGHT.

C.Walshe 1922

during the interval had convinced her that the exercise was well called for:

> "Visitors to the Regent Theatre may be roughly classified as follows: students of mysticism and folklore who are able to understand the great truths behind this gossamer curtain of faery (a small clan, but they come frequently and every time discover some new aspect of illuminating significance); a large number of people who think the play beautiful but sad; and many for whom the whole drama is so elusive and incomprehensible that they irritably demand of each other, 'what on earth the fellow can be getting at,' and are frankly bored; and there is a fourth class who, while keenly appreciating the artistic beauty of the performance, also sense the existence of a deeper meaning, but are hopelessly baffled by the intricate symbolism employed."

Those who found the drama incomprehensible might not have been any more the wiser after trying to digest Ms Fornario's analysis:

> "...The second scene shows Etain sheltering from a storm in the hut of two peasants who represent animal instincts, and who are terrified both of her and of Eochaid, who seeks shelter from them also. The lower instincts are as much afraid of the desire principle, when that is seeking its higher self, as they are of the soul, knowing full well that such an attempt towards unification, if successful, will inevitably be followed by an attempt at their own extinction."

This might not be all nonsense, but it is not any easier, either.

Oddly, Netta Fornario complains that the line, "There is no dream save this, the dream of death" was left out of Boughton's libretto:

> "It is unfortunate that this pregnant sentence was omitted; but the wonderful music of the closing bars, based on a re-statement of the Dalua theme, explains it with extraordinary clarity for those who can understand, and one watches the descent of the curtain convinced that in spite of the apparent tragedy, and notwithstanding struggle, illusion and mistakes, the end is peace and fulfilment for all."

Like we shall see with Mary Bligh Bond, Netta seems to have had a preoccupation with death as the gateway into the Other World, literally and symbolically; the moment of deliverance into Light. But did she fall foul of the same 'danger' that Goodchild had perceived in the kind of beauty Fiona Macleod was seeking?

In her *Psychic Self-Defence,* Dion Fortune recorded that the naked body of Netta Fornario had been found in the middle of the winter of 1929/30 on a hillside on the island of Iona, covered in scratches. She was laying over a cross which had been cut into the turf. The knife used was next to her. A cross on a chain was around her neck. Much occult speculation followed, but it seems to have been a rather bizarre suicide with death ensuing from exposure.

Others went to The Regent even more times than poor Netta. Princess Marie Louise attended on fifty-two occasions. But no-one surpassed the record of a Miss Parker who saw it through 133 times.

Not only the public and the critics, but leading musicians sang the praises of Boughton's achievement, among them Holst, Bax and Elgar.

Boughton remained indifferent to its success, let it go its own way and carried on with the things that interested him.

He still applied himself to composition and still regarded the Glastonbury Festival and the touring circuit associated with it the natural home for the performance of his works. To date, only two parts of Buckley's Arthurian cycle had been set and performed, *The Birth of Arthur* and *The Round Table.* Boughton lay that question to one side, went forward with the performance of *Alkestis* and rose to the challenge of setting Thomas Hardy's play *The Queen of Cornwall.*

This was performed at the Summer Festival of 1924. Hardy attended the second performance with his wife, and was remembered as being as much concerned about the amount of logs burning on the hearth at the Assembly Rooms as he was with the artistic proceedings, although he did report that he was very pleased with the musical re-working of his play. T. E. Lawrence was also observed to be there with them. That year also saw the introduction of Laurence Housman's *Little Plays of St. Francis,* and marked the start of the author's involvement with the organization of the festivals.

Boughton became more involved with the touring aspect of the work. His last active year at Glastonbury was 1925. Housman was by then living in Street, and the last Glastonbury Festival of all, in 1926, consisted entirely of his own plays.

It was also the year that Boughton joined the Communist Party. This marked no special change in his attitude, simply a desire to take a more direct role on behalf of a cause which he had upheld from his earliest years.

It was no coincidence that 1926 was the year of the General Strike and the Miner's Lockout. Boughton was one among many socialists who saw it as the advent of the ultimate revolution, Britain's emulation of the Russian *bouleversement* of 1917. He was rising to the call. Even such an innocent production as his musical nativity play *Bethlehem* was re-vamped to serve the mood of his increasing politicization. The winter tour of the performance of the play by the Glastonbury Festival Players was scheduled to end at Church House, Westminster. He made a private decision to perform it on that occasion in modern dress, with Christ born in a miner's cottage and Herod, the embodiment of capitalism, wearing a tuxedo and smoking a cigar.

But Boughton was in no position to act on his own in such a matter; the Glastonbury Festival Players were a registered company. A huge row blew up among the other directors and only by a narrow margin was the production allowed to go ahead. This week long London series of performances was a financial failure and marked the end of the life of the Festival Players.

It was also the time of a watershed in Boughton's own life. As Michael Hurd observed, "What he did not know was that he had reached the zenith of his public career and had already begun the slow descent into obscurity".

Glastonbury was over. Boughton and his family moved to a small-holding at Kilcot in Gloucestershire where they were to remain until the end of his life. The dream of the rural artists' community was never realized, but at least, here, he could do it on his own. He could compose, study, write articles and subsidize these activities, when necessary, with the income from the farm.

He organized a festival at Stroud in 1934 on the lines of the Glaston-bury events. It was a success, and saw the performance of two new music dramas, *The Ever Young* and *The Lily Maid*. An attempt to follow this up with another festival at Bath the following year was a financial disaster, with Boughton incurring considerable personal debt in spite of the support of his guarantors, including the ever-present Shaw.

Boughton had the pleasure of seeing one of his daughters, Joy, become a leading oboist. He composed a concerto for her which was first performed in Oxford in 1937. It was probably one of his most successful endeavours outside the field of his stage works.

The remaining parts of the long-delayed Arthurian Cycle were completed during the war. They have never been performed. Michael Hurd has had the opportunity to study the scores of both *Galahad* and *Avalon* and is of the opinion that, though competently executed, they suggest the work of a composer whose powers are in decline. Perhaps we should not be surprised that the climax of the whole

Cycle in *Avalon* ends with a choral realization of the peasants' 'Song of Revolution'.

Here and there were revivals of Boughton works after the war years. These were mostly small affairs and show some measure of the extent to which the musical public had forgotten this very significant composer. As for the man himself, he seems to have been relatively untouched by this indifference. His life went on to the full; he was devoted to his family and friends and they to him. Like many members of the Communist Party he was dismayed at the way the Russians had put down the Hungarian popular revolt of 1956; he resigned from the party along with many others.

On 24 January 1960 Rutland Boughton died peacefully in his sleep while on a visit to his daughter in London, having celebrated his eighty-second birthday the day before. In retrospect his most creative period coincided with the time of his collaboration with Christina Walshe. She had provided the designs for the stage sets and the posters and programmes for the festivals. It should not be forgotten that it was Christina who had introduced him to the writings of Fiona Macleod. Apart from *The Immortal Hour,* Boughton set several Fiona poems as songs. These were four of the *Six Spiritual Songs* (1910); four of the *Six Celtic Choruses* (1914); and the *Five Celtic Songs* (1910). The music-drama *The Ever Young* (1928/29) seems to have been intended as a sort of sequel to *The Immortal Hour* and is notable for Boughton's own libretto very much on the lines of Fiona Macleod's Celtic quasi-folk tales. He has the third scene set in the 'Dome of Bride, the Moon Goddess'. In the five *Songs of Womanhood* (1911) Boughton set some of Christina's own poems, including *Prayer to Isis* and *Woman's Song of Creation* (now available on CD – see below).

Boughton's eclipse is usually attributed to the uncompromising stand he took on political issues. Was he cold-shouldered simply because he was a Communist? There are many examples of artists in all fields who have been successful in spite of being affiliated to the 'far left'. The alternative view has it that his music simply was not good enough. This might be true of some of it. But no less than Sir Edward Elgar wrote that, "Mr Boughton's music-drama 'The Immortal Hour' is a work of genius". No English composer of the twentieth century could have hoped for a better-qualified commendation.

Bernard Shaw stuck by Boughton through every phase of his career, joining with him in rejoicing that the 'amateur' spirit of the Glastonbury productions was so much more satisfying than the slick professionalism of the London theatre-machine.

There were volumes of correspondence between the two, and Shaw was a very frequent visitor to the events at Glastonbury. His book *The Reluctant Wagnerite* has a chapter on Boughton. In recent years there have been signs that Boughton is at last getting the recognition he deserves. There were a number of broadcasts at the time of the centenary of his birth in 1978, and in the 1980s the first CD recordings of his music became available, including *The Immortal Hour.*

Michael Hurd's biography of Boughton, *Immortal Hour* (Routledge & Kegan Paul, 1962), has been up-dated, greatly expanded and published as *Rutland Boughton and the Glastonbury Festivals* (Oxford University Press, 1993).

In recent years The Rutland Boughton Music Trust (website: **www.rutlandboughtonmusictrust.org.uk**) has gone from strength to strength in its promotion of Boughton's music through recordings and public performances, including world premières of some works. In 1996 a group of local enthusiasts decided to organize a Glastonbury Arts Festival in the spirit of the earlier events, mindful of the appropriation of the name 'Glastonbury Festival' by the massive annual pop-event actually located some miles from the town. It was opened by the actor Edward Tudor-Pole, grandson of Wellesley Tudor Pole, and was a great success. The highlight of the programme was a full stage production with orchestra of *The Immortal Hour,* presented on 29, 30 and 31 August at the Strode Theatre, Street. It was acclaimed in the national press and there was a full house every night. The 1996 festival also included a chamber concert at St. John's Church, Glastonbury by the Razumovsky Quartet with the oboist Sarah Francis performing Boughton's *String Quartet No. 1,* his *Oboe Quartet* and the *Somerset Pastoral* and *The Passing of the Faerie* for oboe and string quartet. Rutland Boughton's biographer Michael Hurd gave a talk on his life and work at the Assembly Rooms. This was also the venue for a talk by Geoffrey Ashe, *Glastonbury and King Arthur.* An exhibition of British art at the Rural Life Museum included a painting by Christina Walshe of a Glastonbury scene. Building on this success, another festival took place the following year that again included the Razumovsky Quartet at St. John's, this time performing the *String Quartet No. 2 in F.* At the Strode Theatre, the local Glastonbury Festival Orchestra gave an excellent performance of Boughton's *Concerto for Flute and String Orchestra* and on 11 September the Bournemouth Sinfonietta gave the world première of the *Concerto for String Orchestra.* Subsequent to these 1997 events, the Glastonbury Arts Festival ran out of funds and did not resume. However, a few diehard local enthusiasts were determined to continue to promote

Boughton's music in the community. Under the banner of Avalon Music, Brendan Sadler, who had conducted *The Immortal Hour* in 1996, and professional artist Paul Branson, were responsible for staging a recital at the Strode Theatre on 30 November 2004 by young members of the Singh String Quartet, which included Boughton's *String Quartet No. 2 in F* and a talk by the composer's grandson, Ian Boughton, who has sung as a baritone on recordings as well as performances of his grandfather's works. A performance of *Bethlehem* was given at St. John's Church on 5 and 6 January 2005 involving amateur and professional singers. Again the national press was there; a review in *The Independent* for 13 January summarized it as, "gorgeous music; gorgeous occasion". Following these performances of *Bethlehem,* Ian Boughton, in his role as Administrator of the Boughton Trust, and the Mayor of Glastonbury, Cllr Nick Cottle, unveiled a commemorative blue plaque at the Assembly Rooms. The inscription reads: "Rutland Boughton, English Composer. Established and Directed the original Glastonbury Festivals in these Assembly Rooms, 1914-1926". On 24 September 2005, also at St. John's, mezzo-soprano Louise Mott accompanied by Alexander Taylor presented an evening of songs by notable English composers, including Boughton's settings of *Five Celtic Love Songs* by Fiona Macleod, *Songs of Womanhood* by Christina Walshe, *Symbol Songs* by Mary Richardson and settings of a series of poems by Edward Carpenter. Also included was a song by Eleanor Farjeon, *Sweet Ass,* dedicated to Boughton's third partner, Kathleen Davis, and her babes. The occasion saw the launch of a new CD of these same songs.

Many other performances have been given of Boughton's works elsewhere, including *Bethlehem* at Holy Trinity Church, South Kensington, London, on 16 December 2005. World premières continue to emerge from 'bottom drawer' oblivion. The *Reunion Variations* (1945) was given a first performance with its alternative 'orchestral-ending' by the Hitchin Symphony Orchestra at Hitchin Town Hall on 27 November 2004. It had been stipulated that this work should only be performed after the composer's death and in many ways can be seen as a sort of 'farewell' to his family. The orchestra was conducted by Paul Adrian Rooke, who has overseen the resurrection and re-scoring of a number of works, including the as-yet unrecorded opera, *The Queen of Cornwall,* based on the play by Thomas Hardy. As we have seen, this had originally been performed at Glastonbury in August 1924. Another recovered early work, Boughton's character symphony for baritone and orchestra, *Oliver Cromwell* (1904-5), was heard for the first time ever, again at Hitchin, on 26 November 2005.

So the work proceeds, and the creations of a worthy composer are now in less of a dark corner than before. In his musical style, Boughton may not have been a man before his time, but in his vision of the role of the artist in society and his talent for galvanizing the enthusiasm of ordinary people to make a contribution to great creative events, he certainly was. For this reason alone we can rejoice in his rediscovery in a different, if somewhat more desperate, age. As we have just noted, his *Reunion Variations* was very much intended as a message from the beyond after Boughton had departed this life. He wrote this work with two alternative endings: one orchestral, the other sung to a poem of his own. Let Rutland Boughton have the last word here with this final verse of the song-ending version of the *Variations:*

> *So pour your songs love-hearted*
> *Throughout the stelline blue.*
> *When you on earth make music*
> *I shall be there with you.*
> *My love to all my dear ones,*
> *Wherever they may be;*
> *Or on the earth yet singing,*
> *Or in the air with me.*

CHAPTER TWELVE

The Architect

W HILE THE YOUNG Wellesley Tudor Pole was making his early pilgrimages to Glastonbury, and while Dr Goodchild was still watching over St. Bride's Well, a well-established Bristol architect was preparing the ground for his own entry upon the Avalonian stage.

Frederick Bligh Bond was a man of great sensitivity, intelligence and charm. His profound sense of history and his practical understanding of architecture fostered in him a life-long love of ancient church buildings. He was an acknowledged authority on medieval church woodcarving and, as an active member of the Somerset Archaeological and Natural History Society, much sought after as a lecturer or conductor of guided tours to various sites in the county. Here and there he would deliver up his thoroughgoing, yet witty, accounts of the history and construction of this or that church or manor-house, to the delight of his attentive followers.

For someone so disposed it was perhaps inevitable that he should find his way to the one place that could afford him the chance of exercising his many-faceted talents to the full: the ruins of the great Abbey Church at Glastonbury. It was to become the centre of his life's quest; the object of an obsession that would carry him through thick and thin, pain and triumph, and, ultimately, humiliation.

His ample personal credentials for the task may well have been, in part, the gift of natural inheritance. The Bond family history is nothing if not interesting.

Frederick's father, the Reverend Frederick Hookey Bond, was Headmaster of Marlborough Royal Free Grammar School, where Frederick Bligh Bond was born on 30 June, 1864. His mother, Mary (née Dela Fosse), was the daughter of a Major in the Army.

The Rev. F. H. Bond's father was Rear Admiral Francis Godolphin Bond, whose mother was the half-sister of Vice Admiral William Bligh - Captain Bligh of Mutiny-on-the-Bounty fame. Therein lies a rather complicated tale.

The Australian historian George Mackaness has done much to unravel the family relationships which have been preserved in the name Bligh Bond. The greatest clue came from the record of births all on the same page of a Family Bible, entered between the years 1754 and 1765. Here, William, the son of Francis and Jane Bligh, born 1754, is listed along with the names of several children of John and Catherine Bond of Plymouth.

It seems that Jane Bligh had previously been married to one Richard Pearse, who had died leaving her a widow with five children. One of these, Catherine, married a naval surgeon from Cambridgeshire called John Bond. Francis Godolphin Bond, their youngest child, was born in 1765. It thus turns out that, through *her* mother, Francis Bond's mother was half-sister to William Bligh, although she was some twenty years his senior. It is almost certain that the Bonds and the Blighs all lived together in the same household, particularly as John Bond would have been away at sea for much of the time. The entries in the same Bible support this.

Although Francis Bond was helped along in his naval career by his half-uncle Bligh, he was not on the Bounty and so not involved in the mutiny episode of 1789.

According to naval records, Francis Bond joined the Royal Navy when only nine years of age. In fact he was not sent away to sea, it being a common practice to register minors while still at home as the period thus served could count towards the stipulated six years of apprenticeship.

In 1779 Francis, then aged fourteen, was promoted to midshipman and served several postings afloat. On one of these he was badly burned in an explosion of loose gunpowder, disfiguring his face and partly crippling his hands. Yet when still only seventeen he was certificated as Lieutenant by the Lords of the Admiralty.

When Captain Bligh returned to England from the South Pacific after the mutiny, he had to face a Court Martial for the loss of the *Bounty*. Fortunately their findings exonerated him from all blame and he was able to resume his career. He was given command of *H.M.S. Providence* and charged with completing the task originally set for the *Bounty*. This had been to carry the breadfruit plant from the Pacific to the West Indies, where it was thought it might offer a more interesting and nourishing alternative to the plantain customarily the staple diet of the plantation slaves. Bond was Bligh's First Lieutenant on that voyage.

Also on board was Lieut. George Tobin, related to Nelson's wife through his mother.

A secondary objective of the *Providence* expedition was to investigate and chart some of the hitherto unexplored coasts around Tasmania and to visit the Barrier Reef. The Bond family gift of draftsmanship shows up well in the excellent charts Francis executed of such places as Adventure Bay, Tasmania. Capt. Bligh gave the name Bond's Reef to part of the Barrier Reef, near Bligh's Entrance. The vessel progressed to the West Indies without serious incident.

A quantity of letters between Bligh and John Bond and Francis Godolphin Bond has been collected and published in the Australian Historical Monographs Series, edited by George Mackaness. Some of the communications were terse and official; others were more personal in tone, such as might be expected between those sharing common family interests.

After sailing under Bligh, Lieut. Bond undertook several more appointments until given command of *H.M.S. Netley*, a fast gun-brig, in service against the French and also in the protection of British convoys against the depredations of Spanish privateers. As a result of actions off the coast of Portugal in the year 1800, the *Netley* brought in a total of forty-five Spanish vessels, often without a shot being fired. At about this time he was promoted to the rank of Commander. In gratitude for his services, the merchants of Oporto presented Bond with an Address of thanks.

One of the signatories to the document was Thomas Snow of Oporto (later of Exeter). The next year, at Oporto, Commander Bond married Snow's nineteen-year-old daughter Sophia.

Francis and Sophia had seven sons and daughters, although not all survived. Frederick Bligh Bond's father, Frederick Hookey Bond, was born to them in 1820.

After schooling at Winchester and Exeter College, Oxford, Frederick Hookey Bond entered the ministry of the Church of England. He married Mary Isabella Dela Fosse in 1852. He was fascinated, and even proud, of his father's association and blood-link with William Bligh. What with the mutiny and Bligh's reputation as a nasty piece of work, we might wonder why. But a deeper investigation of the facts of the case can reveal Bligh as a slightly more reasonable and conscientious commander than is generally supposed. In 1886 the Rev. Bond prepared a manuscript account of his father's life and service for the family papers. With his interest in the past it is understandable that he chose to give at least one of his children the second name Bligh.

The Bond family were fond of keeping all sorts of records and memorabilia, perhaps spurred on initially by a sense of responsibility towards the documents they held of their sea-going forebears. Many of the contributions which they added to the collection were in the form of their own drawings and paintings. All of the family were exceptionally talented in this respect, including the Rev. Bond's wife Mary. Frederick Bligh Bond could thus have inherited his artistic propensity from either side of the family. Later his only daughter, Mary (there was a preponderance of Marys associated with our Avalonian families), would reveal similar gifts - and without formal training.

Bond's childhood at Marlborough was marked by a desire to be alone, dreaming and seeing things which he presumed others could see too. It was a gift common to the early years of several people in our study. For all of them it came as quite a shock when they eventually realized how unusual these powers were.

FBB's Anglican religious upbringing was conventional enough and he seems to have always accepted the substantial truth of Christian doctrine. Yet even in his earliest years he sought to probe the more obscure byways of the spiritual world. The handbook which inspired these psychic adventures was *The Night Side of Nature* by Catherine Crowe, first published in 1848, which he read while still in his teens. Mrs Crowe's work was unique and far ahead of its time in its carefully reasoned and objective treatment of such topics as apparitions, the after-life, precognition and trance states. Significantly, much of the spirit of her approach was later embodied in the aims of the Society for Psychical Research, of which Bond was to become a life member.

In 1876 the Rev. Bond had to retire to Bath from his job at Marlborough Grammar School owing to his wife's ill health. Here his son Frederick completed his schooling at Bath College before going on to study architecture in London. He eventually gained his FRIBA and also became a Member of the Institute of the Royal Academy.

In 1894 he married Mary Louise Mills. It was a disaster; its ramifications were to blight his life and even contribute to his removal to America in later years. Their one child, Mary Theodora St. Vincent Bligh Bond, was born in 1895. By 1898 Bond had left his wife, taking the child with him. Mrs Bond immediately initiated proceedings against him for a legal separation on the grounds of his cruelty in taking away the daughter. The High Court granted a separation and ordered that the child should spend equal periods with each parent until she could be sent away to a boarding school. Unfortunately this legal action was only the first of many. Problem piled upon problem. Mrs Bond often broke the custody agreement and reportedly filled Mary's mind with all kinds of slanders and accusations against her father. Understandably the child became disturbed in these unsettling circumstances. As she grew older she turned more and more to a psychic visionary world which she found she could enter and leave at will. But this realm of experience was not only an escape from the tug-of-war going on around her; she had been aware of such things from her earliest years:

> "Often in the dark of my night nursery, long after my nurse was asleep, I, as a mere babe, watched the little living lights of the fairies, flaming like tiny fire-flies, lives almost unbearably active, swarming like a miniature firmament of restless stars upon the dimness of my counter-pane. And these small folk would continue to keep me company, dancing over the bed, and sometimes one would lie for a second, nestling in a fold of the coverlet, or in a hollow where my knees would be tucked up, and perhaps once or twice they would alight upon my face, and I would feel, for a tiny space, their frail impalpable warmth rest upon my skin. They did not come every night, but if I wanted them badly, or if I had been sad in the day over some childish misdemeanour of my own, when I called them, they would come, bouncing, light as feathers, all over the place! I do not know how I called them - but it was by some mysterious process known to my childhood state that brought them and quite impossible to put into words. I only know that I called them with a wiser and older 'something' within me - this 'something' was very familiar with them, prenatally familiar, and could summon them by that remembered kinship it had with them."

When, in her innocence, she resolved to tell her elders about these secret visitations, she unwisely picked the wrong ones and met with scoldings and rebuffs. The one person who would have understood so well, her father, was simply not within reach at that time. The dominant figures of her early life were her mother and her nanny.

Although she knew nothing of her father's ideas or his involvement with psychic research, it is remarkable how closely her disposition followed his. Indeed, as she grew older, Mary must have seemed something of a marvel to Frederick Bligh Bond; as if his innermost soul stood in flesh and blood before him. She was the one good thing to come out of a most unfortunate marriage and ever a great joy to him. Of course, she came to share and co-operate in his various endeavours very fully - but not without attracting jealous opposition from her mother.

Mary ever lived in two worlds. We must be grateful that she has left us this somewhat bizarre recollection of her school-days:

"At my boarding school once when I was playing tennis, a huge blue genie shot like a cerulean meteor, high in the sunny air, over the tops of the tall trees surrounding the grounds, and I was silly enough to utter an exclamation and drop my racquet! He was a person colossal in size, and his passage was exceedingly swift. I got the transitory impression of that cyclonic passage of his tremendously elongated limbs, and his splendid and flaming blue head before he was gone. And he was one of many such - denizens of that magical hidden supernature that so few will willingly look upon, or acknowledge even if they have eyes to see it - these sons of the fabulous hierarchies of space..."

The terms of the custody order and the claims of his investigative work on his time prevented Bond from seeing as much of his daughter as he would have wished. He viewed her precocious artistic talent with a good deal of paternal pride - if not astonishment. More so because she often depicted her extraordinary visionary encounters in her creations.

Worries about Mary and the need to fend off his estranged wife's constant efforts to undermine his public reputation provided an uncomfortable backdrop to the years of his association with Glastonbury. Yet being alone brought its benefits. He had time and freedom to lose himself in his quest for hidden knowledge - especially with regard to the past of the Abbey.

The appearance of the ruins was rather different in 1907 from what it is now. The ground was rougher and sheep clambered over the crumbled masonry around the great arches. The wind washed along the creeper-covered north and south walls with a noise like the sea-shore. Only the curiously-shaped Abbot's Kitchen on the south-western corner remained intact. Today everything has been tidied up in surroundings looking more like a well-kept city park. Bond's two main interests were architecture and research into the paranormal. At Glastonbury they could be brought together.

Early in 1907, there was a rumour going around that Stanley Austin, the local owner of the Abbey grounds, was planning to sell up. Not wanting to miss out on the opportunities this might bring, Bond applied to the Somerset Archaeological and Natural History Society for permission to excavate on their behalf in the Abbey grounds. Taking on trust these evident portents for his future destiny with the place, he set about making preparations well before either fact was confirmed. His imagination was fired. Yes, he was equipped to handle the normal excavation work well enough - but he would also extend the potential for success by means of some kind of psychical experimentation. If this

CAPTAIN JOHN ALLEN BARTLETT (JA) AND HIS WIFE MAUD.

had to be in secret, so be it.

Bond had already made an exhaustive study of all known references to the construction and history of the Abbey, ancient and modern. Several questions arose, but he decided to give priority to a search for the lost foundations of chapels believed to exist beyond the main body of the church. It invited an alternative approach.

The ideal collaborator was on hand. Captain John Allen Bartlett was a West-Country songwriter and lover of history and legend, and, like Bond, in his mid-forties at that time. He had been in touch with Everard Fielding, Secretary of the Society for Psychical Research, after he had discovered, quite by accident, that he seemed to be able to produce automatic writing; that is, written statements, or 'messages', obtained through the movement of the hand of the writer without conscious control or awareness of what was being set down, as we have seen before when Christine and Janet Allen visited Glastonbury in November 1905 (see Chapter 5).

As a member of the SPR, Bond confided with Fielding that he intended to use psychical methods in his investigations at Glastonbury. Bond was at that time living in Bath; Bartlett, who was a near neighbour, would be brought in to assist. It was quite a 'hot potato'; no one else should know about it.

The first sitting took place at 4.30 pm. on 7 November 1907, in Bond's office at Star Life Chambers, Bristol. Bartlett held a pencil over a sheet of foolscap paper while Bond placed his right hand fingers lightly on the back of Bartlett's writing hand. They propelled their first question out into the unknown and illimitable:

"Can you tell us anything about Glastonbury?"

CHAPTER THIRTEEN

The Gate of Remembrance

MANY MORE SITTINGS were to take place before clearance was given for work to start at the Abbey. Yet the most striking piece of information, and the one by which Bond has been most remembered, came to light on that very first occasion at Bristol.

As the two men deliberately tried to keep their attention away from whatever might be written, Bartlett's pencil traced a spidery course across the paper to spell out this rather generalized message:

"All knowledge is eternal and is available to mental sympathy."

followed by:

"I was not in sympathy with monks - I cannot find a monk yet."

There next appeared a sketch of the ground plan of the Abbey, with a rectangular addition at the east end drawn over three times for emphasis. Down the centre of the plan was the signature 'Gulielmus Monachus' (William the Monk).

More plan-sketches followed, both of the new discovery to the east and the more familiar St. Mary's Chapel to the west. Both were named - and the one to the east turned out to be the lost chapel dedicated to King Edgar.

As is well known, Bond went on to excavate and uncover the foundations of the Edgar Chapel after further sittings which provided more precise details and measurements. At the time it was simply attributed to good detective work; nothing was known about Bond and Bartlett's automatic scripts, and it would remain so until Bond revealed the truth in *The Gate of Remembrance* in 1918. But even here one detail was still concealed; Bartlett was merely referred to as JA, the initials of his musical and literary pseudonym, John Alleyne.

The Abbey had been sold by auction in the summer before the

sittings began. The prospect of the sale had attracted attention from all around the world months before the set date. The Catholics, with their base at Chalice Well, were hoping beyond hope to make a grand return to their former House of Glory; a coterie of Americans, under their spokesperson, Mrs Isabel Inez Garrison, had plans to set up a boys' Chivalric College on the site; the Church of England was interested too.

The day came, 7 June 1907, and a large crowd gathered in the Abbey grounds to witness the bidding, which started at £24,000 and rose slowly to £30,000. The man of the day turned out to be a Nottingham manufacturer, Ernest Jardine, prospective Unionist candidate for East Somerset.

Mr and Mrs Jardine had stayed overnight at the George and Pilgrims Hotel, secure and certain of surpassing all possible challengers. But what could this man who had made a fortune out of lace-making machinery want with a ruin? For one, he played a masterstroke calculated to bring political advantages: he offered the whole site to The Church of England on very reasonable terms of repayment; also, he gained for himself the lease of the fine Abbey House as his home in the district for at least five years.

His intention to re-sell was not immediately made known, and there was some astonishment when Dr Kennion, the Bishop of Bath and Wells, eventually announced that the Church would be taking up ownership of Glastonbury Abbey subject to an appeal for the funds required to pay off Mr Jardine. The King and Queen and the Prince of Wales and other notable figures subscribed. By October 1908 the Church was in full possession and Jardine its tenant. There was complaint in some quarters that the Abbey House ought to be put to some religious use, but the Trustees saw that it was prudent to let Jardine do as he wished - and it was not often that he did otherwise! From his new base he exercised his considerable entrepreneurial skills in both vote-catching and extending his business empire. Modesty was not his style. He brought brass bands down from his works at Nottingham to entertain the locals; he addressed the town football club and told them that he had played for seven years for the Nottingham Forest team and never missed a single game; he refused to employ union labour but claimed to pay at least twenty-five per cent above the normal rate. The small factories he set up brought employment and it was not hard to drum up support for his campaign in the run-up to the 1910 General Election. He was pleased to quote one of his work-force as saying: "If all employers were Jardines there would be no need for unions."

He won the seat, but one wonders if he could have secured his majority of 1,027 votes without the prestige engendered by his performance at the Abbey auction.

The change of ownership of the Abbey did not obstruct the plans to excavate, and in May 1908 Bond was given licence to dig at the site as representative of the Somerset Archaeological and Natural History Society. By that time there had been twenty-nine automatic writing sittings, both at Bristol and Glastonbury. Not all concerned the Edgar Chapel, nor even the Abbey, and some introduced the curious errant figure of the monk Johannes whose natural simplicity won the hearts of all who got to know him. Bartlett's wife, Maud, who composed pieces of light music under the name Carlyon de Lyle, had a set of seven impressions for the piano based on the life of Johannes published at the same time as *The Gate of Remembrance* and given the same title.

Bond's brief was for excavation alone; initially the restoration of the fabric of the buildings was solely the concern of the Church Commissioners and their architectural advisor, William Caroe, a much bigger man in the profession than Bond.

Plans were afoot for a grand ceremonial inauguration to be attended by royalty and the bishops of the land. In the spring of 1909 all the walls were made safe and the area extensively tidied up. The old entrance from the High Street was closed and part of the Red Lion Inn in Magdalene Street opened up to form the broad archway still used by visitors to the Abbey today.

The opportunity afforded by the coming royal visit was not lost on Bond. The guests of honour were to be the Prince and Princess of Wales. He and Bartlett decided that they should present them with an illuminated parchment manuscript in the style of a greeting from the monks of old. It was a commendable gesture, but not without an element of self-interest. As the first product of the Guild of Sacred Art which Bond had recently set up in premises in the High Street, it was likely to bring some useful publicity.

What they concocted was a piece of 'archaic' writing similar in vein to some of the automatic scripts but not in any way derived from them. However, in the course of its preparation, Bartlett came up with some genuinely automatic verses which they decided to append to the main text:

> "Then ye grasse schal bee as glasse
> And ye schal see ye mysterie
> Deepe downe hit lyes ffrom pryinge eies

> And safelie slepes, while vigil kepes
> Ye Company
> (Howe doe) ye dry bonys stir and shake
> And eche to eche hys fellowe seekes
> Soone comes agayne what once hath bene
> And Glastonys glory shal be seene."

According to the *Gate of Remembrance,* these verses were "incorporated in the Address in a form slightly modified from the original".

It was meticulously executed. The illuminations were done by one of Bond's friends, the Reverend R. Jeffcoat; the rest was the work of the newly founded Guild. Fortunately some copies are understood to have survived, although the original document, presumably entrusted to the keepers of the royal archives, was destroyed in 1920 during a general clear-out.

The unfavourable weather of Tuesday, 22 June 1909, may have caused a few empty places among the invited guests in the roofless Abbey, but it did not dampen the excitement in the town streets, decked out once again with all the trappings of the Jubilee and the Coronation. At the service that afternoon, the Archbishop of Canterbury formally received the Deeds of the despoiled shrine on behalf of the Church.

With the ceremony over, the royal couple and dignitaries repaired to Abbey House, home of Mr Jardine, for tea. Here a number of presentations were made. The occasion was recorded in a report in *The Central Somerset Gazette* for 25 June:

> "...Miss Mary Bond, the pretty little daughter of Mr Bligh Bond FRIBA, of Bath, the well-known architect and antiquary, who has done so much excellent exploration work at the Abbey on behalf of the Somerset Archaeological Society, handed to the Princess a most handsome souvenir of a day which will be historic, not only in the annals of Glastonbury, but in the annals of the Church of England..."

Albeit surreptitiously, those who would the following year accede to the Throne as King George V and Queen Mary, became the recipients of a small item plucked from the storehouse of what Bond liked to call the Greater Memory.

To all intents and purposes anyone can be forgiven for thinking that Bond and Bartlett imagined they were communicating with the spirits of departed monks. It is not so simple. Bearing in mind that Bond was a member of The Society for Psychical Research, and on close terms with its President, Sir William Barrett, a distinguished physicist and pioneer researcher into hypnotism and telepathy, and that he had been persuaded by the ideas of Catherine Crowe from an early age, it is not surprising that he preferred a more sophisticated explanation of the processes involved in obtaining the automatic script material.

The spiritualistic medium is generally understood to be a totally passive instrument - simply a channel for whatever is trying to 'come through'. In Bond's view, both his and Bartlett's mental contents were *actively* involved in – and even necessary for - the transmission of the scripts, although on an unconscious level. In other words, the life-knowledge invested within each of them was acted upon by an impersonal agency to articulate historical and philosophical truths. Even in the case of such a definite human personality as the overweight truant-monk Johannes, Bond questions the conventional spiritualistic interpretation:

> "Is this a piece of actual experience transmitted by a real personality, or are we in contact with a larger field of memory, a cosmic record latent, yet living, and able to find expression in human terms related to the subject before us, by the aid of something furnished by the culture of our own minds, and by the aid of a certain power of mental sympathy which allows such records to be sensed and articulated?"

Note that the term 'mental sympathy', which Bond uses here, appeared in the very first sentence of the first sitting in November 1907. It seems crucial to his view. His vision is of a subtler level of communication that transcends time and space. He aspires to raise the 'little limited self' to

> "...the dignity of a mystical fellowship in which isolation ends, and Past and Present are seen as parts of a living whole; points on the circumference of a circle whose radius is Life beyond these limitations... ...Not by our own power, but through the unseen Gate of the subconscious mind, will these memories link themselves with ours - not through the evocation of the 'spirit' of Johannes, but by the power of the Universal Spirit, whose life permeates all the regions of Time, and in Whom we and Johannes and all who are in mental kinship with his thought, are as one."

What is striking here is the parallel to the extraordinary perceptions of Bond's erstwhile mentor, Catherine Crowe, writing more than half a century earlier:

> "...to the great Spirit and Fountain of life, all things, in both space and time, must be present. However impossible it is for our finite minds to conceive this, we must believe it. It may, in some slight degree, facilitate the conception to remember that action, once begun, never ceases - an impulse given is transmitted on for ever; a sound breathed reverberates in eternity; and thus the past is always present, although, for the purpose of fitting us for this mortal life, our ordinary senses are so constituted as to be unperceptive of these phenomena."

To compare these two quotations is to realize how much Catherine Crowe must have influenced the direction of Bond's life and work. They are really saying exactly the same thing.

The question as to the reality or otherwise of such 'entities' as Johannes is never wholly answered. Bond would prefer us to consider the monkish image as 'something furnished from the culture of our own minds'; an artifice of the Unconscious mediating the Voice of the Past more readily to us. Someone like him - even very like him - could have once lived, or he could be a composite of several people - or no-one in particular at all. The appearance of Johannes in the scripts came as a surprise. The sole intention of the sittings was to elucidate facts that might aid the work at Glastonbury. His was an alien presence, and an interference to the task in hand. Yet the breath of fresh air he brought was not unwelcome:

> "...He ever loved the woods and pleasant places which lie about our house. It was good, for he learnt in the temple of nature much that he would never hear in choro. His herte was of the country and he heard it calling without the walls and the Abbot winked at it for he knew full well that it was good for him. He went a-fishing, did Johannes, and tarried oft in lanes to listen to the birds and to watch the shadows lengthening all over the woods of Mere..."

The period of the first series of automatic scripts spanned the years 1907 to 1912. They were mostly about the Abbey, although Johannes and other extraneous interpolations cropped up from time to time. Bond preferred to call the script-seances 'psychological experiments', no doubt in deference to his belief that his and Bartlett's minds were intrinsic to their production. Some pointed an accusing finger and declared it to be all 'psychological' and therefore a delusion. If so, how can the apparently involuntary movements of Bartlett's writing hand spelling out coherent statements in Latin and old and modern English be understood? We must take it that both men were scrupulously honest and utterly dedicated towards producing what they deemed were authentic results. If they say that they kept their minds and eyes away from the paper while the script was emerging, then we must believe it.

Bond certainly had an acute awareness of his own mental processes, and could probably play tricks with them. In support of this there is an intriguing reminiscence of a local resident about a Glastonbury dentist who knew Bond, and often invited him to his home. Here the visitor would greatly amuse the children of the house by being able to tell them one story while at the *same time* writing down another! Was this merely an exhibition of adroit mental gymnastics or were the children privy to a rare solo performance of automatic writing by Bond himself? The latter seems unlikely as an accomplice was always required to produce the script. Nevertheless, it bears curiously on a device often used by Bond and Bartlett to divert their attention away from what was being written. In *The Gate of Remembrance* Bond tells how he

"...used to read aloud to JA (Bartlett) during the whole course of the writing, from a novel or other entertaining or amusing book, calculated to retain his attention, and the script resulting has proved to have nothing at all in common with the subject matter of the book..."

An instance is given in a letter of 1919 to the secretary of the Society for Psychical Research:

"...Lady Barrett was in Clifton last week, and I took JA to see her and we had a sitting, the result being three pages of curious script relating to philosophy. I was reading aloud all the time from Jerome K. Jerome's 'Idle Thoughts of an Idle Fellow'."

In another work, *The Hill of Vision* (1919), the various diverting readings were recorded with their respective scripts - and not always particularly lightweight material. Perhaps this was deliberately done to test for any influence.

However, even if Bond could pull off a few party tricks, it is hard to see how he could have managed to control Bartlett's hand. The degree of physical contact was too slight - as far as can be judged from his own account of the conditions at the sittings.

Inevitably alternative theories to Bond's time-transcending 'Greater

Memory' were put forward.

Around the time that *The Gate of Remembrance* was being published, the Reverend F. T. Fryer of Bath seems to have appointed himself the local watchdog over the activity at Glastonbury on behalf of the Society for Psychical Research - although he was apparently not a member of that body.

Fryer would visit Glastonbury or meet with Bond in Bath and report back to the SPR secretary in London. He was friendly but mostly critical. His acceptance of any paranormal activity went only as far as the telepathic possibility. He felt that Bartlett was unknowingly picking up all sorts of odds and ends from Bond's mental storehouse. That these, even, could have transferred themselves through Bartlett's writing hand remains a remarkable enough possibility in itself.

Not long after the first scripts emerged giving details of the Edgar Chapel, a manuscript had come to light which also showed a chapel existing at the eastern extremity of the Abbey. Bond did not divulge this to Bartlett, who apparently continued to give out automatic data which could now be confirmed by the manuscript. Fryer contended that Bartlett had been influenced telepathically by what Bond already knew about the chapel and that this undermined some of the claims made.

Bond was quick to respond:

"...JA was unfamiliar with the Cannon MS which I borrowed, made extracts from and returned. I resided at Glastonbury, and JA was only at this time an occasional visitor. He would come down for two or three days at a time and on these occasions he would learn in a general way what I was doing, assist me in an excavation, and act as automist.

...even assuming my knowledge, there remains the fact that it is in my knowledge and not JA's, but that it is JA's hand that writes. Is telepathic action assumed? I have not found the writings follow any thoughts of mine..."

Fryer was unimpressed:

"It is not assumed that any ideas in Mr Bond's mind were orally communicated by him to JA. Judging from our present knowledge and most probable theories of telepathy, I have concluded all through that the originating mind is Bond's, JA being his emanuensis... It is impossible for any human being to say what, or what not, is among his mental possessions..."

There was one occasion when Bond accepted that telepathy could have been involved. The sitting took place in Oxford on 27 March 1918 in the presence of Bond's publisher, Basil Blackwell, and a young writer, Dorothy L. Sayers, later to become well-known as the creator of the character of Lord Peter Wimsey in her detective stories.

The day before, Bond had spent the morning in the Bodleian Library looking at Dugdale's *Monasticon*. He made a note of the following extract concerning the election of the last Abbot of Glastonbury:

> "On Beere's death, forty-seven monks devolved the election of their Abbot to Cardinal Wolsey, who declared Richard Whiting, then Chancellor of the House, their Abbot."

No questions were asked at the sitting, and Bartlett's hand proceeded to scribe something very much in line with what Bond had been reading the day before:

> "Wolsey the Cardinal housing me with the King, and did appoint me Abbot, olde man that I was. Here was the Hall that he built in this town in Chancellorium. I have said I came to Oxford, and Wolsey the Cardinal did make me Abbot in ye Hall that he had builded... Would God I had not been so; then had my death been otherwise."

It is interesting that Bond quite openly admits that on this occasion he could have transferred the material telepathically to Bartlett. This might put in doubt the involvement of the individual spirit of the long-dead Abbot, but does not unduly disturb Bond's idea of 'tuning-in to history'. Of course, it could also be postulated that Bond's reading in the library had opened the way for the Abbot to communicate on the same kind of wavelength the next day. But such arguments are open to endless variations and possibilities. Bond's view is what matters here.

As time went on other 'psychics' entered the field apart from Bartlett, who seems to have fallen out with Bond in the early 1920s (see T. H. Hopkinson-Ball, *Visions of Glastonbury: The Automatic Drawings of John Allen Bartlett - Light,* Winter 2003, Vol 123, No. 2). The newcomers still produced automatic scripts, but with a different emphasis and not always requiring Bond's presence at the sittings. However, there is a common thread running through all of them: submission to the directives of an unseen fraternity calling itself variously The Watchers, or The Company of Avalon, or simply Ye Company. Here Bond seems much more prepared to forego his normal reservations and allows that a group of 'souls' or 'departed spirits' is present and concerned to make contact with us through the medium's pen. Yet he is still careful to draw the line between this kind of communication and 'normal spiritualism'. To illustrate this he brings in the traditional teaching of the after-life states of Purgatory and Paradise. Those who find themselves in Purgatory are too self-centred and worldly to rise to the level of Paradise where they could have "become apart, integral and symmetric, of the greater spiritual Units co-ordinated in overruling Intelligence and Sympathy." The facts of what is termed Spiritualism reflect the narrow human limitations of Purgatory; 'The Company of Avalon' belongs to the more exalted realm of Paradise:

> "So it is, we are told, with the Company of Avalon, a group of souls who are impregnated with the devotional ideal which was translated into architectural symbol by the Benedictine brethren of old time. These, the 'Elect of Avalon', combine as a united spiritual force in an effort which is really one of response to those of us who, of our own volition, have attuned ourselves to their 'vibrations'. But being themselves for the most part so far removed in condition from modes of physical expression of the truths they would seek to convey, they choose as spokesmen some who, though liberated in spirit, and of their Company, have retained such sympathy with earth and the dwellers on earth that they are able through this mutual sympathy to creep to us across the 'bridge of Love' and, entering our atmosphere and conditions of consciousness, speak to us through the mediumship of one or other whose organism is attuned to a psychical responsiveness."

This quotation is taken from the preface to Bond's book *The Company of Avalon* (1924). This is noteworthy in that most of its scripts are given through a lady named 'S', and purport to come from one Brother Symon, Sub-Prior of Winchester in the twelfth century. The oddity here is that not only do the communications come from Brother Symon, but that S is herself the reincarnation of him! Bond seems to accept this, but points out that it should be seen as "an exceptional thing connected with the mission of certain souls". He regards S as a "practical Churchwoman" who had never "been at all influenced by current theosophical doctrines of rebirth". Exceptional or not, in one of her scripts we find a Brother Romauld of Glastonbury stating that Robert, Abbot of Glastonbury 1171-1178, is he

> "...who seeketh in Glaston now... But our Abbot - Robertus Abbas - was

cutte off from his worke in his strength, by a greate fever. Yet Romauld
saith he cometh agayn for love of Glaston, yet not a prieste."

Not a priest? - well not yet. He 'who seketh in Glaston now' is of course
Bond, the twelfth century Abbot Robert de Jumièges (the younger) - or
at least some aspect of him - returned. Bond passes over this revelation
lightly, and I have not come across reference to it elsewhere. However,
Robert is accorded a much larger potted biography in the list of
'Dramatis Personae' with which he prefaces the scripts in *The Company
of Avalon,* than any other character. There are resonances of the twelfth
century in the twentieth with bittersweet implications for Bond. We are
told that it was during the abbacy of Robert that the first fatal quarrel
arose with Wells, "on account of the episcopal encroachments". Bond
had had his own differences with the Diocese of Bath and Wells,
especially since the publication of his psychic work in *The Gate of
Remembrance.* According to the script, Robert was responsible for much
building work and fine chiselled Romanesque ornament. Before his
death he was visualized as a man of 'sad countenance, eyes dark, hair
iron-grey'. With good reason this was an apt description of Bond at
that time, too.

CHAPTER FOURTEEN

Friends and Foes

FREDERICK BLIGH BOND was a small, thin man, rather bird-like. As a child he had been intimidated by his more robust peers. Yet he craved recognition; he wanted to *be* somebody. There is no doubt that he had great gifts - and he knew it. Unfortunately this led to a sense of self-importance marked by an obstinacy characteristic of those who feel they do what they do by Divine Decree. Caution in others about his claims was seen as opposition. Inevitably, there was trouble.

He was not one to appeal to the dull or the unimaginative, nor to the professionally defensive. But such people are the mainstay of the boards and committees of small provincial towns and cannot be ignored or offended. It is they who hold the purse-strings. To say that Bond fell out with the ecclesiastical administrators of the Abbey over his psychic methods alone is an over-simplification. There are signs that certain of his temperamental quirks gave rise to some discomfiture well before that time.

In Kenawell's biography of Bond there is a chapter entitled 'Real and Imaginary Battles'. Sadly, it is a fact that after such a happy and promising start, the years of the work at the Abbey were progressively punctuated with disputes and doubts which reached a climax on the publication of *The Gate of Remembrance*.

It is curious, for Bond was not a prickly customer to meet socially. Everyone spoke of his good humour and the enthusiasm which informed his communication with others on the subjects he loved. In more recent years professional field-workers have acknowledged that the excavations and reports he prepared for the Somerset Archaeological Society were good and thorough enough by the standards of the times. So what went wrong?

The reasons lay with power and politics at a most petty and parochial level in collision with Bond's near-obsession to pursue his spiritual quest at Glastonbury come what may.

In 1909 Bond acquired the post of Diocesan Architect. It was not connected to his work at the Abbey, which was unpaid, but certainly gave him a greater sense of authority in that regard. But the appointment had not been without rancour in the Diocesan chambers at Wells. An anti-Bond lobby, that included the bishop, remained, watching and dissatisfied. They had wanted the formidable William Douglas Caroe for the job - the man in whose London office the young artist and calligrapher Eric Gill had once been so bored. As the renovator of the Abbey, Caroe quite probably passed unfavourable observations back to his friends at Wells. Plainly, Bond was now sailing very close to the wind. However much he succeeded in keeping the secret of his psychic investigations, the fact is that he was largely motivated and directed by them: he was adamant about the existence of an apse at the east end of the Edgar Chapel, because the script had said there should be; he seemed concerned as to the 'true length of the Abbey' beyond the point of reasonableness.

By 1912 the untidy look of the place was giving some cause for concern. Tons of excavated soil were lying around the site to the extent that there was not enough money to pay for its removal. The Abbey Trustees decided to step in. Bond was becoming too much a free agent; a committee was set up to control the finances and to monitor Bond's future activity.

In 1913 a change in the organization of the Diocesan administration caused Bond to lose his cherished appointment as Honorary Architect. To add insult to injury, the post was advertised once again, and awarded to William Caroe.

Bond had long accepted that Caroe had been behind the bishop's rejection of some of his schemes for church restoration. The character of the bishop's comments bore the mark of professional advice - such as could only have come from Caroe. Bond was too small to hope to take on these important adversaries alone; he sought support from all manner of associations and individuals, convinced that the injustices of his treatment were sell-evident.

As always, there was sympathy, probably genuine, but no useful action. Perhaps they saw what Bond could not see, that some responsibility for his misfortunes lay with himself.

By the time of the hostilities of 1914 things were getting desperate and Bond was almost bankrupt.

It must be remembered that incessantly, year after year, Mrs Mary Bond had been waging a campaign of extraordinary ferocity against the character of her husband, in spite of the fact that they had separated in the previous century. No-one was spared the fury of her claims of his dishonesty and wickedness: relatives, friends, clerics, business associates, psychical researchers and others. Quite why this poor woman was driven to such lengths could be a case-study in itself, but there would be little to go on, save for the press reports of her various court actions against him - which she usually lost.

What is certain is that some of her efforts were very successful. Friends of Bond even found themselves wondering if some of her allegations might be true. Kennawell reports that a brother in India, Major-General Sir Francis Bond, refused to communicate with him for years after reading one of the court hearings, but the evidence for this is unavailable. Mostly Mrs Bond complained that her husband was not sending her money to maintain herself and her daughter, although in fact he did, to the best of his ability.

Private detectives were sent to spy on him in the hope of verifying some of Mrs Bond's worst suspicions. The man was hardly ever left in peace. She accused him of poisoning her daughter's mind with spiritualism and using her as a medium. All this came to light in a court case in 1922. The absurdity of the position was highlighted in the response to the judge's enquiry as to the girl's age. She was twenty-six.

This at least gives some clue towards understanding why the wife of this psychically-absorbed architect should have turned against him with such explosive hatred. Plainly, she was not as dedicated to this kind of thing as he was; the number of hours in the day and night taken up with these interests worried her tremendously; she could not deal with it. Had he made the mistake of not divulging fully to her the facts of his abiding preoccupation before they married? Perhaps his strong romantic sensibilities got the better of him and he saw her too much as his dream-princess before waking up to the reality of her human frailties and the force of her individual personality rather late in the day. Whatever, her quest to get even with him was as dedicated and persistent as his own at Glastonbury. She damaged his career - most of his commissions were from the clergy - by appealing to Christian righteousness and sense of justice. Her remonstrations may well have been the main factor in getting Bond eased out of his Abbey appointments, probably more than the 'spiritualist' epithet.

William Kenawell summed up the position:

> "The picture, a familiar one to psychiatrists and judges, seems to be that of a wife who as the victim of an unsuccessful marriage relation turns her frustrated energies into becoming a destroying fury. Bond's attempts to cope with her seem to have been courageous and responsible on

the whole, but in the end he did not have enough strength and psychological insight to deal with her adequately and so bring him a quiet mind. And a quiet mind was an outstanding necessity for the pursuit of his life's main work at Glastonbury. It is ironic that the Abbey, set among the green fields and hills of Somerset, had an aura of great peace against which his tumultuous marriage stood out in such dramatic contrast."

He would have had no mind for the task at all had there not been those who stood by him and who understood something of the wonder of his inner world. Yet, just like his foes, many of these were church people. Notably, the most sympathetic were often those more aligned to the Catholic tradition - or at least to the spirit of that tradition.

At that time most Anglicans regarded 'Roman' Catholics as an alien species, somehow the representatives of a foreign culture on their soil. Even the Anglo-Catholic branch of the native church had to face fierce opposition from within its own communion. Yet Bond had no difficulty in meeting Christians of either persuasion. The glorious days of the life of the Abbey to which he looked so fondly were of the time before Henry VIII set about his destruction of the nation's monasteries. All Britain was Catholic then.

It was a Catholic monk, Dom Bede Camm, who was co-author of Bond's first published work, *Roodscreens and Roodlofts* (1909). This former Anglican was a member of the Benedictine community at Erdington Abbey near Birmingham, and, like Bond, well-versed in ecclesiastical architecture.

It was while on a visit to Erdington in 1908 to confer with Dom Bede that the guest master, Dom John Chapman, introduced Bond to a friend of his who might share common interests with him. The fellow visitor was the American architect Ralph Adams Cram.

Cram was a major figure in his field, more a transatlantic counterpart of William Caroe than Bond. But on a personal level he showed himself very much in tune with what Bond was doing. Their intense tobacco-fuelled discussions ran on into the night in that Abbey guest room. In his preface to Bond's *The Hill of Vision* (1919) Cram recalled that he was invited to meet Bond "that he might tell me of certain very wonderful happenings then in process at the ancient and holy ruins of Glastonbury". In fact he was appreciative of both Bond's professional and psychic capabilities. It was a friendship that would last through to the time, many years later, of Bond's stay of some ten years in America. Cram was not a Catholic, but on the pro-Roman wing of the

American Protestant Episcopalian Church. Born in New Hampshire in 1863, he was a champion of medievalism, advocating closeness to the land, the feudal stratification of society and autocratic government. In his work he was an exponent of the Gothic Revival. Among the buildings he designed were St. Thomas' Church, New York City; Emmanuel Church, Cleveland; and The First Baptist Church, Pittsburgh. He died in 1942.

Another enthusiast for Bond's operations was Dom Aelred Carlyle, Abbot of the Anglican Benedictine community on Caldey Island, off the coast of South Wales.

One day in the summer of 1910, a chauffeur-driven limousine sporting highly polished brass and paintwork pulled up near the Abbey at Glastonbury. An unofficial royal visitor? No. The figure that emerged was clad magnificently in ecclesiastical garb. A large pectoral cross hung on a chain around his neck. Dom Aelred had arrived.

Aelred was the name in religion of Benjamin Fearnley Carlyle, cousin to Janet and Christine Allen. His one ambition was to oversee the revival of Benedictine monasticism within the Church of England. He had achieved this insofar as the Caldey community teetered from year to year ever on the brink of financial ruin. The anomaly of his lavish life-style incensed his many critics; his benefactors were more than a little uneasy too. For Aelred nothing was too good for God; the dream must be realized regardless of spiralling costs and bankers' ultimatums.

Each year it was one of his duties to visit the Glastonbury area to call on a small contemplative community of Benedictine nuns which fell within his jurisdiction, at their convent of St. Anne in the nearby village of Baltonsborough. He had come to the Abbey to find Frederick Bligh Bond while on this visit.

In December 1908 Bond and Bartlett had produced a script which indicated that the bones of Richard Whiting, the martyred last Abbot of Glastonbury, had been secretly interred behind the altar. It reported they were subsequently removed at the time of the destruction of the buildings and deposited nearby, their identity unknown. Bond had unearthed some remains and the revelation of the script was the response to his question about their origin.

The meeting between Bond and Carlyle concerned these bones. Both men seemed to accept the validity of the information in the script without reservation. Surprisingly, perhaps, in the case of Carlyle. But less so with an understanding of his background.

Ben Carlyle had revealed his psychic gifts at an early age. At his public school he had formed a sort of esoteric brotherhood which met in secret in a room in a farmhouse. His lifelong interest in psychical experimentation and occult phenomena began at around this time. His ability to hypnotize his schoolmates did much for his prestige. All this in spite of a commitment to Christianity and the Church. He happily accommodated these disparate elements in his outlook throughout his life without any sense of conflict.

So it was that Dom Aelred returned from Glastonbury to his brethren at Caldey, bringing a casket of old bones.

The relics were set in a magnificent reliquary in the choir of the chapel surrounded by every available candlestick and engulfed in clouds of incense. Richard Whiting was honoured at Vespers, Lauds and High Mass. Aelred had told his community to be satisfied with the witness of the automatic writing.

Both Dom Bede Camm and Ralph Adams Cram made visits to Caldey. In the case of Dom Bede, he was summoned urgently in 1913 to prepare the way for the conversion of the Community to Catholicism.

With this change the bones had to be quietly hidden away in the sacristy. Dom Aelred and most of his monks had severed their allegiance to the Church of England and placed themselves under the authority of Rome. For their new masters automatic writing was not an approved means for the validation of holy relics.

Six years later a more humbled Dom Aelred left Caldey for Canada to work as a parish priest near Vancouver. His monks remained on their island for a while before resettling themselves at Prinknash Abbey, in Gloucestershire. In his old age Fr. Aelred returned to England to join the rank and file at Prinknash. He was buried there with the full honours due to an Abbot.

For Bond, Aelred was no more than a ship that passed in the night, for all his goodwill. Others kept their loyalty over many years. These knew him well enough not to be taken in by Mrs Bond's hate campaign and included Everard Fielding (secretary of SPR), Sir William Barrett (SPR president), Lady Barrett, John and Maud Bartlett, and numerous Anglican ministers appreciative of the quality of the professional work he had put in on their parish churches. Several of these had supported him vigorously at the time of his Diocesan appointment. It is also quite certain that he knew Dr John Goodchild.

As we know, Goodchild was often in Bath at the Francis Hotel. Bartlett lived in Bath and Bond was sometimes given as having a Bath address. With their community of interests it would be strange if they had never met.

In fact Goodchild's opinion about an inscription on a small baked-clay medallion which had been found during the excavations was quoted in Bond's first report for the Proceedings of The Somerset Archaeological Society for 1908. Bond sometimes sought Goodchild's views and had considerable respect for his antiquarian knowledge. He had less regard for the part Goodchild had played in the Cup episode at Bride's Well, as was clearly shown in a letter to the Reverend Hayes of the SPR, dated 5 December 1916:

> "The Holy Grail was a *chimera*. There was self-delusion and an element of unworthy ambition in the exploiting of it. The vessel may have been quite of old time, but it was bought by an Englishman at Bordighera, buried by him at Glaston, and dug up twenty years or so later by young people with whom he had been in touch. The fictitious miracle did harm to many young and impressionable girls who were drawn into the web. But the original purchaser of the vessel was free from blame. He was an idealist and his error was of that order."

Perhaps Bond never knew the full story of the recovery of the Cup, or did not choose to believe it. He is wildly wrong in saying that it was buried for twenty years - it was actually eight. His defence of Goodchild is curious. Plainly he is trying to blame somebody else: but who? Quite probably it was Wellesley Tudor Pole. If so, he seems to be suggesting that there was some kind of attempt to hide the fact that the vessel had been placed in the well by the doctor prior to its recovery. That was never the case. True, the young group did originally identify the object with the Grail of legend, and so did Archdeacon Wilberforce. But Goodchild was at pains to disassociate himself from any such claims, pointing out that the Paris 'voice' had at no time connected the Cup with the Holy Grail.

In his letter to Hayes, Bond is careful not to betray the feelings of loyalty he held towards his friend. He had much to thank him for and it is certain that they shared a common interest in the study of gematria.

It is a subject that seems to have passed Bond by. He claimed that he had never heard of William Stirling's book, *The Canon*, prior to 1913, even though it had been published fifteen years previously. We know that Bond saw quite a lot of the doctor in 1913, and at that time Goodchild probably had more knowledge of sacred numerology than anyone in the country. He would have introduced Bond to both Stirling's work and his own corrections and refinements to his thesis. Significantly, it was in that year that Bond published his observations on the geometrical system underlying the Abbey construction for the first time, in the Proceedings of The Somerset Archaeological Society. He claimed he had discovered a module of 37 feet recurring throughout the buildings and showed a plan of the church overlaid with a grid of 74 foot squares. He is careful to remark that 74 feet is 888 inches. Normally this would seem a superfluous comment. But students of symbolic numerology might see the point: by gematria the Greek for Jesus, Iesous, adds up to 888. Also 74 x 9 gives 666, the number of the Sun - or the Great Beast, depending on one's persuasion.

Bond's Abbey plan is contained precisely within the length of only eight of his 74 ft squares, but it could be projected to nine to include St. Dunstan's Chapel, standing apart at the west end, although not to the exact limit of the extra square. Wisely Bond kept quiet about any connection of the Abbey with the number 666, although anyone sharp enough could make the deduction. Instead, he preferred to make an issue of the length of the main body of the church, including the Edgar Chapel. This was 592 ft (74 x 8) but only if the existence of an apse at the east end of the chapel be allowed. It was this question of an apse that drew so much criticism from his opponents. They looked for any chance to undermine his theories of sacred geometry, especially once it became known that the indication of the chapel and its supposed apse had first been given to Bond by automatic mediumship. Although the foundations of the apse were exposed and made good, it was suggested that he had interfered with the stone rubble to falsify the effect he wanted.

Some time after Bond had left Glastonbury, the footings east of the chapel were removed by those who thought they knew better, much to his dismay when he returned years later.

Was it Goodchild who encouraged Bond to look for measures in the Abbey to the module of thirty-seven (or seventy-four) in the first instance? It is hard to be sure. The same Report of 1913 gives a lengthy account of a visit that the two of them made to the Abbey in July of that year.

Goodchild had become interested in the subject of egg-stones used by various primitive cults. He felt that such a cult-stone must have existed at any place bearing the name *Avalon*. He asked Bond if he had come across such a stone in the neighbourhood of Glastonbury. In fact he had come across a large unusual boulder in the Abbey grounds three years before. Bond had not yet properly looked at this stone, and so arranged to have it turned over for Goodchild's benefit. They found a hollow cavity on the under-side, giving the appearance of what Bond described as a 'pecten-shell' with several chiselled grooves radiating outwards from it. They found a lot of markings on it, some of which seemed natural - perhaps glacial - while others were clearly artificial. Goodchild even went so far as to suggest that these were possibly hieroglyphs. Bond ends his article with the speculation that the name *Avalon* could be derived from two Celtic words, *aball* and *onn,* meaning *apple* and *stone.*

The subject was still in the air three months later when Goodchild wrote to Janet Allen:

> "You asked me what was in the Pecten on the Cult-Stone and I did not know, but I have just had a neat little snapshot from Miss Brodie, and on examining this with a glass it appears to me that the object inside must have been intended for the Mollusc itself with its Mussel (or possibly a fish), and it may hint that the foundation deposit within it was a Pearl, possibly a large British Pearl (of Gt. Price) like that in our English Crown. Possibly there may have been merely a carving of a pearl."

Miss Brodie, mentioned here, was one of the many associates of the group at Clifton and a frequent visitor to Glastonbury.

The next time we find Bond and Goodchild together is in the December of the same year at the doctor's hotel in Bath. Bond was presumably Goodchild's guest and, according to the guest-lists published in the local paper, stayed four weeks in all, not leaving until the second week in January. This arrangement might have been obtained on favourable terms as there is evidence that the doctor had family connections with the owners.

Bond had hit hard times and was short of money. His sojourn at the hotel may have been just an act of simple generosity on Goodchild's part; but, more likely, there were other considerations.

Goodchild was past sixty and not well. Twenty-eight years of pulmonary tuberculosis must have taken its toll. He may even have sensed that his days were numbered. He had in his possession the fruits of a lifetime of antiquarian research in the form of notes, papers and gematric calculations. In his estimation, Bond was the only person he knew with enough dedication and understanding to make good use of his accumulated knowledge. It is not difficult to suppose that many of those days at the Francis Hotel were spent absorbed in the intricacies of Goodchild's deliberations on these matters of mutual interest. By the time the visit was over, Bond must have left, effectively Goodchild's successor - at least from the doctor's point of view - carrying with him ample material to further his own researches. It was not a moment too soon: a month later his good friend had departed this life.

The fact that Bond's next published works were on the Cabala and Gematria respectively and that the first of these appeared within three years of Goodchild's departure adds weight to the thought that the doctor's work was one of Bond's primary sources.

But why did Bond keep quiet about this liaison? Did he want all the credit for himself or was Goodchild's connection with the Cup episode an embarrassment to him, and possibly a threat to his own credibility? The latter seems the more likely proposition.

The externals of life in the year after Goodchild's death were difficult for Bond. Money was in short supply, and his reputation somewhat sullied. And this while the clouds of a dark and terrible war gathered, and finally broke, over Europe. Things of the mind, things of the spirit; these were a welcome refuge at times of such adversity. Glastonbury still claimed his heart and soul, but practically there was little that could be done in his new-found seclusion. He played and toyed with the mysterious numerical combinations generated by applying the rules of gematria to the Greek of Biblical words, names and phrases and to the Creed. Here was an oasis of harmony and order in the chaos of life.

While looking through a periodical called *The Guardian* (not the newspaper), he was impressed by the tone of a letter from the Reverend T. Simcox Lea of St. Austell in Cornwall. He made contact at once and found a willing enthusiast for his researches into scriptural numerology. The upshot of this was that Lea became the collaborator with Bond on his next two books.

The title for one of them, 'Apostolic Gnosis' says something about Bond's spiritual position: 'Apostolic' in the sense of being identified with a Church which claimed an unbroken line of succession of its priests from the first Apostles; 'Gnostic' in the sense that the mystic can grow in the knowledge of the inner laws of the Creator-God expressed in the concordances of sacred numerology and geometry.

Lea became interested in the archaeological work and made several trips to Glastonbury. As a cleric he was a useful ally, taking Bond's side in his difficulties with the Anglican hierarchy. But even he was not untouched by the vindictive efforts of Mrs Bond. He was worried enough to write to his collaborator in 1923:

"A full statement of your position would be a great advantage to me... Already I have had hints, from sources I may not name, that you are thought not to be straight... When one does not know the facts, it is difficult to meet such intangible insinuations."

Simcox Lea's sources were most likely colleagues encountered at Church conventions. One of these might have been the Reverend J. H. Wilkins, vicar of Redland and Westbury-on-Trym in Bristol. Mrs Bond's pleadings for her righteous cause had thoroughly won him over. The abhorrence she instilled in him against her husband seems to have set the minister on a quest to undo him by whatever means available. That he was someone Bond had regarded as a friend made his actions all the more reprehensible. In January 1922, this 'friend' who was a member of the Society for Psychical Research and a former client tried to publish a sixty-six page pamphlet arguing against Bond's Abbey measures and the claims in *The Gate of Remembrance*. It contained libellous imputations. Acting on advice, Bond successfully moved to get the first edition withdrawn. It was published in a revised form as *A Further Criticism of the Psychical Claims Concerning Glastonbury Abbey, Etc.* The old issue of the apse of the Edgar Chapel and its incorporation in the 'true length' of the Abbey was raised yet again. Wilkins' arguments were so weak that Bond suggested he get out of his armchair and come down to Glastonbury and measure the buildings himself. No doubt he declined the offer.

The short works by Bond and Simcox Lea have remained the preferred source material for Bond's later apologists. Lea had the job of ferreting out likely pieces of biblical text to which Bond applied the necessary calculations and drew up comparative tables.

We have already outlined the role of Dr Goodchild in setting Bond on the road which led to the books in co-authorship with Lea. It is interesting to find, in the same letter to the Rev. Hayes, already quoted in connection with Bond's opinion of the 'Cup', that the publication of these works is also discussed. Bond tells Hayes that the key to the *gnosis* recovered in the Greek texts will be shown in a forthcoming issue of *The Guardian* and that:

> "...it exhibits a perfect body of sound Christian knowledge in being three centuries before the great Church Councils. This will be given to the Church in a book to be published in January next by Blackwells, offering a new language for the interpretation of the Creed of Athanasius by expressing it in mathematical terms."

Note that these books are addressed primarily to the Church. Notwithstanding his psychical and metaphysical leanings, Bond saw everything he did within the context of the Christian tradition. But the Church he had in mind was something larger and more universal than the modern denominational divisions. Historically he looked to medieval Catholicism before its decline, but perhaps more to the earliest beginnings and the supposed foundation at Glastonbury of the first Church in the world after the crucifixion.

The Church of the day was another matter. Worried by Bond's possessive attitude towards his appointment at the Abbey, the Diocese of Bath and Wells had been keeping him at arm's length for some years. His gnostic and cabalistic ideas found little favour with them. *The Gate of Remembrance* was the last straw. To add to Bond's problems, the Dean of Wells, Joseph Armitage Robinson, had become active in the Somerset Archaeological Society and was also concerning himself with developments at Glastonbury.

No excavation was carried out during the war, but was resumed in 1919. It had been Bond's intention to search for the foundations of the Chapel of Our Lady of Lorretto on the north side of the main church. Soon he was claiming success. Certainly, as far as could be judged from the vestiges uncovered, a building had once been there, although not strictly in the position indicated in the automatic scripts. Passing over these discrepancies, Bond announced that he had 'proved' the reality of the psychically communicated data.

On 4 September 1919, the Rev. Fryer reported to the secretary of the Society for Psychical Research more sceptically:

> "On Tuesday last I went to Glastonbury to see the excavations made on the supposed site of the Lorretto Chapel. Mr FBB has been at work there for some days and so far has discovered what he believes to be the western wall foundations of the chapel. But this wall is 10ft or so nearer the transept, that is eastward of the chapel, than he thought it should be... So far as I could see there is nothing yet found to substantiate any of the statements of the script beyond the measurements of the walls."

That year another of Bond's works appeared. *The Hill of Vision* comprised more communications through the hand of Captain John Allen Bartlett of a prophetic nature in connection with the Great War. It would be the war to end all wars, ushering in an age of peace and world enlightenment. On the face of things, nothing could be more preposterous, unless we allow that the Second World War and its aftermath be regarded as a continuity of the First.

From 1920 onwards the campaign intensified: the embarrassing little man at the Abbey had to go.

Bond's sense of being the high steward of the mysteries enshrined in the ruins at Glastonbury for the age to come was absolute. He would countenance no effort to usurp him from this conviction.

Objectively, in the antagonism that arose over his future position, fault can be seen on either side. Bond frequently overstepped the mark in a way that was galling to ordinary level-headed folk; but the Diocese of Bath and Wells was equally guilty in its mean-spirited and under-handed manoeuvrings against him, much of which stemmed from the high-handed attitude of William Caroe and his advocates. There was little openness in the debate. It all became rather like some complicated game played in a maze.

In 1921 Bond was informed that Sebastian Evans had been appointed by the committee as co-director of the excavations. It was a crafty move designed to give Bond only a fifty-per-cent say in all future operations. Understandably he was outraged. A year later came the decision to dissolve the committee itself. If it no longer existed, then neither did Bond's appointment. He was told that the position had become untenable as he had been unable to co-operate with Evans - a foregone conclusion from the start, no doubt.

As ever, Bond sought allies in high places which again generated some sympathy but nothing of practical use. A token permission was given to him to have access to the Abbot's kitchen. Here he was limited to sorting small artifacts, falsely deeming this one concession as an indication of a change of heart on the part of his ecclesiastical over-seers. Even when the responsibility for future excavations passed to the Society of Antiquaries, Bond thought he might still be in with a chance. Vain hopes. In April 1924 he received official word that he could no longer hold a key to the Abbey ruins and would have to enter on the same terms as the public. He duly complied, but a further row blew up when it transpired that he still had a copy of the key in his possession. It had all become a very shabby business indeed.

The final card that Bond tried to play was born as much out of expediency and desperation than from a devotion to research.

According to one of the automatic scripts, church treasures had been buried at various places around the grounds to protect them from the despoilers at the time of the dissolution of the monasteries. Bond set up a couple of independent experiments using a dowsing rod which gave a positive indication of something under the ground at the very spots shown on his script plan. He made an approach to the trustees at Wells for permission to excavate at these locations. They refused without giving a reason. Bond then tried to override their authority by writing directly to the Archbishop of Canterbury in a very complaining letter of 30 April 1924:

> "...There is urgent need for a full enquiry if treasures of antiquity are to be saved from the hands of those who would if they could obliterate the record of all that has resulted from my work over the years. Much is already spoiled, much is not available for public view, and there has been mishandling, waste and confusion."

In all three letters were sent to the Primate through the Dean of Canterbury. The response was not unexpected:

> "I cannot see that I have any status which would call for, or indeed justify, my intervention in a matter of controversy which has arisen between the Administrative Trustees and yourself. In these circumstances you will, I hope, pardon me if I do not go into the matter."

Bond also sought the approval of another 'higher authority' in the form of an appeal to the council of the Society for Psychical Research. Here again the fair-minded Rev. Fryer was on hand to back him up:

> "Mr Bligh Bond... is anxious that the SPR authorities should come to the rescue and approach the Trustees with a request for the experiment to be made. The awkward part of the matter is that the Trustees dislike countenancing, in however small a degree, what they consider mere 'spiritualism'. But if approached by the SPR on the ground that the desired experimental excavations are for the purpose of verifying the assertions of two 'dowsers', the Trustees may be willing to give the consent asked for..."

Bond followed this up with a letter to the President of the SPR, Sir William Barrett, of 29 April 1924:

> "I thank you for the opportunity of perusing Mr Fryer's letters which I return to you with this, and would say that I am cordially in favour of a move on the part of the SPR shortly, as I consider that the matter is one which should be tested under the auspices of the leading authorities both in Psychical Research and in the realm of Archaeology...
>
> The prejudice to which Mr Fryer refers is believed to have its ground entirely in the intense dislike of the constituted authorities to anything savouring of 'psychism'. No other reason is known to exist, and I have been repeatedly told that if I gave this up, my course would be a smooth

one. I have in fact been 'bribed' to do so, with offers of a professional kind, but I have not responded to these, nor shall I..."

For another year Bond pursued his intentions with some zeal but to no avail. More experiments were carried out using various dowsers with mixed results. Then came the death of Sir William, and with it little hope of getting the Abbey Trustees to look at all favourably on his request for leave to excavate for lost treasure. Despite his despondency over this, he was still counting on a change of fortune once the agents of the Society of Antiquaries were fully in control. On 21 September, 1925, Bond wrote:

"...I never thought the Dean of Wells meant business, and with Sir William's death faded any hopes that I might have cherished. And as Sir Hercules Read was also conveniently out of the way, the old Dean thought it worth his while to make a final move and exclude me even from the Abbot's Kitchen. I had no recourse but to retire and leave the Trustees to 'stew in their own juice' - and a pretty mess they have made of it. Next year I hope we shall see a great change. The Antiquaries are men of sense and do not entertain prejudices, or at least do not allow their work to be subordinated to them."

In the event it seems the Antiquaries had no use for him either, and this in spite of the efforts of some of Bond's friends to get him elected a Fellow of the Society.

Even with the writing so plainly on the wall at Glastonbury, Bond went doggedly on in the vain hope that events might somehow still turn in his favour. But there was not much more he could do than bide his time and wait goodness-knows-how-long for any respite from his accumulated troubles.

Things might have seemed a lot worse in this time of extreme frustration had Bond not been able to make an escape at intervals to the more amenable atmosphere of London. Here the Kensington-based British College of Psychic Science was happy to employ him as editor of their journal *Psychic Science*: a congenial labour which placed him among like-minded and sympathetic friends and probably saved him from total nervous collapse. Inevitably he lost no time in using the pages of this journal to ventilate his grievances against those who had so unjustly curtailed his work at the Abbey.

In 1923 Sir Arthur Conan Doyle, who was by then President of the Council of the College, began making contributions to the journal and reportedly shared an interest with Bond in his investigative and theo-retical work. More than anyone, it was the creator of *Sherlock Holmes* who encouraged Bond to make plans for a lecture tour of America.

Bond's first links with that country had been forged back in 1908 at the time of those memorable late-night discussions with Ralph Adams Cram in the smoke-filled haze of the Guest Room at Erdington Abbey. They had kept in touch ever since, and Cram effectively became Bond's chief advocate in the United States. Perhaps it was due to his good offices that an anonymous benefactor had come forward in the early 1920s. The initial help that came from this member of the American Society for Psychical Research probably consisted of assistance with touring expenses and some publishing costs; the wherewithal for day-to-day living was still a matter for his own concern.

By coincidence it was from America that Bond had been surprised to receive a bundle of automatic scripts through the post that had much in common with his earlier work with Bartlett, and the more recent sittings with the medium known as S. They were written in a strong, colourful literary style which amplified and extended the material that Bond already had to hand. These new communications were said to be through the hand of a medium called KL in company with his friend Philip Lloyd. The latter seems to have been a pseudonym of the English-teacher and poet Thomas S. Jones, who died in 1932 and whose works were published posthumously in New York in 1937. A recurring theme of these scripts was the Grail, through different phases of time. This brought forth from Bond some comments which carry more than a hint, yet again, of criticism of that other 'Grail' episode at St. Bride's Well in 1906:

> "Its symbol is the Cup, or Chalice, and men have been prone, in their ignorance and folly, to idolize the actual vessel which was never more than the symbol of a deep truth living at the heart of the Faith... But the time is not yet right for the recovery of the concrete symbol, and will not be until men and women are strong enough and pure enough in faith to resist the temptation to idolize it."

The whole material was collected and privately published in nine small volumes as *The Glastonbury Scripts*.

Although he somehow managed to maintain a flat in London, Bond still lived mostly in Glastonbury during the unfortunate years of his decommission at the Abbey, first at Elton Cottages, near Edgarley, and then at a property in Magdalene Street called Abbots Leigh, which he

BLIGH BOND BY THE EDGAR CHAPEL AT GLASTONBURY ABBEY

set up as a guest-house, advertising it internationally as suitable for visitors wishing to explore the ancient Avalon.

It was a short-lived enterprise. Bond seems to have been placing too much store on the possible immanent receipt of a legacy from an ancient, ailing aunt. But this stalwart lady, a daughter of Admiral Francis Bond, survived well into her nineties against all expectations.

With everything going wrong in England, the chance to escape on a lecture tour far away in America was too good to miss.

Bond arrived in New York at the beginning of October, 1926. The tour took in the north-eastern states and Canada, and was a great success. He was so gratified with the warmth and generosity of his hosts that he returned for another tour in 1927. This time he met up with his old friend Ralph Adams Cram and even put in some part-time work for him as a woodwork designer. He was also introduced to the Most Reverend William Henry Francis Brothers, Vicar General of the Old Catholic Church in North America. Bond warmed to the combination of rigorous traditionalism and freewheeling liberalism that he found in this somewhat offbeat, yet inspired, prelate.

There were many other new friends; America was good to him. He decided to extend his stay, but took a short break of three weeks or so that summer to visit England to see his sister and daughter and to have a look at things in Glastonbury. He was content to find the Antiquaries doing a spot of useful excavation but noted little of special interest.

On his return to America he began to consider the possibility of applying for citizenship. But this would have required a year's sojourn in England according to the regulations. It was out of the question.

In November he was offered the post of 'Educational Director' for the American Society for Psychical Research, the prospect of which caused him to ease off his work with Cram.

Bond spent the winter lecturing and accepting the hospitality of a chain of hosts. He began to use the headquarters of the ASPR as his personal address. Meanwhile, back in England Mary had married and was expecting a child. It seemed a good enough reason to make another trip. This he did in July 1928 with his patroness footing the bill. Things were not good. Although he was pleased to now have a granddaughter, he was dismayed to find his daughter initiating divorce proceedings against her husband. He had to step in to help her and delayed his return to America by some weeks. He arrived in New York once more in September.

There were more lectures and he became increasingly involved with the ASPR, causing some consternation by his tendency to spot trickery in psychic cases which others accepted as genuine. In 1930 he became editor of the ASPR journal. Yet even here he got involved in a wrangle with the British SPR over the wholesale reproduction of large chunks of their exclusive material. Bond could not see that he was doing anything wrong: surely the furtherance of knowledge surpassed such petty considerations? The matter was eventually resolved but the London society withheld its exchange of journals with the ASPR for several months.

In August of that year, Bond wrote to Everard Fielding of the SPR:

"...Mary is coming out next month to pay me a visit here. She is very happy now with her little daughter Gabriel (now just over two years old) and her new husband Alan Saunders who is all that I could wish as a son-in-law."

Mary had married this young London schoolteacher not long after her divorce was settled. It was to be a permanent liaison although they were to have no children of their own.

These were happier times. Bond was no longer troubled by the citizenship question; he had been accepted as a non-quota immigrant, which meant he could stay in the United States indefinitely.

CHAPTER FIFTEEN

The Priest

BOND WAS NOW IN HIS LATE SIXTIES and still looking for a new direction in his life. The Right Reverend Brothers opened the way for him.

Churchmen are not usually at all happy with the techniques of psychism or any attempt to make contact with the discarnate spirits of the deceased. Brothers did not feel at all bound by such constraints and welcomed Bond's experience in these fields with the same openness as his dedication to such causes as women's rights, divorce, birth control and pacifism. As Archbishop and Metropolitan of the Old Catholic Church in America, Brothers was a free agent while remaining faithful to the core of Christian belief and practice. He had no superiors.

The Old Catholic Church in America was one of many smaller denominations in the western world which, although in varying degrees independent of each other, claimed the true apostolic succession of their bishops and priests, and were at pains to show the validity of their orders, often seeking re-consecration from as many available sources as possible to allay all doubt.

One of the primary centres of these separated apostolic lines arose when a section of the Roman Catholic Church in Holland broke away from the Holy See after the declaration of Papal Infallibility by the Vatican Council of 1870. This new body became known as the Old Catholic Church. The idea of being free from the authority of Rome readily found acceptance further afield, and Old Catholic jurisdictions soon sprang up in other countries.

Brothers was born William Henry Francis on 7 April 1887, to a Roman Catholic family living near Nottingham, England. In 1901 they moved to Waukegan, Illinois, where his father helped to establish the first mechanized lace-making factory in the country, quite probably using equipment imported from the Nottingham factory of Ernest Jardine, the purchaser of Glastonbury Abbey at the 1907 auction. Brothers was untainted by the wealth of his upbringing and had but one ambition: to lead a life devoted to religion and service to others. In 1904, Aelred Carlyle, already mentioned with regard to Bond and the bones of Richard Whiting, came over from England to seek ordination at the hands of Charles Grafton, Episcopalian (American Anglican) Bishop of Fond du Lac, Wisconsin. The ceremony was meant to be secret because the Anglican Church in England had not been willing to do it. Brothers was said to have been a witness to the covert event and was reportedly very impressed with Carlyle's vision to found an American Benedictine House at Fond du Lac. However, Dom Aelred and his monks soon returned to England and Brothers decided to form a Benedictine community of his own back in his home area of Waukegan. This was established as The American Order of St. Benedict under the protection of Bishop Grafton. At that stage it was effectively an Anglican order of a similar status to the community under Dom Aelred in England. In 1909 the community moved to Fond du Lac to be nearer to Grafton and the financial and practical support he offered. Their new building was named St. Dunstan's Abbey and Brothers was appointed Prior. Soon after this he was ordained a priest, although there is some question as to which bishop was employed. The suggestion that this might have been the French-born Old Catholic Bishop Joseph Villate seems unlikely, as he had fallen out with Grafton some years before after refusing to submit to his oversight. Other reports indicate it could have been Bishop Jan Tichy of the Polish Old Catholics in Chicago whose church was in full communion with Grafton. In 1911 St. Dunstan's Abbey was formally received into the Polish Old Catholic Church. However, the sudden death of Grafton caused the community to separate from the Anglican Episcopalians and move back to Waukegan in 1913 with Fr. William Henry Francis Brothers its Abbot. In 1916 the Old Catholic Prince-Bishop de Landas Berghes et de Rache arrived in America and took up residence at the Abbey, and is believed to have consecrated Fr. Francis (as he was generally known) as a bishop within a matter of weeks. When de Landas died in 1920, Bishop Francis was elected Archbishop and Metropolitan of the Old Catholic Church in America and set about successfully uniting all the disparate national elements into one body. In 1924 Archbishop Francis moved to New York City, from where he presided over congregations extending throughout the East and Midwest. His next move was to Connecticut.

In spite of all these ecclesiastical and monastic appointments, it might seem surprising to learn that Archbishop Francis was married, and it was in the home of this kindly Archbishop and his wife on Valley Road, Cos Cob, Connecticut, that Bond gratefully took up residence in the early 1930s.

BLIGH BOND AND ARCHBISHOP WILLIAM HENRY FRANCIS
AT COS COB, NOVEMBER 1933.

There was an affinity between the two men beyond circumstance and personality. Both reached back into the past, the one to the holy place that he believed was the birthplace of the British Church, the other to the holy tradition in its pure and primitive form as it would have been practised in those ancient times.

That was how Bond saw it: the religion practised by his Archbishop friend was as close as one was ever likely to get to the essential and authentic 'Glastonbury Christianity' of his best dreams. With a whole ocean between him and the green hills of Somerset he prepared himself for the vocation of priest in the Old Catholic Church.

The ministry was hardly a new thing in his family. The denomination might be different, but his own father had been a man of the cloth and his first cousin no less than the Reverend Sabine Baring Gould, among whose many achievements had been the composition of the hymn *Onward Christian Soldiers*. He was also a leading folklore collector. In his *Book of Cornwall*, Gould records the tradition among the tin miners that their ancestors had been taught to extract tin from the rock by Jesus, when on a visit to Britain with his uncle Joseph of Arimathea.

Up until that time Bond had been a rather lukewarm Anglican, preferring to indulge his taste for ritual within Masonic Lodges, including meetings of the *Societas Rosicruciana in Anglia*, a brotherhood of Christian Freemasons which had essayed to revive the original Rosicrucian Brotherhood of the seventeenth century.

There is a photograph of Bond and Archbishop Francis vested in priestly attire standing in the open air before a wooden Calvary and a background of winter trees. The date is given as November 1933, but this would not have been the occasion of his ordination, which is understood to have been on Trinity Sunday, 1932.

It is unlikely that Bond ever sought to exercise his ministry on behalf of any 'parish' or other community of ordinary lay folk. He could not hope to emulate the pastoral zeal of his Archbishop. He probably looked upon the office more as a kind of initiation into the deeper mysteries of the faith, the fulfilment of some long-held intellectual quest.

While still involved with the 'Benedictine' Abbey at Cos Cob, Bond was also occupied with his spiritualistic and 'psychical' interests. As Editor of the *Journal of the American Society for Psychical Research* he was having a rather bumpy ride. His opinions were not in line with the Trustees, whom he criticized for their gullibility in considering certain doubtful cases as genuine. Bond demanded they should all resign for the sake of "the reputation of the ASPR as a serious scientific body". He was probably right, but how typical of him to get into this kind of predicament. In 1935 he took the more sensible course: he resigned and they stayed.

After this he was invited to take on a new editorial post with a magazine called *Survival*. This was the journal of the Survival Foundation, Inc. which existed to assist 'the reconstruction of the spirituality of America'. Bond's finances were severely impoverished at the time. The promise of a salary of £2,400 per annum in the depressed 1930s came as a godsend. He started with high hopes which were soon dashed when the number of subscribers failed to rise above 134. There was an extended period when all efforts were made to save the venture through appeals to promoters, benefactors and others. These failed. Bond went for many months without drawing a salary. With the situation untenable, he withdrew, leaving his co-worker sort out the debts and demands for non-payment of rent and other services.

A longing to return to Glastonbury still burned within him. He began to claim that he had finished with the 'phenomenal' aspect of spiritualism. His activities belied this. If anything, the 'communications' which he considered seriously at that time were far more within the conventions of 'orthodox' mediumship than any of his earlier experiments at Glastonbury. There were even messages from his mother, telling him not to be so obstinate and get back home to England.

There was never any acrimony in Bond's church life, as far as can be judged. Archbishop Francis was too much 'his sort of person' to allow for the kind of deterioration of relations that seemed to bedevil most of his liaisons at a certain stage.

The Archbishop's further career very many years later came to have a strange, if indirect, connection with contemporary happenings at Glastonbury. If anyone deserves the title 'Honorary Avalonian' it ought to be Archbishop Francis. He was an outspoken pacifist and a campaigner for racial equality. His radical views may seem highly eccentric in the light of the sort of company he kept, hobnobbing with the richest in the land, officiating at weddings of such infamous families as the Vanderbilts and the Astors. He once told Mrs William Randolph Hearst that she ought to grant a divorce to her husband who had left her and was living with another woman. But Mrs Hearst returned to him the saying, "What God hath joined together, let no man put asunder". "Well," he replied, "obviously God didn't join you together, or you would have stayed that way."

Among the people he befriended over a huge span of years - he lived to be ninety-six - were Frank Lloyd Wright, Franklin D. Roosevelt,

Father Divine and Bob Dylan. He is said to have turned down a request to perform the marriage of Edward Prince of Wales and Mrs Simpson.

Typical of his frank speech was a comment on the position of black people in American society: "...They are discriminated against in every way, and denied most of the opportunities for culture - and then condemned for their lack of it. I find them to be a most delightful people - simple, real and profoundly religious. They have so many virtues that the white man has lost - if he ever had them."

For two years the poet Kahlil Gibran shared William Henry Francis' home at 109 East 10th Street, New York City. Francis helped him translate his work *The Prophet* into English from the Arabic.

In 1937 he moved to Woodstock, a small town host to a community of artists in the heart of New York state. He took over a former Episcopalian chapel on Mead's Mountain and began a new ministry. Later, he built a 'cathedral' lower down, and more accessible, but this was destroyed by fire along with many of its treasures. He was a skilled woodcarver, making his own church screens. It goes without saying that he and Bligh Bond found common cause here. After the fire he built a new church, mostly with his own hands. The Church of Christ on the Mount, as it was called, also became his home. In the 1960s, in the era of 'flower power', there was an influx of a large number of young 'hippies', attracted to Woodstock for its setting, its art and music, and easy-going life-style. 'Father Francis', as they called him, became their friend and confessor.

The rest of the world began, rather scornfully, to refer to Father Francis as the 'Hippie Priest'. He loved the newcomers. He wrote to one of his priests in Australia in 1963: "Awhile ago I had the church filled with young people until a quarter to ten at night. It is interesting - but very tiring."

It was still fashionable in select circles to call on Father Francis' services. In the same letter he reported that: "I have two weddings this week. One is a showy affair with many bridesmaids, etc. The groom is the brother of Updike, one of America's best-known writers. The groom is connected with the theater, hence many of the Broadway people will be here."

What William Francis found so special about the hippies was that they were just like him – at least, in their attitude to society. "They condemn militarism, materialism and competition," he wrote, "and glory in life, love, and individuality." He felt convinced that at last the Kingdom of God was coming among men.

Woodstock had become what he called 'the Hippieopolis of America'.

He was scornful of the opposition this generated in the town, of the city council working overtime enacting powers to outlaw the newcomers, of shop doors bearing signs 'No bare feet'.

Quite the same thing happened in Glastonbury in the 1970s and there are more points of similarity yet. The hills and mountains around and beyond Woodstock were sacred to the Native American people. They called them 'The Land in the Sky'. There is an Indian tale that tells of a 'Great Flood' coming down from the sky to close off the earth from the heavens. The 'breasts' of these Catskill Mountains are said to ensphere a window on to the galaxy. On this legendary terrain Archbishop Francis built his church just below the peak of Mead Mountain.

In a gesture of thanks for their friendship, and as an expression of solidarity with their ideas, Father Francis helped his hippie friends to organize a massive love, peace and music festival at Woodstock in 1969. It was the time of the Vietnam War. The compulsory drafting of all young men into the armed services was a major issue. There were endless demonstrations, protests and public draft-card burnings. The Woodstock Festival should be understood against this background. As a consequence, the congregation at the Church on the Mount grew - and so did 'Father' Francis' reputation. The scene in his church on a Sunday morning could be quite extraordinary. Nothing pleased him more than to look across the pews to see the singer Bob Dylan there, flanked by a shaven-headed Buddhist monk and an orange-robed devotee of Hare Krishna.

It is a curious fact that, silently biding their time in the archives of this rustic wooden 'cathedral' while all this was going on, was a collection of 'automatic scripts' relating to Glastonbury Abbey which had once belonged to The Right Reverend Monsignor Frederick Bligh Bond, OSB.

All sorts of other parallels with Glastonbury abound. We need look no further than the following extract from an article by Janet Day Sankey that appeared in the *Woodstock Times* for 27 September 1973. It might well be about Father Francis' Church on the Mount, but it has all the flavour of other people's thoughts on its Somerset counterpart:

"As I stood there, my speechless and spellbound state melted into something more like a feeling of perfect peace. It seemed this was a structure built to shelter the one spot on earth where all lines converge, all points intersect and, that, therefore, to simply stand there in the middle of it was to become fully integrated, at rest, and to actually experience, for a moment, Eternity."

The Woodstock Festival of 1969 is now a piece of venerable North American folklore. In 1971 came the Glastonbury Festival. It had all the stamp of the one-off Woodstock event, from which it took its cue. Originally a 'free' festival, it has since become entrenched as a more or less annual ritual; a midsummer city-size intrusion of well over 150,000 souls into a few fields around Worthy Farm, on the edge of the village of Pilton.

What was interesting about the earlier Pilton festivals was the underlying New Age mythos which provided a sense of metaphysical approbation for the event. The site was said to be on the ley line between Glastonbury and Stonehenge. But the freaky weirdnesses and casual nudity of some of those attending in the early years has long been surpassed by the vastness and international prestige of its successor – mega-bucks generated in a few days that would send a Boughton, Bond or Buckton reeling in disbelief.

In *The View over Atlantis* (1969), John Michell had shown that there was a concordance between the measures of Stonehenge and Glastonbury Abbey. This was directly extrapolated from Bligh Bond's conclusions about the gematric 'grid' at the basis of the structure of the Abbey. But it would be wrong to presume that Bond himself had failed to observe that his findings could also be applied to the proportions delineated by the old stones on Salisbury Plain. Recent research indicates that although he did understand the possibility, it was the architect Keith Critchlow, a dedicated student of Bligh Bond's work, who first set down a properly drafted plan of the measures of Stonehenge. Michell elaborated and extended Critchlow's thesis. He also explored the proportions and significance of the Great Pyramid using the same measures, and these were embodied in the famous pyramidal stage at Pilton, on which all the major performances at the festival took place. Unfortunately, this first pyramidal stage burnt down in 1994, and its replacement was built with total disregard for the original proportions. There was therefore at one time a posthumous link of Bond with the Glastonbury Festival that resonated very well with the living involvement of his old friend in the Woodstock happening.

Archbishop Francis died in July 1979 aged ninety-six. His friend, the late Orthodox Christian writer and pacifist, Mariquita Platov, had in her possession his copy of William Kenawell's *The Quest at Glastonbury*. Inside is an inscription which reads: "Frederick Bligh Bond was ordained as a priest by me and lived at my home on Valley Road, Cos Cob, Conn. W. H. Francis."

There is a certain vagueness about the extent of Bond's ecclesiastical appointments. In his book *Bishops at Large,* Peter F. Anson (one-time monk at Caldey Island, Bro. Richard Whiting), indicates that a document was drafted stating that Bond *would be* consecrated 'Vicar General of the English-speaking Congregations on the North American Continent'. Archbishop Francis saw no anomaly in the proposed appointment, and as the document implies:

> "In the enrolment of a professed psychic researcher as a member of the Apostolic Hierarchy may be seen the intention that the ancient Church now recognizes its responsibility in regard to the custody and teaching of all that pertains to the Science of the Soul and the cultivation and dispensation of the spiritual Gifts and Inspiration of seer and prophet."

Perhaps the photograph of Bond and Francis was on that occasion - presuming that it did take place.

In January 1936 Bond left America for good, returning to England full of dreams that everything was about to work out perfectly once and for all as regards Glastonbury. He believed his requests for excavation rights would be granted; the final discoveries would be made which would vindicate his claims; his life's ambition would be fulfilled and universally applauded.

For a man of his mature years it is remarkable how little any sense of realism informed his outlook. He was no doubt spurred on by promises of financial backing from his benefactors, the Van Dusens of Excelsior, Minnesota.

But he was aghast, on his return to Glastonbury Abbey, to find the ruins 'neglected' and that the apse at the end of the Edgar Chapel had been removed. Angry letters flew about to government offices, various societies, and (once again) the Archbishop of Canterbury. To be fair, the authorities did seriously consider his application to excavate once more - until someone with a longer memory reminded them of the furore his psychic methods had caused in the past. No permission was given.

After spending some time with his daughter and her family at Wimbledon, it seems he spent his remaining years in poor health living near the town of Dolgellau in North Wales, apparently sharing his accommodation with a number of other persons to whom he was known affectionately as 'Father Abbot'. Perhaps these people shared his 'Old Catholic' outlook and there was an element of seriousness in the appellation. He started painting and sketching again - accomplished and confident images of the countryside and its older buildings. It gave him much pleasure, and he confessed that it took him away from the 'Glastonbury groove' in which he brooded sadly when unoccupied. It was a time of war. At least he was far away from the air raids suffered by the major cities in those same years.

As ever, it seems he was provided-for by the charity and goodwill of others. He died of a heart attack in the Cottage Hospital, Dolgellau, on 8 March 1945. After some technical deliberations caused by his status of priest in another denomination, Frederick Bligh Bond was buried in Llanelltyd churchyard according to the rites of the Church of England. A friend recalled it as being a lovely spring day, his resting place being beneath a brilliant hedge of rhododendrons. He was eighty-two.

It might be thought that he should have been interred at Glastonbury, as had his friend, Captain John Allen Bartlett, according to his own wishes, in 1933. But such an undertaking would have been too great during the war years.

He can hardly have guessed that there was destined to be a significant revival of interest, amounting almost to a 'cult-following', in his work within a later generation.

According to most reports of his activities in England and the United States, Bond was always on the threshold of poverty. Such assessments can be very relative to different people's values. In fact, when he died, he owned a house in Wimbledon, had a quantity of furniture and held shares in the London Tin Corporation, British Plastics Ltd., EMI, Scophony Ltd., and Vine Products Ltd. He knew a thing or two about 'ordinary life' after all!

CHAPTER SIXTEEN

Avernus

FBB's daughter

W HILE MANY PEOPLE may wish for dreams or visions, Mary Bligh Bond was positively assailed by them for the whole of her life. Every thought and emotion coalesced for her into some kind of sharply defined form, burning in her mind with a force and reality greater than any object of the natural eye.

We have seen the part her visionary world played in her unsatisfactory childhood; the curious night-time visitations in her nursery and strange happenings on the school tennis court. This power of spontaneous visualization expressed itself in her great gift of draughtsmanship which she manifested without any formal guidance. She also had a way with words and a fine sense of drama; conspicuous enough talents and yet somehow the world passed her by. But a closer look at her work offers a likely explanation: the content is bizarre and almost too uncompromising in its self-authenticity, making no concession at all to the trends and tastes of the day. She had little concern for these anyway. Ecstatic deliverance into the realm of the spirit from our material world-life was her sole object; a fallen angel seeking her return. Yet she was no simple quietist contemplating an easy nirvana; the ascendant path was laid stiff with barbs and traps and menaced by unpleasant astral entities ready to drain the soul of its life and lure it from the straight and narrow path with hedonistic temptations. It was not of the mood of the times.

There was one aspect of her life that did bring at least some recognition of her gifts. This was in the field of puppetry and puppet-making. Here she won several awards and was privileged to have her creations accepted in permanent exhibitions.

There is no doubt that Mary had to endure a great deal of suffering all through her childhood years. The normally traumatic experience of being sent away to a boarding school was, for her, a welcome break from the strain of the terrible emotional battles that she found herself caught up in endlessly and uselessly even into her adult life. How good Bond ever was at consoling and reassuring his daughter is uncertain, but the impression is given that Mary much preferred his company to her mother's. Yet as she matured in years she came to judge both of them with an equally critical eye. By her own understanding of the terms, she saw her father as 'occult' and her mother as 'astral' in their inner modality. In neither case was this in any sense a compliment. In the teachings that she had taken up with such passion and devotion, these two states represented everything inimical to the spiritual progress of the soul.

Unfortunately Bond had a tendency to parade his daughter's psychic and artistic qualities to enhance his own prestige, perhaps stemming from his relatively innocent use of her at the age of thirteen to present his parchment 'Address' to the Prince and Princess of Wales on the occasion of their visit to Glastonbury for the ceremonial inauguration of the Abbey in 1909. More worrying was his fascination with her ability to act as a medium for strange music; drumming could sometimes be heard in her vicinity. She was evidently uneasy about being introduced to members of what she regarded as pretty dubious secret societies. She claimed that one of them told her she would be 'blasted to death' if she ever revealed its identity. Later, in America, she met up with what she described as 'hoodlums and gangsters'. It is hard to imagine that Bond would have knowingly placed Mary into such unwholesome company, and there was almost certainly an element of paranoia on her part.

Whatever the case, it is clear that she was far from happy with some of the experiences arranged for her by her father. There were fewer such difficulties within the field of her drawing and painting. She often staged exhibitions, hopefully to raise funds for their day-to-day needs. There would have been only a very sporadic income from such sources, yet she seems to have been unwilling to take up any kind of more mundane employment while she still lived with her father, apart from operating a small shop for a while with some friends.

As to her way with words, she was exercising herself here, too. In her early twenties she began to set down a novel based on her visionary experiences but extended into a fictionalized story form. Much of the material for this came from the time she had spent in Glastonbury. It was a period of intense activity, inwardly and outwardly. She caused a stir by decorating the walls of their cottage with extraordinary paintings of the beings that populated her psychic world. Dion Fortune was particularly impressed with Mary's work, and had the opportunity to see both her sketch-book and the mural paintings:

"Although the figures she drew were anatomically accurate, they were far from human. Strange ethereal forms of nature-spirits and demons with uncanny eyes like star sapphires flew and writhed across her pages... Strange psychic experiences, too, visited her there under the shadow of the Tor, and she has told of them in a very remarkable book, *Avernus*, a book remarkable both for its psychic record and for its literary quality."

As far as Mary was concerned, these creatures were actually *there* moving around outside herself, and not extravagant projections of her imagination. The following makes this clear:

"Then there are the people who spring from what I learned was a Saturnian hierarchy... They did not understand pain - they had no knowledge or experience of it, and compassion was not apparently of their scheme of things... In a way they were a joy, for in them was a fundamental and rich god-like humour... I remember on one of the rare occasions when I went to church, in the middle of the service I suddenly became conscious of a fiery somebody pressing against my side, whispering absurdities into my ear, bending down over me and inter-penetrating my next-door neighbour. Luckily I was kneeling and could hide my face. This was fortunate as I also had to hide my mirth."

We might well wonder how these 'Saturnian' people could make themselves understood, but Mary speaks of them as using all the 'tongues of mankind' and picking up her language from her 'brain-mind' and using it to talk with her - a process not so very different from her father's earlier theories of mediumship as being 'something furnished from the culture of our own minds'. It was the response he used to give if challenged about the unauthentic character of the language of the automatic scripts.

The impression might be given that Mary was all alone in her strange world. It was not the case; the need to share and communicate with others was strong in her. Inevitably she sought out sympathetic company - except in matters of the heart where her scorpionic temperament could lead her into difficulties. She reports that one of her closest friends was another girl who could also 'see' things. In the years after their schooldays they would go off together into wild places to watch the spirits of nature. But who was this friend she described as a 'Celt' and who had also been in touch with the other-world creatures since her babyhood, seeing them dancing over her bed at night and being able to call them? Although there is no hard evidence, it has been surmised that it might have been the young Dion Fortune, subject of our next chapter. It was a view reportedly held by at least one of the older members of her Society of the Inner Light. It has even been suggested that they could have attended the same school, each becoming a window for the other on to the spiritual world. Certainly we know they met in adulthood, and that Dion Fortune had a high regard for Mary's visionary powers, and that some of her art works are still displayed on the walls of the London headquarters of the Society of the Inner Light. But a possible youthful association would add a whole new dimension to their story.

Whether it was Dion Fortune or some other girl, the two friends often saw the same things together. Mary claimed they would go into the heart of the New Forest, away from any roads, to play with the many fauns that lived there. These seemed about three feet high, rushing lightly over glades dappled with shades and sunlight, mixing into the colours of the forest, the greens and browns of bracken and trunks and mosses and leaves. Some were transparent and some were almost invisible although quite tangible. At night their hoofs could be heard on the gravel outside their cottage or on the stairs. One even tried to pull her friend out of bed, but as she resisted him "he got tired and scuttled away".

Mary had long learnt to keep such things to herself. She could only satisfy her desire to make her experiences known to others by relating them in the form of a novel. Thus *Avernus* had its beginnings. It was a work conceived and developed, as Dion Fortune would have it, 'under the shadow of the Tor'.

Avernus is the name of a lake near Naples, the modern Lago di Averno, close to the home of the Roman poet Virgil, who died in 19 BC. It was once held to be one of the entrances to the world of the dead. Mary prefaced her book with a Latin quotation from Virgil's *The Aeneid*.

> "Easy is the descent to Avernus
> …but to retrace one's steps
> …this is the labour, this is the hard task."

Mary was very much taken up with the whole question of death. That her book should take the name of an entrance to the abode of the dead is not at all remarkable. In her puppet plays the association was continued. Her two prize-winning dolls were of Ophelia (who drowned) and Charles Stuart (who was executed). Also much commended were her dolls for the Victorian horror-story, 'Sweeny Todd, the Demon Barber of Fleet Street'.

The story in *Avernus* is strangely convoluted, and the language rich and intense and at a constant pitch. In a way Mary makes out the storyteller to be much like herself: a girl, about her own age and confronted by all manner of psychic revelations.

The other main character is another girl who first enters her life as a fellow pupil in her boarding school. This pale, fragile new friend seems to harbour many portents of her own doom. It transpires that she carries within herself an unspeakable burden of bad karma accumulated in incarnations lived in aeons long past. The story moves to the years after they have left school - perhaps at about the time when the real Mary and her friend were investigating the woodland sprites together. Does that make *Avernus* biographical? Certainly not in any literal sense, although it is possible that something of the spirit of the relationship of the two friends could be encoded in the text, particularly if extended to encompass previous incarnations. But conventional analysis is seriously skewed by the introduction of discarnate entities into the tale. By any reckoning we are in a weird and unfamiliar environment.

In the novel, the story-teller, Ignatia, has to help her stricken friend, Amelia, through the time of terrible spiritual tribulation due to be visited upon her at the coming equinox, all the while haunted by a vision she has had of her as a lifeless corpse.

The drama heightens as the fateful day draws near. The two become dominated by spirits from the past. Ignatia searches for some way of deliverance, watching and attending to her twin-soul companion as best she can:

> "Utterly ungirlish was she now, and her speech started to go away from its usual phraseology. Old, old, and yet there was about her that which was not, and never could be, age as humanity knows it - that which was young of a daedal youth, not of mortality...
>
> 'Go on, my darling,' I insisted softly; my eyes had wetted, and I saw but dizzily her brooding face.
>
> 'I have so many things to tell you,' she resumed. 'Many things - a pile of isolated scraps to piece together, and also another thing I think will happen to me, but I will tell you later. I need you, my Personage, for when the time comes (and this will be soon, for the equinox is passing), in its wake the things which will be the sum of all the other things that have happened in the past will come...
>
> She regarded me intently for a few seconds, without speaking, and

then resumed:

'You look like a medieval Spanish prince lying there, Pedro! Perhaps I am going to shock something in you when I tell you this - that it is your *sexlessness* that is so familiar? When I say 'sexlessness' I suppose I mean duality, for you are both, but you are more of a man than a woman, and to that dual You belong those things I seem to see in your face, and hear in your voice, not to 'Ignatia Muir'."

The more the two become their spiritual selves the less they keep their physical gender. They do not dispose of it altogether, but judge it differently and are less bound by it. Reincarnationists have always believed that they can be born male or female in different lives.

As the day of reckoning comes upon them the past ages are re-lived.

Angels and devils, beings of every quality, hideous and beautiful, contend for the soul of Amelia. It is up to Ignatia to urge her to resist the terrible fascinations that have always been her ruin:

"She told me of blasphemies, of orgies of unspeakable sin, outrages done, devilries, the bringings of pestilences, cruelties done to the minds of many, and to the bodies of many - she told me of flesh bred of obscene matter, of degradations, and animal victims used for hideous purposes...

Inevitably the physical body of Amelia dies, her spirit once and for all redeemed and restored to the angelic plane, the final battle won. Ignatia feels the loss of her soul mate and dwells darkly on her own demise - the one gateway to their re-union. When she goes she will leave Ignatia, her name in this present incarnation, behind her:

"Soon I think I shall depart from Ignatia. Although the time has not been given me, it is apparent in this rapid decline... I thought at first that it might be years, but with this wasting came the knowledge that it was no far-off day They meant, when They said I should see Them in the dawn... The tonic I need is the unlatching of a door and the relief of a heavy overcoat removed.

I think of so many things as I sit here. Of the numberless races of the universe, and the smallness of this planet. Of the nameless lovely things that people label with small names, and of little silly laws laid down by man, or with one fraction of himself that he sees and thinks the whole! Devils, angels, shee: all are the same in that great Source, for one is the other, and yet each can be apart and separate.

Nine days have I counted since the day of Poppy's burning. Nine days have I been writing this. It is the ninth evening, merging into the tenth morning...

Somehow I think I may open eyelids upon a dawn I long to see. Through my window I catch a glimpse of a royal dim heaven, remote and majestic; and in its imperial blue the Milky Way has spread its carpet of stars. It is frosty tonight. May the dawn be one painted by the gold-mist of great Helios, as he rises smiling over the ball of the world, bringing day, and light, warmed by his breath. I have just looked in the glass again. Hypolyte is very evident, and Ignatia looks like dead!

Nine days! Is not nine the number of the sons of God?"

So ends Mary's strangely beautiful and somehow primordial tale, *Avernus*. Uncomfortably self-centred and yet expansively universal - dare we say 'cosmic'? - at the same time. It distils the mythic scale down to the level of individual soul-experience. It is also a 'confession': a statement of that stage in her life before moving forward to fulfil herself as a woman and mother - and to seek to embrace a more spiritual dimension of *being*.

However much she sought to gain the spiritual heights, Mary was never wholly released from the spell of Avernus. It was herself, her own nature in high relief.

When her father moved to America Mary became free to make her own way in the world. But she entered into a marriage which went wrong very quickly. It was a liaison which Bond may not have liked. He seemed very ready to extend a visit to England in 1928 in order to help her through her divorce. Even so, Mary born him his only grandchild, Gabriel Heliodora Angela.

Two years later there was a second marriage. Bond looked upon this new relationship far more approvingly.

Alan G. P. Saunders is remembered as a good-looking, 'hearty' individual with a liking for rather ferocious sports cars and a tendency to make fun at other people's expense. He humoured, but distanced himself from, his wife's spiritual interests and evidently indulged her eccentric taste in home-decor.

In this same year of her marriage to Alan Saunders, Mary became a member of The Order of the Cross, a mystical fellowship founded some years before by the Reverend J. Todd Ferrier, a Scottish Congregation-alist who had to forsake his ministry at Paignton, Devon, after experiencing revelations which compelled him to redefine the whole of Judaeo-Christianity in terms of the human soul and the spiritual history of the planet. Mary identified totally with Todd Ferrier's 'inner' illuminations and found his insistence on the necessity to adopt a vegetarian diet to be quite in line with her own feelings about animal exploitation.

It was the parting of the ways for Mary and her father; her spiritual position was now radically different from his. For all his interest in psychical research, Frederick Bligh Bond was a traditionalist in church matters; his quest was to seek the heart of the apostolic faith - and to show that Glastonbury had played a part in that faith from its earliest beginnings.

Todd Ferrier's teaching was superficially not unlike Theosophy, but different in important aspects. Its starting point was the Bible, both the Old and New Testaments, but in a 'restored' form, re-interpreted to show its original purpose: to reveal by means of allegory and symbol the pathway of the soul towards the transcendent realization of its divine birthright. A full acceptance of the doctrine of reincarnation was essential to any understanding of this esoteric revision of familiar sacred texts. Just as the characters in Mary's novel had interacted and worked through their destiny in countless lives in the past, so Todd Ferrier taught that all souls had lived through many aeons of time. It might suggest some affinity with Eastern thinking. However, his view of the material world accorded more with the presentation in the book of Genesis of something having 'gone wrong' with creation, causing a 'fall', or loss of contact with the divine source, than with the oriental supposition that matter is necessary as a sort of proving-ground for souls. He held that, through an abuse of the gift of free-will, an element of the angelic hierarchy had de-polarized the spiritual life-stream that nourished our planetary system with disastrous consequences for all. Life ceased, and the previously vitalized elements of the planet were reduced to a state of fixity leading to the geological epochs and the evolutionary development of life forms understood by science.

Mary attended Todd Ferrier's lectures and the services of worship of the Order with great devotion as often as she could. The Order was totally egalitarian in the sense that it had no appointed ministers. Members simply took turns to act as ministrants in the services, which followed a pattern similar to that of many Christian churches. There was a dressed altar, with a central cross and candlesticks, and familiar hymns, prayers and psalms were employed - albeit with some modification to the received versions.

God, as the 'Father-Mother', was both male and female. Woman was exalted as the representation of the intuition and the human soul.

Everything was placed on a new level of meaning. Christ and Mary symbolized, along with most of the personal names given in the Scriptures, spiritual qualities and not historical figures. Christ was the 'Divine Principle' within the being of Mary, the Soul - or 'Maria', as Todd Ferrier usually gave it. This Latinized form gave the name a poetic edge which appealed to Mary Bligh Bond. After her marriage she preferred to be known as Maria Saunders - particularly within the fellowship of the Order of the Cross.

In 1931 Mary (Maria, if you will) took her small daughter with her on a six-week visit to America. Grandfather Bond was naturally delighted to see them both. This successful trip seems to have prompted them to return the following year. This time Mary left Gabriel with her grandfather and arrived back in England alone. The child was away for nearly a year. It may seem a long time for such a young child to be without its mother, but certainly she would have been made a great fuss of. By then Bond was thoroughly involved with the small 'Benedictine' community at Cos Cob. In a letter dated December 15, 1933, he wrote to a friend: "I have the satisfaction of having my little grandchild with me and we shall probably go out to the Abbey for Christmas Day."

Once back in England, Gabriel would be taken along to Todd Ferrier's special children's services; any discrepancy between his esoteric view and the more traditional practices she had witnessed at Cos Cob being lost on one of her tender years.

For her part, Maria Saunders, a regular attender of meetings and gatherings', had become something of a 'character' among the Order members. Her highly individual temperament and manner of dressing - even her preference for wearing slacks caused raised eyebrows - contrasted with the more 'spiritual' diaphanous attire favoured by most of the female membership. Above all, her art works were held to be too 'astral' and not enough 'spiritual'. Members of the Order used to warn each other to avoid reading Avernus, seeing it as something all too dark and sinister and a threat to their spiritual wellbeing. She was not too dismayed by these attitudes, and in turn privately regarded most of *them* as being too fundamentalist and meekly passive to Todd Ferrier's teaching. In time, some of the more independent free spirits of the Order sought each other out. Among these was John Foster Forbes.

Forbes hailed from a minor aristocratic Scottish family with its seat at Rothiemay Castle in Aberdeenshire. He had joined the Order after being greatly helped through an illness and some sort of mid-life crisis by some kindly members who had befriended him in Scotland. He was very taken up with prehistory, and sought to apply what he had learnt from Todd Ferrier about the Fall of the planet and the magnetic potency of ancient rocks to the question of the true purpose of the stone circles and megaliths of pre-Roman Britain. This interest alone tended to set him aside from the rank-and-file membership, but gave him common ground with the interests of Maria Saunders. The two of them could always be found chatting earnestly on the sidelines at any social gathering of the Order.

Todd Ferrier died in 1943. In the years after the founder's passing, Maria, Forbes and one or two others tended to become even less involved in the life and administration of the Order at its headquarters at 10 De Vere Gardens, Kensington. They made the acquaintance of Antony Bates, a young artist member who provided the illustrations for one of Forbes' books, *Ages Not So Dark*. Indeed, art was a common interest.

In her own work, Maria did not invent the scenes or figures she depicted: she drew or painted what she *saw*. In this she had something in common with that other great artist of vision, William Blake. It even prompted some to make the suggestion that she might be the reincarnation of Blake. Maria was quick to refute this - only to re-open the speculation by intimating that she had a much greater affinity with Blake's close friend, the writer and painter Henry Fuesli. In yet another 'life' she felt she had been the great woman poet of classical Greek times, Sappho of Lesbos.

Forbes, too, was a passable watercolourist, and privately published a book on his wet-paper technique, *The Art of Atmospheric Landscape Painting*. He was also a poet and self-taught organist. For many years he lived by schoolmastering, but gave this up in later life for anything that came along: odd-jobbing, gardening, and even working as a costume model for art students. He would hold forth - while the 2B pencils worked earnestly over his remarkably bony profile - in cultivated, resonant tones that belied his Scottish origins, on whatever subject took his fancy: UFO's; the diet of his corgi dog; phrenology; the risk to the equilibrium of celestial bodies by space travel; and more. He published a small-circulation-journal, *Avalon*, devoted to metaphysics and prehistoric research.

Like all members of the Order of the Cross, Maria, Forbes and Antony Bates were strictly vegetarian, teetotal and non-smoking. They were dedicated anti-vivisectionists. Here Maria employed her artistic talents to serve the cause. She and Antony worked together on puppet shows and staged a joint exhibition of their paintings in an art shop in Barnes, which was opened by Annette Mills, creator of the popular

MARY BLIGH BOND (LEFT) WITH ANNETTE MILLS AND ANTHONY BATES

television puppet, *Muffin the Mule*. This was in 1953. By that time Forbes was chiefly exercising himself on the current debate about UFO's and extraterrestrials. He was probably one of the first to speculate on the significance of UFO sightings in close proximity to prehistoric sites. He moved to Brighton where he somehow survived on next-to-nothing in a caravan. Independent in the extreme, he even refused to draw his state pension as a point of principle. He spent his last year in a one-room flat in Regency Square overlooking the West Pier and the sea. He died in 1958 aged 69.

Maria and Alan Saunders lived all their married life together in a house owned by Frederick Bligh Bond at 2, St. Johns Road, Wimbledon. "The sort of place where you might be given a cup of coffee in a flower pot", was how one member of the Order of the Cross remembered it. Quite a bit of Bond's own furniture was kept there, but inevitably Maria put her stamp on the interior scheme. The walls of the sitting room were covered in red silk; a sedan chair stood in the corner; 'Atlantean masks', which she had herself made, added to the strange atmosphere, together with an extraordinary lampshade depicting the drowning Ophelia.

Maria always used her maiden name in her artistic work. Mary Bligh Bond was prominent in the puppet theatre world in the post-war years. Her puppets of Charles Stuart and Ophelia won the Davidson Trophy in the national competition for glove puppets in 1946/7. Photographs of her Sweeny Todd puppets were included in the Puppetry Year Book for 1947. She also performed puppet plays with her husband at such events as the Annual Exhibition of the British Puppet and Model Theatre Guild.

As a sculptor she occasionally undertook commissions for various church authorities. She used to colour the finished pieces in the manner of the ancient Greeks.

The dichotomy between the astral and the spiritual is one which has vexed and challenged mystics and visionary artists for generations. The one is so often confused with the other. Maria was as troubled as many in this regard. It was something she never resolved. Her friend Antony Bates observed this dilemma: "Poor Maria was always seeking the sublime and coming up against the most terrible opposites. She said one of her main tasks in this life was to distinguish the Divine and Celestial Voices from the merely Astral. Todd Ferrier told her that when her time came to arise she would know with certainty." That time came for Maria in 1969. Her husband Alan followed her a year later soon after retiring from Rokeby School, Kingston-upon-Thames.

CHAPTER SEVENTEEN

The Changeling

I T WAS DION FORTUNE who coined the term 'Avalonians' for the particular generation of Glastonbury seekers that she found herself among.

She arrived rather late on the scene: the people of the Cup had long since gone; Bligh Bond was in the throes of his despair with the Abbey authorities; Alice Buckton had been at the Chalice Well for some seven years; Rutland Boughton's festival movement would soon be an item of history.

Bond, Buckton and Boughton were people she knew. She saw the worth of what each was achieving. How they viewed her is unsaid.

Dion Fortune was a complex and powerful occultist who was moved to make her inspirations known to a wider public. She was dedicated to a degree that leaves little else to discuss in connection with her. Her life revolved around her magical groups and her writings. Her real name, until her marriage to Dr Penry Evans in 1927, was Violet Mary Firth.

Just around the corner from Kitty Tudor Pole at Tudor Cottage was Sollershott Hall. Originally named Homesgarth, it was a venture of Letchworth Cooperative Houses Limited and consisted of a number of sensible two- and three-storey gabled brick-built terraced houses arranged around a quadrangle with one side partly open. There was originally a shared central heating system and a communal dining room. Ebenezer Howard had lived in one back in the early days. In the 1920s a retired couple made their home there. The woman of the couple told Kitty a strange tale.

Evidently, very soon after the birth of her daughter something had happened to convince her that the child was a changeling: as if its soul had been snatched away and replaced with another. This mother was Sarah Firth; her child was Violet Mary.

There had long been a rumour in occult circles that Dion Fortune was the result of such an act of fey intervention. It was not a story always seriously believed outside her inner circle - but few people had had the opportunity to meet Mrs. Firth. Had they done so they might have viewed this extract from DF's novel *Moon Magic* as something more than fiction:

> "…I was supposed to have died as a baby. I was declared dead and lay dead for many hours in my mother's lap, for she could not be persuaded to put me down; and at dawn I revived, but the eyes that looked at my mother, she told me many years afterward when I asked her the cause of my strangeness, were not the eyes of a child, and she knew with the unerring instinct of a mother that I was not the same one."

Violet was a Firth of the Firth Sheffield Steel family - or at least her grandfather was. It was something she liked people to know. She always thought of herself as a Yorkshire woman even though she had never lived there.

Her father, Arthur Firth, practised for a while as a solicitor before marrying Sarah Jane Smith, daughter of a fellow Yorkshireman who ran a hydropathic therapy centre at Limpley Stoke near Bath. Arthur threw in his lot with his in-laws in Somerset, but before long moved with them to operate a similar enterprise in North Wales.

Violet was born on 6 December 1890 at the seaside resort of Llandudno. Yet for all her early years spent there and the fact that she later married a Welshman, she never identified herself with the land of the dragon. She took the simplistic line that the British were neatly divided into Celts and Saxons. She distinctly placed herself with the latter (although the Firths were more probably of Viking descent). She felt that the two races were so far apart temperamentally that it was 'almost impossible for the one to judge the other'.

The call to write came early to her. She had acute powers of visualization, describing 'brightly coloured pictures' rising in the 'magic lantern' of her young mind. She saw strange places and strange people, and came to believe that these were visions of the lost land of Atlantis.

When she was still quite young the family moved back to Somerset, and Weston-super-Mare, the town where Mary Tudor Pole had canvassed for the cause of animal welfare. Here she completed her schooling and became aware of the magic of the West Country landscape and coastline. At the age of sixteen, Violet and her family moved yet again - to London.

The Firths were followers of Mary Baker Eddy's Christian Science, and Violet was well-grounded in its precepts, but once she began to make her own way in life she was soon drawn away to alternative sources of spiritual sustenance.

At the age of twenty, Violet entered Studley College, a horticultural training centre for young women in Warwickshire. Although in some respects it was a useful and formative time for her, the experience was far from being a happy one. Within eighteen months she had satisfactorily completed her studies and readily accepted an invitation to join the staff. It was about this time that she began to be seriously troubled by the controlling and bullying temperament of the warden, Dr Lilias Hamilton. Things reached such a pitch that she was brought to a position of almost total nervous collapse. She was only saved from further distress by removing herself from the place in 1913. She later declared that it had taken her a full three years to recover from the ordeal.

In matters politic and patriotic Violet was a traditionalist. In 1914 she willingly offered her services to the national war effort and, with thousands of other young women, joined the Land Army, replacing the farm workers who had been sent to the Front in Europe. After a spell on a farm she was assigned to a laboratory job, where she had to watch over bacterial cultures brewing in an incubator. Here she discovered a method of making cheese from soya bean milk. Her widely acclaimed book, *The Soya Bean: An Appeal to Humanitarians*, published in 1925, gave an account of the process and its ethical merits as a vegetarian protein substitute.

Even after the war, Violet was still troubled with the emotional damage she had suffered at the training centre. To try to get to the bottom of her malaise, she started to study psychology. In a remarkably short time, after training in London as a lay analyst, she felt she was sufficiently prepared to take on her first patients. Anyone could do this in those days. There were no formal controls on what was regarded as a slightly 'weird' activity on the margins of conventional medical practice. In no time she was making quite a bit of money for herself.

Perhaps it was a natural progression - at least for Violet Firth - from psychology to occultism. Although both defer to the hidden forces that inform the appearances of life, the phenomena of psychology emerge from the depths of the individual psyche; the phenomena of the occult are understood as invisible forms and powers *outside* and *beyond* the psyche - although they may primarily engage it at the unconscious level. For Violet the two were quite compatible. She learnt to interpret 'occultism in the light of psychology and psychology in the light of occultism, the one counterbalancing and explaining the other'. It was not always so. She admitted that when she first encountered members of the Theosophical Society she regarded nearly all of them as pathological cases, much in the way of her own patients.

There were three groups that offered Violet what she was looking for in the field of occult knowledge. The first was a small band of neophytes gathered round 'Dr' Theodore Moriarty, an Irish-born Rosicrucian Freemason who had arrived in England from South Africa during the war. The second was the Hermetic Order of the Golden Dawn, still flourishing in 1919 despite internal wrangles and the demise of some of its earlier members. Thirdly, and notwithstanding her first impressions, there was the Theosophical Society.

Moriarty taught a kind of westernized Theosophy which made much of the Atlantis story and believed in a 'Christ Principle' which had manifested itself through 'advanced souls' down the ages; Horus, Buddha and Mithras were 'Christs' by this analysis - as well as Jesus.

There were numerous stories about Moriarty's powers, how he could ward off demons and disperse malevolent astral entities. He conducted magical rituals before his small group of followers dressed in elaborate 'Egyptian' and 'Atlantean' garb.

Moriarty died in 1923, a lasting influence on Violet's life and work. Her novel, *The Secrets of Dr Taverner*, is acknowledged as a respectful exposé of her mentor and his methods.

In 1919 Violet was initiated into the Alpha and Omega Temple of the Hermetic Order of the Golden Dawn. It meant she had to take a magical name for herself. Those who already had a motto in the family would normally use that. For the Firths this was 'Deo non Fortuna' - and that was how Violet was known to her fellow magicians from that point on. It was just a very small step to modify it to Dion Fortune - neater, tripping better off the tongue, but no longer translatable as anything in particular.

One of the most worthwhile benefits of her time in the Golden Dawn was the instruction she received in the Hebrew Kabbalah, or Tree of Life, a glyph of the chain of creation, or, conversely, a system defining the return path of the soul to its creator. This specifically 'western' approach to meditation which came out of Jewish mysticism is well documented elsewhere, including DF's own *The Mystical Qabalah* (1935).

DF (as she was known from then on) was a spiritual pragmatist: she would only extract out of any metaphysical system those bits of it which she judged *real* and useful to her. In the case of Theosophy there was plenty to question and dispose of. It is surprising that she went into it at all considering her refusal to accept that Madame Blavatsky's

Himalyan 'Masters' had a physical existence from which their spirit-forms journeyed around the world giving their teachings through chosen adepts who just happened to be senior luminaries within the Theosophical Society. But the call had come from the Inner Planes; she had to obey.

Most members of the TS at that time had been taken in by the claim that a young Indian, Jiddhu Krishnamurti, was the 'World Teacher' for the coming age. Plucked from his family in his boyhood by C. W. Leadbeater and other Theosophical birds-of-prey and subjected to a special programme of 'education' appropriate to his calling, he later rebelled against the whole charade. Many were profoundly disillusioned, attacking Leadbeater for the *bête-noire* that he had always been. But DF had shunned him all along.

As regards Blavatsky, DF was more ambivalent. She saw that they had fought a common battle against the same prejudices and for the same ends. Both had campaigned for the Women's Mysteries. After all, HPB's seminal work, written in the previous century, had been called *Isis Unveiled.* Isis, the goddess within the Egyptian trinity of Isis-Osiris-Horus was judged the intuitive gateway to all secret knowledge. During the gestation of her opus, Blavatsky described 'living in a kind of permanent enchantment' while she watched the 'fair goddess'. Dion Fortune's biographer, Alan Richardson, has shown engagingly how much DF, too, was in the thrall of the goddess, resurrecting her in a temple dedicated to the 'Mysteries of Isis' in London in the late 1930s.

Amid the tangles and schisms of the TS, there was one pillar of light for DF: the Christian Mystic Lodge.

The Lodge was established in 1919 with the object of 'Interpreting Christianity in terms of Theosophy and Theosophy in terms of Christianity'. Over the span of its life it gradually became more Christian, more mystical and less Theosophical. From January to July 1927 DF found herself President of the Lodge, using the pages of its journal to lambast the cliques and hypocrisies she found within the TS, particularly as regards Leadbeater and the Liberal Catholic Church and its attitude to the World Teacher movement. What she was looking for was a kind of 'Protestant', even Quaker-style, reformation of TS esoteric Christianity as practiced by the Liberal Catholic Church, free from its male priestly intermediaries and awe of the Apostolic Succession. Quite a bit of trouble ensued. DF left the Theosophical Society and The Christian Mystic Lodge to form her own, independent, Community of the Inner Light in 1927. By 1929 she had left the Golden Dawn, too.

Someone who saw, and helped, DF through all these vicissitudes was Charles Thomas Loveday. Sixteen years older than his friend, he was her planner and provider over many years. Employed as some kind of fairly senior functionary within London Tramways, he also had property - and money. He had been with her in the Christian Mystic Lodge (taking the motto *Amor Vincit Omnia*) and was effectively, with DF, a co-founder of the Community of the Inner Light. They first met by chance in Glastonbury in 1922, while each was paying a moonlight visit to Chalice Well.

In *Avalon of the Heart,* her personal view of Glastonbury and its spiritual history, DF tells of walking to the Abbey one morning with Frederick Bligh Bond after seeing some automatic scripts the night before. She claims she watched pegs being put down in the turf according to the instructions and saw the excavator's picks strike the lost footings of an ancient chapel "in less than twenty minutes". Allowing that *Avalon of the Heart,* for all its real value and poetic appeal, is chock full of charming inaccuracies and simplifications, we must take this account with a fair pinch of salt. It could suggest a date of around 1919 or 1920, when Bond was still excavating the Loretto Chapel.

Interestingly she deals with the story of the Cup and Bride's Well. Something of the general line of events is there, but the details are hopelessly compounded and confused.

DF wrote elsewhere that the Atlanteans had a 'Moon-Bowl' which had within it a substance 'in actual contact with the Supernal'. Through man's sins the Cup or Bowl was withdrawn to become the object of the Eternal Quest presented in the Grail legend. One would have thought she could have made more of the possible connection with Goodchild's Cup. Of course, she may well have done so. It would not necessarily have been put into print; possibly it was more a subject for her inner circle of initiates to consider.

Sometimes DF stayed at Alice Buckton's Guest House at Chalice Well, and other times at an old farmhouse opposite, in Chilkwell Street. Here she once encountered a salamander, or 'fire-spirit', which appeared out of the fire in the hearth, "two and a half feet long from nose to tail, of an elephant-grey colour, the ridges of its neckfolds and back edged with glittering ruby light". It even flopped down the stairs after her exactly "like a dachsund". Back in London, its presence was with her for several weeks, but it disappeared for good when the time came for her to pack for the next visit to Glastonbury.

However close DF was to Loveday, theirs was not the sort of relationship that would lead to marriage. The person that she *did* marry was

<u>Thomas Penry Evans,</u> a medical practitioner and son of a South Wales tin-shearer.

Evans was a bright-minded Celt, a Christian to a degree but with a strong leaning towards Pagan magic. However simplistic DF's division of the British into fair Saxons and dark Celts, they exemplified it. The marriage breathed new life into her work but brought antagonism into her life. They were two impossibly strong characters. <u>By 1938,</u> after almost twelve years together, <u>he had left her.</u>

DF was always on the move - but not to many places. Usually only two places: <u>London and Glastonbury.</u> By a rather circuitous route one used to be able to get to Glastonbury by train from London. But in *Avalon of the Heart* it is plain that she knew it better as a road journey:

> "The long road from London spans the breadth of England and leads from one world to another. The narrow and difficult streets of the city give place to the Great West Road - a name magical in its very syllables, and magical too in its great undulating breadth for those who have eyes to see. It turns off from the heavy traffic of Chiswick, lifts to a bridge, and London is left behind...
>
> The road leads for a time through the flat valley-bottom of the Thames. Elms are its trees, and the country is unlovely with the marshalled utility of market-gardens, sad because they are falling on decay, for the tide of houses is sweeping over them, and no one cares to tend the worn-out trees when next year's crop may never be gathered."

DF's description rhapsodizes lovingly over the swift-changing features of the countryside. Like the climax of some great symphony, she closes on her final cadences:

> "The last barrier of hills is climbed, and the road descends in three great steps towards the alluvial levels that were once all salt-marsh and tidal-estuary. The wide flat plain stretches out in the evening light. Smoke hangs over the clustering hamlets that lie thick in this rich land. Here and there on its expanse rise sudden hills, still called islands hereabouts, where some eddy of the slow Severn tide laid down its silt. Upon one side the line of the <u>Poldens</u> guards the levels; upon the other, the <u>Mendips.</u> Beyond is the sea, hidden by the grey mist of distance. In the middle of the plain rises a pyramidal hill crowned by a tower - the Tor of <u>Glastonbury!"</u>

Loveday was the proud possessor of one of those large, powerful

PENRY AND VIOLET EVANS (DION FORTUNE) AT CHALICE ORCHARD.

Harley-Davidson motorcycles that were sometimes a feature of our roads in the 20s and 30s. The late Harry Carter, of Chilkwell Street, remembered it shuttling to-and-fro past his house, its sidecar loaded with provisions from the town. It would be yet another noble example of the total chivalric devotion Amor Vincit Omnia had for his High Priestess to picture them both thundering along the road to the west past the dread 'temple of blood' at Stonehenge (that was how DF saw it), faces set towards the setting sun in grim anticipation of some sure encounter with the Old Gods on the Hill of Vision at Avalon. Perhaps, if she went with her husband, Penry, DF enjoyed the luxury of a car-ride.

Loveday had already provided the needful funds for DF's London base at 3 Queensborough Terrace, and, despite the credit she seems to claim for herself in *Avalon of the Heart,* was also responsible for getting hold of the forty-foot wooden army building that became her Glaston-bury base from 1924 onward. He watched over its eventual installation on the lower slopes of the Tor, just over the way across Well House Lane from Chalice Well.

People living nearby found cause for gossip. Groups would arrive, spend the weekend there and disappear off again, leaving it empty. It was thought they came there to have 'parties'. The truth of it might not have been any less strange.

By 1928 it was being generally advertised as The Chalice Orchard Club, open throughout the summer season as a hostel and pilgrimage centre.

Glastonbury was everything to DF, but she still needed to work from her London headquarters. She was never permanently at Chalice Orchard and not at all a contributor to local community life in the way that Alice Buckton was. She was there more for her own purposes. She often spoke of how the 'veil was thin' at Glastonbury, and that more had been revealed to her within the bounds of Avalon than anywhere. She visualized a polarity between Glastonbury and London. The 'Inner Adepts' had told her that 'Glastonbury supplies the force for the forms that are built in London'.

While visiting with Loveday in the winter of 1922/23 she believed she had found her own 'western' Masters. Unlike the adepts of the Theosophists, there was no suggestion that these presences had any kind of contemporary physical existence elsewhere. But they were an oddly assorted trio: the philosopher Socrates; a former Chancellor of England in the sixteenth century, Lord Erskine; and a young officer killed in the Great War, David Carstairs. Thomas Erskine was considered to have been a reincarnation of Henry VIII's adversary, Sir Thomas More. Before that he had been Thomas a Becket.

From Socrates issued *The Cosmic Doctrine*, DF's intricate presentation of the obscure processes at the beginning of Creation, through to the laws governing the spiritual powers which overshadow our planetary existence.

Loveday was only ever a grudging pagan; his greatest loyalty remained with the Master Jesus, as esotericists called Him, and in the 1930s he helped to form The Guild of the Master Jesus within the Fellowship of the Inner Light, which offered 'adoration and service to our Lord, and seeks to know Him as the Risen Christ, the Unseen Companion of the Heart, the Master of Love and Compassion, the Great Initiator of the West'. Quite in the tradition of Christian Orthodoxy, save for the final endowment.

If Loveday was her companion on the Christian path, DF shared her pagan sentiments with Penry Evans. Here she seemed to find greater energy, particularly as a fount of inspiration for her novels. In *Priestess,* Alan Richardson has shown how a strand of autobiography runs through these tales, drawn from her life's experience both on the inner and outer planes:

> "Had Dion devoted her formidable and considerable talents to writing, pure and simple, she would have been a great novelist by orthodox standards; or if not a novelist in the first division, at least a promotion challenger from the second. As it was, in her last two novels, *The Sea Priestess* and *Moon Magic*, she achieved greatness within the genre. Quite simply these are the finest novels on magic ever written. Really, looking around at the competition, they are the only novels on magic ever written.
>
> In order, her output was as follows: *The Winged Bull* 1935; *The Goat-foot God* 1936; *The Sea Priestess* 1938; *Moon Magic* 1939/40. It was reputed that the latter was begun shortly after *The Sea Priestess*, but not completed until a year or so after her death, thanks to the mediumship of a woman who, originally, had started off in 3 Queensborough Terrace as a maid."

Granted DF was an occultist, but within that persuasion was she more Christian or Pagan? It seems she needed both. The power and attraction of the energies of Nature and the Old Gods had a great appeal to her, but one always senses the ascendancy of the power of Christ. She says as much in her handbook, *Psychic Self Defence*.

"The occultist does not ignore the Christ-force, however; he recognizes it as among the hierarchy of supreme forces of the universe, although he may not be prepared to assign to it the exclusive position which it occupies in the heart of the Christian mystic...

It should be invoked in every operation of psychic self-defence where any human element, incarnate or discarnate, is concerned."

Perhaps the clearest exposition of her attitude is found in the following unpublished extract of 1927:

"There are two aspects of force with which the soul functions, astral force and spiritual force. Christianity has for its work the manifesting of spiritual force to mankind, and nature worship has for its task the manifesting of elemental force, and both these types of force are necessary for the full functioning of the soul. Rome forgets this, and therefore crushes the human soul out of shape with her discipline. We, if we want to manifest human life at its highest aspect, must not only be Christians, but also pagans, for these two aspects of religion concern the two aspects of man's nature, the individuality and the personality. It is the task of Christianity to bring the Godhead down into manhood, but it is the task of paganism to bring manhood up to Godhead, and only as the task is pushed from both ends will it ever be completed at the central point of balance."

In Glastonbury she found the two forces in equilibrium: the Pagan Tor and Well; the Christian Abbey and its environs:

"Two traditions meet in Avalon - the ancient faith of the Britons, and the creed of Christ. The older, its relics obliterated, its legends bent to a Christian purpose, is shadowy and veiled. Only here and there do we see clearly the lineaments of the ancient creed; but a veiled figure can be seen in the darkness of the racial memory, and its dim but awful presence is alive...

The Abbey is holy ground, consecrated by the dust of the saints; but up here, at the foot of the Tor, the Old Gods have their part. So we have two Avalons, 'the holyest erthe in Englande', down among the water-meadows; and upon the heights the fiery pagan forces that make the heart leap and burn. And some love the one, and some love the other."

Most of the war years DF was in London. She and her friends were bombed out of 3 Queensborough Terrace and had to move down the road. As in 1914, the plight of her beloved country called for some kind of service. She was not old, but nothing like the fit young woman she had been in 1914. This time, she invoked the 'Watchers of Avalon', the secret guardians of the nation, to its defence. She did this by an inspired act of magical administration, sending an open letter to her membership each week, to be opened simultaneously at a given time. All would concentrate, 'tuning-in' to each other and the group-soul of Britain. Before long they were claiming success; certain national figures began to make influential speeches that seemed to echo the private contents of the circulated letters.

For their invocation, the membership visualized timeless archetypal beings framed within a cavern deep in a mythic hill for which the Tor at Glastonbury was the outer representation: Arthur, Merlin, the Virgin Mary, and, above this trinity, the Master Jesus. DF accepted it was an audacious thing to do, untrained as some of them were. But others were risking far more in the skies, on the seas, and on foreign soil.

Like confronted like. DF believed that dark occult forces were being used by the Nazis which had to be met on their own level. Hers was not the only effort being made to fight this secret war; such strategies as Tudor Pole's Big Ben Silent Minute of prayer and endeavours by other occultists to project a magical shield around the British Isles all contributed, they believed, to the final victory.

London in those years was a place of danger, drama and uncertainty for anyone who chose to remain there. DF had real contact with human tragedy and loss. In such conditions her emotional strength and wisdom served her well, no less than when her friend and solicitor, Harold Rubinstein, told her in August 1943 that one of his sons had been killed on active service in North Africa. There was just one way for her to help her friend and his other two sons in their loss: she made Chalice Well available to them as a place of refuge and quiet for a few days. Rubinstein's hobby was writing one-act plays, many of which were broadcast by the BBC. Later that year he sent DF one entitled *Holyest Erth,* which had been inspired by his visits to Chalice Well and was built around the tradition of the arrival of Joseph of Arimathea at Glastonbury. Her response is noteworthy for its defence of traditional Christian sentiment: "I am doubtful if the play in its present form could be broadcast as it would offend orthodox opinion too much".

Rubinstein's play is set on the lower slopes of the Tor close to Chalice Well. The Druid priest Arviragus and his small family are the sole remaining occupants of this island surrounded by sea-marshes. Others from the community have fled for fear of a Roman attack. News comes that Arviragus' son has died in battle. Soon after this a weary stranger arrives who turns out to be Joseph of Arimathea bringing with him the cup of the Last Supper. He speaks of the death of Jesus and confesses to having removed his Body from the rock tomb himself, giving rise to the false belief among His followers of His Resurrection. In truth he had simply placed It in another tomb. It was on this particular point of heresy that DF became worried. The play unfolds into a discussion about the merits of Ancient British, Jewish and Christian beliefs. In fact, this was the author's motive for writing the collection of eight short plays he called *Hated Servants*, of which *Holyest Erth* is the most significant for us here. For Rubinstein it was part of a personal journey, as he put it, "...to discover, by experimenting in what I will call the dialogue of auto-psychoanalysis, whether I am a Christian as well as a Jew. I have never felt any more at home in the Church which imposes baptism and a man-made creed on its members than I feel in the Synagogue that demands circumcision (and ignores the New Testament)". He admits to being in a no-man's-land where, even if he gets no absolute answers, at least the questions are laid bare. The play has its moment of drama in the attempted suicide by drowning inside the well chamber of Chalice Well of Arviragus' grandson Bran. He is rescued and the play closes with all the participants resolving to build a house of prayer of wattle and daub.

In a footnote to the published edition of the play, the author states that the Guest House where he stayed in September 1943, "...is the property of my friend, Dion Fortune, author of a remarkable book, *The Mystical Qabalah*. The well, which I carefully inspected, forms part of an adjacent property, whose owner will, I hope, forgive me for trespassing".

DF was aware of Rubinstein's standpoint and dilemma; in her reservations she was simply trying to make the play more acceptable to Christians. Considering the content of her own novels and other writings, these cautions may appear rather bizarre. In the event, the published form of the play, as it appears in the collection *Hated Servants* (Gollancz, 1944), seems to have been relatively undamaged by this advice. Theirs was a friendship that has somehow escaped the attention of DF's biographers. It is significant as it is one of the few that existed outside her closed circle of initiates. Harold Rubinstein died in 1976 aged 84 - the end of a long and successful life in law and letters.

DF, determined but physically weak, still served the needs of the membership of the Fraternity of the Inner Light in the war years. Newsletters were circulated, enlightening them on such topics as esoteric astrology and the origins and symbolism of the grail legend.

But the stresses of those dark days seemed to take the life out of her, literally. In January 1946, a few months after the end of hostilities, she died of leukaemia in a London hospital. She would rather it had been Glastonbury. But she soon had her way; before long her spent frame was being laid to rest in the town cemetery.

Loveday, then in his seventies, enjoyed a brief retirement at Chalice Orchard. He died in a Glastonbury nursing home in November 1948. He lies buried a few feet away from DF.

"I am the last of the Avalonians", proclaimed Dion Fortune. And she was, in the sense that she represented the special qualities of a generation whose like will not, and cannot, ever be seen again. But in a more general way she was quite wrong. New 'keepers of the flame' have arrived; some to stay, or, like DF, to commute to Glastonbury from elsewhere. And so they will. It would be rash indeed to propose that any of them might ever be 'the last'.

CHAPTER EIGHTEEN

A New Era

THERE IS A SPACE of about twenty years when not much was happening on the Avalonian front at Glastonbury. The legacy of the people in this book might have been outwardly of small consequence; inwardly, some would say, they awoke and invoked the secret heart of the nation, even influencing the world beyond. Whatever the truth of that, in the Vale of Avalon itself there was definitely a lull in the years after the last war.

There are two further figures of some significance who, on very different levels, passed their own vision on to a later generation. They do not fit so easily into the fraternity of our other Avalonians, who were all connected to each other in certain respects. One was the writer, John Cowper Powys, author of the enormous novel *A Glastonbury Romance.* The other was an artist and sculptor, Katherine Maltwood, 'discoverer' of the Glastonbury Landscape Zodiac. For both of them, the secret they sought to lay bare was held within the place itself and its surrounding lands.

Powys began to pen his novel in 1929. Considering the size of it, it is remarkable that it was published as soon as 1932. He wrote (in *The Modern Thinker,* March 1932): "The main idea was to isolate a spot on the surface of the earth, a spot known to the author from his boyhood, and to write a story about this spot, making the spot itself the real hero or heroine of the tale". For him, a place, a locality, could have a 'psychology'. It could have moods of weather tempered by 'chemical and spiritual influences'; also flora and fauna and geological strata - all these bearing on the unfolding of the lives of the people who lived there.

As well as the cosmic influences of the planets and constellations which poured forth unceasingly on to this particular region of the earth, 'according to the revolution of hours, months, and seasons', there was the ancient and secret influence of the Grail.

As a power within the human drama, within the social order of a small town, the Grail is divisive. However much this would seem to challenge our ideal image of the Grail as a unifying symbol, the truth is that there are always those who will fiercely resist, for reasons of self interest or material gain, all the qualities it represents. In *A Glastonbury Romance* the Grail divides the characters into two hostile camps. There is a reactionary industrialist, bent on converting Glastonbury into a prosperous manufacturing centre; opposing him is a prophetic visionary who looks to bringing about a new consciousness, a change of culture.

There are as many plots and sub-plots as might ever be found in any community in any year. There are 'no less than six major love affairs, one murder, three births, two deaths, and one raising from the dead...' The psychic underlay is always close at hand. In the novel, Powys describes the secret thoughts of the guests at a dinner party rising and floating, hovering, forming and re-forming, "under those glittering candelabra, making as it were a second party, a gathering of thought-shapes, that would remain when all these people had left the room." He then adds his own comment: "All thought-eidola are not of the same consistency or of the same endurance. It is the amount of life-energy thrown into them that makes the difference. Some are barely out of the body before they fade away. Others - and this is the cause of many ghostly phenomena - survive long after the organism that projected them is buried in the earth."

Powys' work was directed towards the ordinary, intelligent 'reading public'; Mrs Maltwood's following was rather different.

In her own lifetime she was appreciated mostly by people like herself: Theosophists, Masons (though many rejected her theories), romantics and those with a penchant for anything mysterious. A few years after her death in 1964 a new generation of the disenchanted young, depressed and oppressed by the prospect of a nuclear holocaust, came to revere her to an extent she would never have dreamed of.

The details of Katherine Maltwood's life vary remarkably from one account to another. Even the spelling of her name is sometimes given as 'Kathryn'. Some say that she and her husband John were childhood sweethearts. In fact he was considerably older than her. Notwithstanding this, she predeceased him by many years.

One thing is certain: they had a lot of money. John Maltwood was an Oxford graduate, a Master Mason, a businessman and inventor. His chief investments had been in beef cattle in Argentina. He is said to have gained most of his fortune through his invention of the bouillon, or *Oxo,* beef extract cube. Like many Theosophists, Katherine may have been a vegetarian - an odd thought, considering how the Maltwoods

KATHERINE MALTWOOD

made their fortune. They were also said to have been closely connected to the Bloomsbury Set, and confidantes of such notables as Virginia Woolf and Lytton Strachey.

From 1917 to 1938, they used to stay at their summer home on the Poldens, on the main road between Glastonbury and Bridgwater. The Priory is a curious mock-gothic structure, looking very much as its name implies. From a vantage point in a small tower, Katherine could look over the countryside towards Glastonbury and draw inspiration for her artwork and writing.

It was from her tower in the summer of 1929 that she had a sudden flash of insight while reflecting on the illustrations she was making for a new edition of *The High History of the Holy Grail*, originally the prose romance *Perlesvaus* written between 1191 and 1212, and translated from the French by Sebastian Evans in 1910. The final stanza of the work gives this indication of its origin:

> "The Latin from whence this history was drawn into Romance was taken in the Isle of Avalon, in a holy house of religion that standeth at the head of the Moors Adventurous, there where King Arthur and Queen Guinivere lie, according to the witness of the good men religious that are therein, that have the whole history thereof, true from the beginning even to the end."

The 'Moors Adventurous' took on a new meaning at Mrs Maltwood's moment of vision. She saw the landscape itself as the subject of the story in the *High History*. The key was in the Zodiac, the system in which the primal forces of life have their symbolic representation in the signs of the constellations through which the sun passes in its annual cycle. Was not Arthur himself the personification of the sun, regnant in the heavens? And the Grail, the age-long object of the questing knights, was the Zodiac, moulded by ancient Sumerians from the watercourses, pathways and hills of the Somerset countryside 5000 years ago.

The secret of the Quest was held in the living symbolism of the Glastonbury Zodiac. It was a concept of immense psychological appeal, 'earthing' the obscure into a more tangible form. Every rock, bush and hillock was pregnant with cosmic power, humming with portents of destiny and high evolutionary fulfilment.

The heyday of enthusiasm for Mrs Maltwood was in the 1970s and 80s. In his *New Light on the Ancient Mystery of Glastonbury*, John Michell, while not accepting the idea literally, still acknowledges a debt to her bold exposition:

> "(The) idea is by no means impossible, and anthropologists recognize that tribal people are inclined to see symbolic shapes in the folds of hills and rivers. The weak point in Mrs Maltwood's vision was her literal expression of it. Many of her effigies seem random and ill-defined and best classified as 'simulacra', examples of the tendency in nature and the human eye, working together, to create apparent symbols and living forms in clouds, rocks and landscapes. Yet through those effigies she created a powerful image, infectious to the imagination, and effective in waking twentieth-century perception of the large-scale, geomantic works of the ancients."

There is something else that sets the character of the work of both Powys and Mrs Maltwood apart from our primary Avalonian group: they are almost exclusively pagan. The others, Goodchild, Tudor Pole, Buckton, Bond and Dion Fortune, all give some kind of recognition to the spiritual ascendency of Christ, albeit as the Christos, the Master Jesus, the Christ within, or whatever.

Only one small clue is given about any possible link between Mrs Maltwood and the other happenings at Glastonbury in the 1930s that we have discussed. It should be borne in mind the 'effigies' she discovered were ranged around a circle some eight miles in diameter with its centre near the village of Butleigh. The 'sign' at Glastonbury was Aquarius, appropriately the emblem of the new zodiacal age (of 2000 years) which we have recently entered. Chalice Well, the 'blood spring', is the living representation of the Water-Bearer. The effigy itself, embracing both the town and the Tor, is in the form of a Phoenix bird, wings outstretched, its beak lowered to drink the waters pouring from the blood-spring. In the following passage from her book *The Enchantments of Britain,* she reveals something of her background in Masonry and also her disdain about the activities of other 'persons unknown' in the neighbourhood:

> "What the Phoenix will bring forth in her anguish during the next two thousand years that the sun inhabits its sacred precincts Time only will prove. Can the fine old Abbey be restored in which to worship the Great Architect of the Universe? Can the little town of Glaston be cleansed by the waters of its once holy 'Chalice Well' (the Aquarius Cup) from the miasma of pseudo-occultism? Can it, by strictly scientific investigation of the Ancient Wisdom, rise on the wings of this 'Evangelistic

Eagle', soaring into the gold and azure of a new sunrise, the clouds of which are even now like a furnace of molten copper?"

Who were the pseudo-occultists? In those days the choice of likely candidates was rather limited; we have probably met them already.

By the time the war had begun, the Maltwoods were already safely in Canada. They had bought a Tudor-style mansion on Vancouver Island, five miles outside the city of Victoria. Their vast art collection and priceless items of Jacobean and Tudor furniture were shipped over from England. Not everything was removed from their London store-house. Unfortunately this remaining part of the collection was destroyed during the Blitz.

Originally called 'The Thatch', the Maltwood's home was adminis-tered for some years by the University of Victoria and known as The Maltwood Museum. Lately it has become a restaurant.

In time as the world began to recover from the war, aspects of Avalonian life at Glastonbury began to return little by little. There was a short-lived attempt to revive the Glastonbury Festivals in 1963 and 1964. Tudor Pole re-convened the Chalice Well Trust on a secure footing in 1959. Geoffrey Ashe's *King Arthur's Avalon - The Story of Glastonbury* first appeared in 1957. The real revival was a little slower in coming.

Around 1967, newspapers began to carry disquieting stories of a mass movement of non-conformity gathering momentum among the young. It started, like all post-war popular trends, in the United States, where the term 'flower-power' caught on as an apt description of the new 'love and peace' revolution.

Possibly the first news that Glastonbury was seeing some of the action in this youth rebellion came as a centre-page spread in the *Bristol Evening Post*. According to the report a group of unconvention-ally attired 'hippies' was living in a gypsy caravan somewhere near the Tor. Their manifesto was beguiling and decidedly 'different'.

What they proclaimed carried a certain coherence while flying in the face of all accepted belief-systems. Glastonbury was a 'power-centre' at the point of intersection of lines of force known as 'leys' which traversed the countryside passing through other centres of power in perfectly straight alignments directed towards points on the horizon where specific celestial bodies arose on specific dates in the annual calendar. They called these lines 'dragon-paths'. The hills lying on the paths were mostly dedicated to the archangel Michael *controller* of the dragon-force rather than the *slayer* of it depicted in Christian mythology.

Along these power-lines travelled UFOs, the vehicles of advanced extraterrestrial beings who were long ago the teachers of the arts and sciences to mankind, dimly remembered as 'Gods' in tribal myths around the world. The Gods were returning, and it was incumbent on mankind to respond with a changed lifestyle and a changed consciousness to meet the new dispensation of the Aquarian Age at the appropriate level of awareness. There were hints that psychedelic drugs had some role to play in this.

There were two organs of information that were very influential within the new 'alternative' community in the late 1960s. These were the iconoclastic bi-weekly tabloid, the *International Times,* and the less regular, more 'beautiful' magazine *Gandalf's Garden,* edited by the well-groomed, wholesome, long-golden-haired hippie-guru, Muzz Murray. Both carried plenty of reports about Glastonbury.

Issue No. 4 of *Gandalf's Garden* was strongly Glastonbury oriented. Appearing in the early spring of 1969, there were three articles of significance. One was by 'Meiwana', headed *Jesus and the Druids,* the main substance of which had been received as a vision at the Chalice Well: Jesus was perceived to have taken his initiation at Glastonbury as a member of 'the highest order of Druids'. The final paragraph was a call to the new faithful to rally once again at Avalon:

"Those who turn to the Light, which is the Truth, in meditation can hear his voice calling to all who love peace to throng to his centre at Glastonbury; to take the pilgrim path, singing their way up the Tor, spiralling from ridge to ridge, quite slowly, to draw the radiation up from the ground and to breathe in the blessing with the air that we may have the strength to take initiation ourselves, that is to die to the old, divisive, demanding ego and to be born into Freedom, Love, Wisdom and Joy."

Another of the articles was by Geoffrey Ashe, *Glastonbury: Key to the Future.* His summing-up at the end of this short piece is yet another assurance that Dion Fortune was not 'the last of the Avalonians':

"But its future is greater than its past. The phase of ruin and silence is ending. Britain will begin to be reborn when Glastonbury is. The Giant Albion will begin to wake when his sons and daughters gather inside the enchanted boundary, and summon him with the right words, the right actions, a different life.

Pilgrimage? Yes, but more than pilgrimage - an enduring community of Avalon, with a constant coming and going, a heart stirring the blood into motion again. The time to found that community is drawing near."

The third article was by Mary Caine. Introducing many people to the Glastonbury Zodiac for the first time, she gave a careful summary of Mrs Maltwood's scheme and her reasons for adding her own refinements. 'Refinements' might be an understatement, for she turned the Scorpio effigy upside down, altered the wings of the Dove at the centre, put a meditating monk next to the 'child in the boat' Gemini effigy at Compton Dundon and changed the outlines of Pisces, Virgo and Sagittarius. In so doing she effectively undermined the whole concept at a stroke. If any of it could be so easily re-drawn, then it invites the prospect that there was nothing there in the first place.

The readers of *Gandalf's Garden* were not to be discouraged; any talk of people being cleverer than us five thousand years ago met with uncritical approval.

There was now a rising tide of migration and pilgrimage to Glastonbury. Like any social grouping there were good and bad among them. In appearance they ranged from the downright dirty to the colourful, beautiful and impressive. Even the occasional 'straight'-dresser was welcome in their ranks. They were not all drug takers and were often very serious indeed about what they thought was the right way to live. Many were careful followers of the macrobiotic diet; others were strictly vegetarian.

This influx was not only 'hippie' in character and not only a response to the ethos of periodicals like *Gandalf's Garden*. A new genre of Glastonbury writing was emerging which included the books of John Michell. His first was *The Flying Saucer Vision* which explored the mysterious association of UFO sightings with prehistoric sites, seeking out evidences from legend and folklore. Next came *The View Over Atlantis*, which brought with it a new acknowledgement of one of the earlier Avalonians, Frederick Bligh Bond. It was also the introduction for many of the new generation of Glastonbury devotees to the principles of geomancy, gematria and terrestrial geometry. There was further discussion of the theory of leys, which, although now regarded as lines of power, were, in the mind of their original discoverer, Hereford trader Alfred Watkins, nothing more than trackways, trade-routes, plotted out by surveyors in continuous straight lines for reasons no longer understood. Watkins could only suggest that they 'thought differently from us'.

Three years later, in 1972, Michell produced another book dealing more exclusively with the Canon of Sacred Measures, particularly as applied to the geometry of Stonehenge and the plan of Glastonbury Abbey. This work was *The City of Revelation*.

Those of the Glastonbury newcomers possessed of an enquiring spirit had the opportunity to discover through the writings of John Michell the legacy of the earlier Avalonians, and particularly the work of Frederick Bligh Bond. There was less a questing for the Grail and Romance among them, and more a fascination with neolithic science and the mystery tradition believed to have been passed down from it to the masonic guilds of the ecclesiastical builders of the Middle Ages.

If this proved too complicated for some, the fantasy world of J. R. R. Tolkien afforded a naive and colourful alternative - extending to both ways of dressing and pet-names borrowed from *The Lord of the Rings* and *The Hobbit*.

While Michell addressed himself to a following of specialists, Geoffrey Ashe was opening up Glastonbury to the wider public.

What is special about Ashe's work is his combination of historical scholarship with an understanding of the relevance of the past to our life today and to the future. This is very much the impulse behind his *Camelot and the Vision of Albion* (1971) which explores the mystique of the British Myth from the Arthurian period through the politics and literature of the past two centuries up to the present time.

Ashe was a founding member and Secretary of the Camelot Research Committee that excavated at South Cadbury, 1965-67. This hilltop site, just twelve miles from Glastonbury, was shown to have been occupied through many different periods from the Neolithic through the Bronze and Iron Ages and the Roman occupation to evidence of a Celtic revival in the fifth century, when the ramparts were refurbished. The hope had been to show that a fifth century chieftain, such as Arthur might have been, could have lived there, giving some credence to the local legend that Cadbury Hill was the original Camelot Castle. They were not disappointed. The site had definitely been occupied at the time in question. All is told in *The Quest for Arthur's Britain* (1968).

Geoffrey Ashe has been active on the Glastonbury scene since the 1970s, supporting, guiding, lecturing, as well as undertaking visiting professorships in the United States. His output of books extends far beyond the brief outline of some of them given here, and includes a Glastonbury novel, *The Finger and the Moon*.

In the 1970s, a local Glastonbury 'alternative' community magazine, *Torc,* appeared in fifteen issues from September 1971 to March 1975. It was a time of some effort in the locality to build bridges and to clarify and inform all parties in a situation that tended to confusion at the best of times. A sense of community evolved, helped by both the magazine and the opportunity to meet in an appointed centre, the long-defunct Abbey Café in the Northload Street car park.

Of our original Avalonians, only Kitty Tudor Pole and Christine Sandeman (née Allen) lived to hear of these developments. Both were full of joy that the place was not dying as they had once feared. Kitty was especially fond of the magazine and regularly ordered copies for her friends.

But was this really the new dispensation envisaged by Goodchild and those who followed him? Obviously it needs more than a few dropouts without gainful employment to bring meaningful changes to our world. But with the larger view, looking at how environmental groups and others are effectively getting things done, in spite of being up against global vested interests, there is cause for hope. Many of the young people of the 1970s stayed to merge happily and usefully into the local community. The Assembly Rooms, once the venue of Rutland Boughton's festivals, have once again been brought to life. There is a café, and concerts and other events are frequently held in the main hall.

Current Avalonian activities are too numerous to mention, but a selective web-search on the name Glastonbury will be sure to bring up-to-date information at any moment far into the future. Be advised that the internationally renowned Glastonbury Festival at Pilton will probably score the most 'hits'. While of admitted significance, it does not bear much relevance to the subject matter of this book, is of short duration and actually some distance from the town of Glastonbury.

Many of the ideas that were once exclusive to the hippie and 'New Age' community have since gained wider currency among the general populace. Hopefully, later generations will see from this story of the earlier Avalonians that the Glastonbury mystique was not an invention of the 1970s, and that the true pioneers were wonderful spirits like Alice Buckton and Frederick Bligh Bond who started with so little to build on after centuries of post-Reformation 'shock' at Glastonbury. Remarkably, they had the power to reach back *before* that time to retrieve the ancient spirit and make of it something to live by.

Afterword

AS I HAVE SAID ELSEWHERE, so much unique information came my way at one time that I felt obliged to try to tell this story. The labour done, I moved away from further Avalonian considerations for a few years apart from responding to occasional enquiries.

The request to revise this book brought with it the need to reconnect once again with the mood of that earlier era. I find that by looking back anew, from a point in time a little later on, the special character and atmosphere of the period has now become even more distinct. As the world changes so the past gains more by way of its own identity. This begs the question as to how it might seem for someone much further in the future.

Books sometimes survive. I have quite a few myself more than a hundred years old. So let me address this to anyone who might pick this up a hundred years from now. Whoever you are, perhaps the child of a child of a child of someone I know, how does it all look to you? If the thoughts of the people in this book are real thoughts, then they will speak to you across the years in a way that can easily be shared with you. You will perhaps sense the difference – maybe the vast difference – with your own world on one level and yet find common ground in the eternal truths that underlie all life and all human thoughts and dreams in all ages.

As I write this there is much unease and insecurity about what the future might bestow on us – or what we might bestow on ourselves. You will now know if we had cause to be so concerned. You may have your own worries. But aside from these global issues, what of the bit of the West Country that has absorbed our interest in these pages? Has the sea risen enough to return to make Glastonbury a near island again? Or is it now a city (God help us!)? All vain guesses, I am afraid. But take a look at the place if you can. If there are groups dedicated to preserving things or honouring its hallowed ways, then please join in and help if you can. What of the Abbey, the Tor, Chalice Well? One last thought. Do some people still seem to be arriving, seeking, trying to find something? Are others homing in to settle more permanently to become, in some way, new Avalonians? I bet they are.

Sources

Chapter 1 Avalon

Robert Brydon (article), *Magico Realism and the Celtic Subversives*, in *Circles*, Magazine of the Theosophical Society in Scotland, Spring 1995.

John Michell, *New Light on the Ancient Mystery of Glastonbury*, Gothic Image, Glastonbury, 1990.

Geoffrey Ashe, *King Arthur's Avalon*, (Collins 1957) Fontana 1973. *Camelot and the Vision of Albion*, Heinemann 1971.

Chapter 2 The Doctor

British Medical Journal, Vol 1, 1877, Page 78.

Private Memo, 1911.

Bob Quinn, *Atlantean*, Quartet Books 1986

John Arthur Goodchild, *My friends at Sant' Ampelio*, Kegan Paul, London, 1890.

Estelle W. Stead, *My Father: Personal and Spiritual Reminiscences*, 1912.

Chapter 3 Light of the West

John Arthur Goodchild, *The Light of the West: An Account of the Dannite Settlement in Ireland*, Kegan Paul, 1898.

Chapter 4 Kindred Spirits

Elizabeth Sharp, *William Sharp (Fiona Macleod) - A Memoir*, Heinemann 1910.

Fiona Macleod, *The Immortal Hour - A Drama in Two Acts*, T. N. Foulis 1908 - also in *Poems and Dramas*, Heinemann 1923.

Fiona Macleod, *The Dominion of Dreams*, Constable 1899/1912, Heinemann 1920.

The Divine Adventure: Iona; By Sundown Shores, Chapman & Hall 1900.

Iona, Floris Classics, Edinburgh, 1982.

Winged Destiny: Studies in the Spiritual History of the Gael,
  Chapman & Hall, 1904, Heinemann 1920.
Rev. E. F. Synge, *Butleigh: A Thousand Years of a Somerset Parish,*
  Butleigh PCC 1974.
Central Somerset Gazette, August 5 1904.
Blue Guide to Sicily, A & C Black, London.
The Spectator, quoted *Central Somerset Gazette,* August 1909.

Chapter 5 Seekers Finders
Elizabeth Sharp, ibid.
Memo 1911.
Goodchild, private letters.
'Triad' Diary 1913.
Oratory Service Book.

Chapter 6 The Pilgrims
Oliver G. Villiers, *Wellesley Tudor Pole: Appreciation and Valuation,* Bells
  of Canterbury 1977.
  Memo 1911
Mary Allen, *Woman at the Crossroads,* Unicorn 1934.
Private letters.

Chapter 7 Deans Yard
Gasquet and Bishop, *The Bosworth Psalter,* 1908.
The Occult Review, August 1907, September 1907.
Diary 1913.
G. W. E. Russell, *Basil Wilberforce: A Memoir,* John Murray 1917.
Chalice Well Messenger, Easter 1976.
Daily Express, Friday 26 July et seq.
Central Somerset Gazette, 2 August 1907 et seq.
The Inner Light (Journal), The Fraternity of the Inner Light, June 1930.
Private Memo. Col. H. M. Farmar, 1939.
W. Tudor Pole / Rosamond Lehmann, *My Dear Alexias,* Neville
  Spearman 1979.

Chapter 8 Builders of Joy
Diary 1913.
Steve Sneyd – correspondence re. Ralph de Tunstall Sneyd
  (allowing corrections to 1993 edition *The Avalonians*)
Tudor Pole/Lehmann, ibid.

John Moss-Eccardt, *Ebenezer Howard*, Lifelines 18, Shire Publications 1973.

Philip Boardman, *Patrick Geddes - Maker of the Future*, University of North Carolina Press 1944.

Goodchild, private letters.

R. A. Gilbert, *A. E. Waite: Magician of Many Parts*, Crucible 1987.

A. E. Waite. Diary-notes.

W. Tudor Pole, *The Writing on the Ground*, Neville Spearman 1968.

Jennifer Uglow (Ed.), *The Macmillan Dictionary of Women's Biography*, 1982.

Mary S. Allen, *Lady in Blue*, Stanley Paul & Co. London, 1936.

Robert S. Ellwood, *Islands of the Dawn, The Story of Alternative Spirituality in New Zealand*, University of Hawaii Press 1993

Chapter 9 Diaspora

Diary 1913.

Boardman, ibid.

Elizabeth Sharp, ibid.

Charles Richard Cammell, *The Heart of Scotland*, Robert Hale 1956.

Report of the Somerset Archaeological & N. H. Society, 1913.

Mary S. Allen, ibid.

W. Tudor Pole, *The Silent Road*, Neville Spearman 1960.

Israel Sieff, *Memoirs*, Weidenfeld & Nicolson 1961.

The Sunday Times, 14 October 1984.

House Chronicle, Stanbrook Abbey.

Mary Bruce Wallace, *The Thinning of the Veil*, Neville Spearman 1981.

D. G. Villiers, ibid.

Timothy Ware, *The Orthodox Church*, Pelican 1963.

Tudor Pole/Rosamond Lehmann, *A Man Seen Afar*, N. Spearman 1979.

Chapter 10 Eager Heart

Journal of the Chemical Society, Transactions, Vol. 91, 1907.

Nature, 12 October 1905.

Proceedings of the Royal Society of London, Series B, Vol. LXXIX, 1907.

Dictionary of National Biography, Second Supplement, Vol 1.

Alice Buckton, MS Poems.

Child Life (Froebel Society Journal) 1899 Vol.1; 1902 Vol.4.

Central Somerset Gazette, 13 June 1913.

Rosemary Harris (Article), *Chalice Well Messenger* 1982.

Alice Buckton, *Eager Heart* (Edition Illustrated by Horace Knowles) Elkin Matthews & Marrot, London 1931.

Edward Carpenter, *Towards Democracy*, London 1884.
Diary 1913.
W. R. Trotter, *The Hilltop Writers*, John Owen Smith 2003

Chapter 11 The Immortal Hour
Muriel V. Searle, *John Ireland: The Man and his Music*, Midas Books, Kent 1979.
Michael Hurd, *Immortal Hour: The Life and Period of Rutland Boughton*, Routledge & Kegan Paul 1962.
Rutland Boughton, *The Glastonbury Festival Movement*, Somerset Folk Press, London 1922.
Diary 1913.
Mac Tyler, *The Immortal Hour: An Interpretation*, Frederick Newman 192_(?)

Chapter 12 The Architect
George Mackaness, *The Life of Vice Admiral William Bligh*, Angus & Robertson, London.
George Mackaness (Ed.), *No. XIX Australian Historical Monographs*, Sydney 1949.
Catherine Crowe, *The Night Side of Nature*, London 1848 (Aquarian Press 1986).
Mary Bligh Bond, *Poems, Visions & Essays*, Ed. A Bates, Renaissance, 365 Sandycombe Road, Kew Gardens, Surrey, TW9 3PR.
William W. Kenawell, *The Quest at Glastonbury: A Biographical Study of Frederick Bligh Bond*, Garrett Publications, New York 1965.
Frederick Bligh Bond, *The Gate of Remembrance*, Blackwell, Oxford 1920.

Chapter 13 The Gate of Remembrance
Bligh Bond, ibid.
Central Somerset Gazette, 10 June 1907 et seq.; 25 June 1909.
Catherine Crowe, ibid.
F. Bligh Bond, *The Hill of Vision*, Constable, London 1919.

Chapter 14 Friends and Foes
Letters.
F. Bligh Bond, *The Company of Avalon*, Blackwell 1924.
Kenawell, ibid.
Peter F. Anson, *Abbot Extraordinary: Memoirs of Aelred Carlyle*, OSB, Faith Press 1958.
Report of the Somerset Archaeological Society, 1913.

Dom Bede Camm, *The Call of Caldey - The Story of Two Conversions,* 1938.

Bath Chronicle December 1913.

Bligh Bond & Simcox Lea, *The Cabala,* Blackwell 1917.
    Gematria, Blackwell 1917.

Chapter 15 The Priest
Waukegan Daily Sun, 6 October 1916.

William H. Francis (Article), *The Churchman,* December 1970.

Mariquita Platov (Article), *The Churchman,* January 1980.

Woodstock Times, 27 September 1973.

Peter F. Anson, *Bishops at Large,* Faber & Faber, London 1964.

Abba Seraphim, *Flesh of our Brethren,* British Orthodox Press 2006.

Chapter 16 Avernus
Kenawell, ibid.

Mary Bligh Bond, ibid.
    Avernus, Blackwell 1924.

Antony Bates, personal recollections.

Chapter 17 The Changeling
Moss-Eccardt, ibid.

Dion Fortune, *Moon Magic*

Alan Richardson, *Priestess: The Life and Magic of Dion Fortune,* Aquarian Press 1987.

Dion Fortune, *Avalon of the Heart,* Aquarian Press 1971.

Unpublished MSS (c. Society of the Inner Light)

Gareth Knight, *Dion Fortune and the Inner Light,* Thoth Publications 2000.

H. F. Rubinstein, *Hated Servants,* Gollancz 1944

Chapter 18 The New Era
John Cowper Powys, *A Glastonbury Romance,* Macdonald 1933 (Picador, London 1975)

The Powys Review, No.9 1981/82.

K. E. Maltwood, *A Guide to Glastonbury's Temple of the Stars,* James Clarke, 1929.

The Enchantments of Britain, Vancouver 1944.

Sebastian Evans (Trans.), *The High History of the Holy Graal,* J. M. Dent 1936.

Hank Harrison (Article), *Our Lady of Glastonbury,* Vancouver Leisure Magazine, August 1974.

John Michell, *The Flying Saucer Vision,* Sidgwick & Jackson, 1967
  The View Over Atlantis, Garnstone 1969.
  City of Revelation, Garnstone 1972.
  New Light on the Ancient Mystery of Glastonbury, Gothic Image Publications 1990.

Geoffrey Ashe, *Camelot and the Vision of Albion,* Heinemann 1971.
  (Ed.) *The Quest for Arthur's Britain,* Pall Mall 1968 (Paladin 1971/72)

Further Reading

Michael Hurd, *Rutland Boughton and the Glastonbury Festivals,* OUP, March 1993.

Geoffrey Ashe, *Avalonian Quest,* Fontana 1984.
  The Glastonbury Tor Maze, Gothic Image Publications, Glastonbury 1979.

Moyra Caldecott, *The Green Lady and the King of Shadows: A Glastonbury Legend,* Gothic Image Publications, Glastonbury 1989.

James P. Carley, *Glastonbury Abbey: The Holy House at the Head of the-Moors Adventurous,* Gothic Image Publications, Glastonbury 1996

Emma Jung and Marie-Louise Von Franz, *The Grail Legend,* London 1972.

Frances Howard-Gordon, *Glastonbury: Maker of Myths,* Gothic Image Publications, Glastonbury 1982.

Konrad Hopkins and Ronald van Roekel, *William Sharp/Fiona Macleod: A Biographical Sketch,* Renfrew District Libraries, Paisley, Scotland.

John Matthews, *A Glastonbury Reader,* Aquarian Press 1991.

Janine Chapman, *Quest for Dion Fortune,* Weiser, Maine 1993

Tracy Cutting, *Beneath the Silent Tor – The Life and Work of Alice Buckton,* Appleseed Press 2004

John Kemplay, *The Paintings of John Duncan,* Pomegranate Artbooks, San Francisco 1994

Lorn Macintyre, *Sir David Russell: a Biography,* Canongate, Edinburgh 1994

Richard Barber (Ed.), *King Arthur in Music,* Boydell & Brewer 2002

Martial Rose, *Forever Juliet – The Life and Letters of Gwen Ffrangcon-Davies,* Larks Press, Norfolk 2003

Currently (2006) *Avalon* – excellent local magazine dedicated to all
aspects of Glastonbury spirituality, prophesy, healing and history.
3 issues annually.
Avalon Magazine, PO Box 3314, Glastonbury, Somerset, BA6 8WZ
email: avalonmagazine@aol.com

Recordings of the music of Rutland Boughton:
Full details on the webpages of The Rutland Boughton Music Trust:
www.rutlandboughtonmusictrust.org.uk

Forthcoming: What promises to be the definitative and meticulously
researched biography of Frederick Bligh Bond by *Timothy
Hopkinson-Ball*, due to be published Autumn 2007 by Sutton
Publishing.

Index

GOTHIC IMAGE

── TOURS ──

**FROM ITS BOOKSHOP AND PUBLISHING BASE AT
7 HIGH STREET, GOTHIC IMAGE OFFERS TOURS TO
THE SACRED SITES OF GLASTONBURY.**

These are guided journeys through the landscape of the Isle of Avalon where we explore the history, myths and legends of this ancient place: the world of the Druids, Goddesses and Celts; fairy folklore; Arthurian legends and the quest for the Holy Grail; the Glastonbury Zodiac; the earth energies, and sacred geometry. We visit Wearyall Hill – the site of the Glastonbury Holy Thorn and the coming of St Joseph of Arimathea; Chalice Well where so many of the events in this book took place; the Tor – site of an ancient three-dimensional labyrinth and the 14th century ruined church tower dedicated to St Michael; Gog and Magog – two ancient Druidic oak trees; the Abbey Ruins - cradle of Christianity and site of Bligh Bond's excavations, and where King Arthur and Guinevere's grave was found.

Tours are by arrangement all year round and take two and a half hours. To reserve a tour contact Jamie George either by phone or email as follows:

Email: jamie@gothicimage.co.uk
Tel: +44 (0)1458 831281 or +44 (0) 7768 087766

GOTHIC IMAGE ALSO ORGANISES HALF, ONE OR TWO-DAY TOURS TO:

**STONEHENGE (with special access if available);
AVEBURY/SILBURY; TINTAGEL/ST NECTAN'S GLEN;
CADBURY/CAMELOT; STANTON DREW STONE CIRCLES
and PENWITH in Cornwall.**

WE ALSO OFFER 10 AND 14 DAY TOURS:

FROM AVALON TO CAMELOT – a journey through the myths of time
SACRED SCOTLAND – the Blessed Isles
MYSTERIOUS WALES – land of Merlin
ENCHANTED IRELAND – land of the faery faith

For full details on all our tours or to order a free colour brochure,
go to our website:

www.gothicimagetours.co.uk